TRADE LIKE A
STOCK MARKET
WIZARD

TRADE LIKE A STOCK MARKET WIZARD

HOW TO ACHIEVE SUPERPERFORMANCE IN STOCKS IN ANY MARKET

MARK MINERVINI

New York   Chicago   San Francisco
Lisbon   London   Madrid   Mexico City   Milan
New Delhi   San Juan   Seoul   Singapore
Sydney   Toronto

15 LCR 21 20

ISBN   978-0-07-180722-7
MHID   0-07-180722-5

e-ISBN   978-0-07-180723-4
e-MHID   0-07-180723-3

The text contains the following, which are trademarks, service marks, or registered trademarks of Mark Minervini, Minervini Private Access, LLC, or their affiliated entities in United States and/or other countries: Specific Entry Point Analysis®, SEPA®, and Leadership Profile®.

Library of Congress Cataloging-in-Publication Data
Minervini, Mark.
    Trade like a stock market wizard : how to achieve super performance in stocks in any market / by Mark Minervini.
    p. cm.
ISBN 978-0-07-180722-7 (alk. paper) — ISBN 0-07-180722-5 (alk. paper) 1. Stocks.
2. Portfolio management. 3. Investment analysis. 4. Risk management. I. Title.
    HG4661.M554   2013
    332.63'22—dc23
                                                                2013005165

McGraw-Hill Education books are available at special quantity discounts to use as premiums and sales promotions or for use in corporate training programs. To contact a representative, please e-mail us at bulksales@mcgraw-hill.com.

This book is dedicated to my mother, Lea, who sacrificed so much of her own life so that my sister and I could have a better one. To my father, Nate, who encouraged me to take a chance and follow my dreams; may they both rest in peace. And, to my wife, Elena, and daughter, Angelia; my beacons of light and promise for the future.

CONTENTS

FOREWORD

I N MY 40 YEARS OF INVESTING I have read numerous investment books, and you would think that I would have a large library filled with them. The truth is that my collection is quite small, because so few investment books are worth keeping. To the handful that are worth reading, one I am adding to my library is *Trade Like a Stock Market Wizard* by Mark Minervini. Mark's book has to be on every investor's bookshelf. It is about the most comprehensive work I have ever read on investing in growth stocks and includes vital details not found in other popular books on that subject. Some investment books cover only the fundamental aspects of investing, and others cover only the technical aspects, Mark's book combines the most important factors that could help you find superperformance stocks in the future. Everyone wants to own the next Apple Computer, Costco, or Home Depot, and Mark shows you what to look for.

Mark took years to research the methods that have made him successful. He has dug up gems of investing knowledge from some of the great investment books and research most investors never knew existed. For example, a source he cites is *Superperformance Stocks* by Richard Love. When you combine that with the experience he gained through many market cycles, you have a book packed with vital advice that will help any investor. In each chapter, Mark clearly lays out the factors that are important for a successful investment. It is one of those books you have to reread to really grasp all that it contains

One of the best sections of the book is Mark's description of the life cycle of a growth stock. You get a fundamental and technical picture of where a stock is along the different phases of its move from the start in phase 1, to the acceleration of earnings and price performance in phase 2, to the topping process in phase 3, to the trip back down in price as earnings slow in phase 4. He shows this not only with price charts but with tables of earnings and sales to show what is happening fundamentally as a growth stock moves over time.

In the last two chapters of the book, which you should probably read first, Mark discusses risk management. This is vital because so many investors seem to get into the right stocks but don't know how to take a profit or when to sell as a position goes against them. He discusses the psychological factors that prevent most investors from cutting a loss. Can you believe that an investor of Mark's stature is right only 50 percent of the time and has still made a fortune! That is due to his use of risk management.

I have always believed that to be a successful investor you have a large tuition bill to pay in hard losses at the University of Wall Street before you can graduate and start making money. Mark supplies the best textbook on growth stock investing, and so you can avoid paying such a high tuition. With his help, a determined effort, and discipline, you can get an Ivy League education for the cost of a hardcover book. If you are a seasoned investor this book is a graduate-level class that will certainly add to your investment knowledge, as it has mine. Mark has also saved me a great deal of time because he wrote the book that I always wanted to write and did it better than I ever could!

Enjoy, and may you all have investment success!

David Ryan
Three-time U.S. Investing Champion

It is true that the market is brutal to most of the people who challenge it. But so is Mount Everest, and that shouldn't—and doesn't—stop people from trying to reach the top. What is expected of a mountain or a market is only that it have no favorites—that it treat all challengers as equals. . . . Trading can be an intellectual stimulation, as well as a way to make money. Played well, it demands skills of the highest order, and skills the trader must work very hard to acquire. A well-conceived and executed transaction is a thing of beauty, to be experienced, enjoyed, and remembered. It should have an essence transcending monetary reward. A piece of each trade should stay with you, forever, because the memory is important. This applies equally to unsuccessful trades, of which there will be many. Even getting out of a bad position, expeditiously, should provide satisfaction not irritation.

—William R. Gallacher

TRADE LIKE A STOCK MARKET
WIZARD

CHAPTER 1

AN INTRODUCTION WORTH READING

> Champions aren't made in the gyms. Champions are made from
> something deep inside them—a desire, a dream, a vision.
>
> —*Muhammad Ali, three-time world*
> *heavyweight boxing champion*

I N THE HEAT OF COMPETITION, champions rise to their strengths, triumphing over mere contenders. Marathon runners win through superior endurance and a keen sense of pacing. The great flying aces of World War I defeated their enemies, winning dogfights by thinking faster and better in three-dimensional space. At the chessboard, victory goes to the player who sees more clearly through the maze of possible moves to unlock the winning combination. Virtually every human contest is dominated by the few who possess the unique traits and skills required in their fields. The stock market is no different.

Investing styles may differ among successful market players, but without exception, winning stock traders share certain key traits required for success. Fall short in those qualities and you will surely part ways with your money. The good news is that you don't have to be born with them. Along with learning effective trading tactics, you can develop the mindset and emotional discipline needed to win big in the stock market. Two things are required: a desire to succeed and a winning strategy. In *Trade Like a Stock Market Wizard: How to Achieve Superperformance in Stocks in Any Market*, I will show you how my winning strategy brought me success and how it can do the same thing for you.

I've been trading and investing in the stock market for most of my adult life: 30 years and counting as of the writing of this book. Stock trading is how I made my living and ultimately my fortune. Starting with only a few thousand dollars, I was able to parlay my winnings to become a multimillionaire by age 34. Even if I had not become rich from trading stocks, I would still be doing it today. For me, trading isn't a sport or just a way to make money; trading is my life.

I didn't start out successful. In the beginning, I made the same mistakes every new investor makes. However, through years of study and practice, I gradually acquired the necessary know-how to achieve the type of performance you generally only read about. I'm talking about *superperformance.* There's a big difference between making a decent return in the stock market and achieving superperformance, and that difference can be life-changing. Whether you're an accountant, a schoolteacher, a doctor, a lawyer, a plumber, or even broke and unemployed as I was when I started, believe me you can attain superperformance.

Success requires opportunity. The stock market provides incredible opportunity on a daily basis. New companies are constantly emerging as market leaders in every field from high-tech medical equipment to retail stores and restaurants right in your own neighborhood. To spot them and take advantage of their success you must have the know-how and the discipline to apply the proper investment techniques. In the following pages, I'm going to tell you how to develop the expertise to find your next superperformer.

Follow Your Dreams and Believe in Yourself

Impossible is just a big word thrown around by small men who find it easier to live in the world they've been given than to explore the power they have to change it.

—*Laila Ali*

Dedication and a desire to succeed are definitely requirements to achieve superperformance in stocks. What is not required is conventional wisdom or a college education. My real-world education began when I was an adolescent. I dropped out of school in the eighth grade at age 15, which means that I am almost completely self-educated. Yes, you read that correctly. I left school at age 15. I have never seen the inside of a high school as a student, let alone attended a university. What I did have, however, was a thirst for knowledge and a burning desire to succeed, to be the best trader I could be. I became a fanatical student of the stock market, its history, and human behavior. I started out by reading the financial news and stock reports at the local library. Over the years, I've read an incredible number of investment books, including more than 1,000 titles in my personal library alone.

In light of my lack of starting resources and formal education, the level of success I have achieved strikes some people as unlikely or even impossible. Along the way, some have even tried to discourage me. You too probably will face people who will try to dissuade you from trying. You will hear things such as "It's a rigged game," "You're gambling," and "Stocks are too risky." Don't let anyone convince you that you can't do it. Those who think it's not possible to achieve superperformance in stocks say so only because they never achieved it themselves, and so it's hard for them to imagine. Ignore any discouragement you may encounter and pay attention instead to the empowering principles I am about to share with you. If you spend time studying and applying them, you too can realize results that will amaze even the most ambitious positive thinkers. Then the same people who said it couldn't be done will ask you the question they always ask me, "How did you do it?"

And the Trade Shall Set You Free

From the very beginning, I saw the stock market as the ultimate opportunity for financial reward. Trading also appealed to me because I liked the idea of having the freedom to work at home and taking responsibility for my own success. In my young adult years, I had tried several different business ventures, and even though I felt enthusiastic, that burning passion was still missing. Finally, I came to realize that what I was most passionate about was freedom—freedom to do what I want, when I want, where I want.

One day it dawned on me: life is rich even if you're not. I realized that things were happening every day, good and bad, and that it was just a matter of deciding what I wanted to be part of. People were getting rich in the stock market. I said to myself, Why not be part of that? I figured that if I learned how to invest in the market and trade successfully, I could achieve my dream of financial freedom and, more important, personal freedom. Besides, who was going to hire a junior high school dropout? The stock market was the one place I could see that had unlimited potential without prejudice. The author and successful businessman Harvey Mackay said it perfectly, "Optimists are right. So are pessimists. It's up to you to choose which you will be."

ACHIEVING THE BEST OF BOTH WORLDS

When I started trading in the early 1980s, I had only a few thousand dollars to invest. I had to make huge returns on my relatively small account to survive and still have some trading capital left. This forced me to hone my timing and learn the necessary tactics for extracting consistent profits out of the stock market day in and day out. Like a pro poker player who grinds out a steady living while consistently building a bankroll, I became a stock market "rounder."

My philosophy and approach to trading is to be a conservative aggressive opportunist. Although this may seem like a contradiction in terms, it is not. It simply means that my style is to be aggressive in my pursuit of potential reward and at the same time be extremely risk-conscious. Although I may invest or trade aggressively, my primary thought process begins with "How much can I lose?" not just "How much can I gain?"

During my 30 years as a stock trader, I've discovered that a "risk-first" approach is what works best for me. It has allowed me not just to perform or perform well but to achieve superperformance, averaging 220 percent per year from 1994 to 2000 (a 33,500 percent compounded total return), including a U.S. Investing Championship title in 1997. My approach also proved invaluable when I needed it the most: cashing me out ahead of eight bear markets, including two of the worst declines in U.S. stock market history. By adhering to a disciplined strategy, I was able to accomplish the most important goal of all: to protect my trading account and keep the profits I made during the previous bull markets.

Invest in Yourself First

When I began trading in the early 1980s, I endured a six-year period when I didn't make any money in stocks. In fact, I had a net loss. It wasn't until 1989 that I began to achieve meaningful success. What kept me going? Unconditional persistence. When you make an unshakable commitment to a way of life, you put yourself way ahead of most others in the race for success. Why? Because most people have a natural tendency to *overestimate* what they can achieve in the short run and *underestimate* what they can accomplish over the long haul. They think they've made a commitment, but when they run into difficulty, they lose steam or quit.

Most people get interested in trading but few make a real commitment. **The difference between interest and commitment is the will not to give up. When you truly commit to something, you have no alternative but success.** Getting interested will get you started, but commitment gets you to the finish line. The first and best investment you can make is an investment in yourself, a commitment to do what it takes and to persist. Persistence is more important than knowledge. You must persevere if you wish to succeed in anything. Knowledge and skill can be acquired through study and practice, but nothing great comes to those who quit.

When Opportunity Meets Prepardness

When people hear my success story, the two questions they ask most often are, How did you do it? and Did you just get lucky? The assumption is that I must have taken a lot of big risks or been lucky along the way.

So how *did* I do it?

For years I worked on perfecting my trading skills, plugging away 70 to 80 hours a week, often staying up to pore over stock charts and company financials until the sun came up the next day. Even though the results weren't there yet, I persevered. I spent years separating the proverbial wheat from the chaff, perfecting my process by analyzing my successes and, more important, my failures. I invested countless hours in learning how great investors approached the market and how they created and executed trading strategies and developed the emotional discipline required to follow their models.

Then something wonderful happened. My preparation intersected with opportunity. I had been honing my skills for years, and by 1990 I was fully equipped to take advantage of a new emerging bull market. With all the lessons I had learned from my trial-and-error days in the 1980s, the pitch was now coming across the plate, and I was staring at my chance to knock the ball out of the park. I was 100 percent prepared, like an Olympic athlete who has practiced and practiced and is now ready to perform with perfection.

Opportunities in the stock market can spring to life on short notice. To take advantage of them you must be prepared and ready to act. **Right now, somewhere out in the world someone is tirelessly preparing for success. If you fail to prepare, that somebody probably will make big money while you only dream about what you could have been and should have done.** So prepare, prepare, prepare, because when opportunity knocks, which it definitely will, you want to be there to answer the door.

Seize Permanent Knowledge

In the following pages, I will share with you a plethora of information as well as specific tactics to help you succeed in stock trading, but there is no substitute for real-life experience. Just as you cannot learn to ride a bicycle from a book, the only way you can accumulate experience is by taking action and producing results and then learning from those results, good and bad. Unfortunately, experience cannot be force-fed; it must be acquired personally over time. However, as you go through trials and tribulations during your learning curve, keep in mind that once acquired, the skill of proficient stock trading can never be taken from you. No one can fire you from your craft the way a boss can from a job; it's just you and the market. All you have learned and the experience you have gained can bear fruit for many years to come. Truly, this is what makes acquired knowledge and firsthand experience the greatest tool to succeed and build upon in stock trading and in life.

Put Passion at the Wheel

The best traders wake up every day excited about trading and speculation. They can't wait to get to work each day and find *their* next superperformer. They are challenged by the markets and feel the same passion and excitement that drives athletes to greatness. Michael Jordan became the greatest basketball player in history because he had passion for the game, not because he was motivated by commercial endorsements. So it is with great traders. They are motivated not just by money but above all by their passion to become the best they can be.

Passion is not something you can learn; it comes from within you. Passion transcends monetary reward. Don't worry; if you are doing something you truly enjoy and you are great at it—whether you're the best writer, lawyer, archaeologist, or basketball player or the world's foremost authority on dung beetles—the money will come your way. **For me, the greatest success came when I finally decided to forget about the money and concentrate on being the best trader I could be. Then the money followed.**

Those of you who enjoy investing and the art of speculation can learn the techniques and disciplines needed to succeed in the stock market. Concentrate on being the best you can be, and the money will follow. The main thing is to let your passion drive you.

The Best Time to Begin

> You don't have to be great to get started, but you have to get started to be great.
>
> —*Les Brown*

Every day we have the opportunity to make choices and shape our future; every day is the first day of the rest of our lives. At some point, those days are gone. You can choose to learn from or regret your failures and also rejoice in your triumphs; however, the sooner you begin pursuing your dreams, the sooner you can achieve them. If you truly want success trading stocks, take action right away. You don't need anyone's permission or any reason other than you've decided to stop wasting valuable time that you will never get back. It all begins with beginning! You can dream, you can think positively, you can plan and set goals, but unless you take action, nothing will materialize. In his book *Possibility Thinking*, Robert Schuller said, "It's better to do something imperfectly than to do nothing flawlessly." An ounce of action is worth pounds of theory. In the stock market, you can make excuses or you can make money, but you can't do both.

It's not enough to have knowledge, a dream, or passion; it's what you do with what you know that counts. Even if you don't become wealthy, by doing what you're passionate about, you will at least be happy. The best chance you have to succeed in life is to do what you enjoy and give it everything you've got. When you get up each morning and do what you love, you never work a day in your life. Those days can begin today. The best time to begin is right now!

A TIME TO SHARE

> If you cannot—in the long run—tell everyone what you have been
> doing, your doing has been worthless.
>
> —*Erwin Schrödinger*

You may wonder why I chose to write this book now. More than a decade ago, I was approached by several major publishers, but I decided not to proceed. Yes, authoring a book gives one credibility and prestige and maybe even boosts one's ego. Although the offers were tempting, I hesitated. I thought to myself, Why should I give away all my hard work for a relatively small sum of money, especially since most people probably won't apply it correctly? Admittedly, I was being a bit cynical. Then I realized that if even one individual put forth the effort that I did in my earlier years, perhaps my book could help that person achieve his or her dreams. Perhaps my work could make a real difference for someone else; perhaps that someone is you.

Since my early twenties, I have been inspired by the words of Dr. Wayne Dyer, the internationally known motivational speaker and author. Not long ago, I reread his book *10 Secrets for Success and Inner Peace,* in which there is a chapter titled "Don't Let the Music Die Inside You." That chapter really struck a chord with me. My father died relatively young, in his fifties. Later, my mother became sick and recently passed after a long battle with an illness. This prompted me to think about my life. Over the years I have accumulated a treasure chest of knowledge and expertise. I came to the realization that it would be a waste to let it all just fade away. Books written by great traders provided me with a foundation to build on—a passing of the torch, one might say. Similarly, I would like others to benefit from and further advance my work.

The stock market provides the greatest opportunity on earth for financial reward. It also teaches great lessons to those who win and those who lose, an education that goes well beyond trading and investing. Without a doubt, the stock market gives you incredible exhilaration when you win and deep humility when you lose. It is the greatest game on earth, and for me it has proved to be the greatest *business opportunity* on earth.

To realize profits from investing in stocks, you must make three correct decisions: what to buy, when to buy, and when to sell. Not all of your decisions will turn out to be correct, but they *can* be intelligent. My goal is to assist you in making these decisions to the utmost of your ability so that you will make *quality choices.* I have spent most of my life perfecting my stock trading methodology, and now, in the following pages, I am going to share these principles with you in detail. Armed with this valuable knowledge, I trust you too will enjoy success in the stock market and pass the torch again.

Most of the examples in this book involve stocks that I traded for myself between 1984 and 2012. This is road-tested research that is very near and dear to me. I hope that you will gain useful insights from this hard-won knowledge and that my story of success will inspire you to accomplish superperformance in stocks and in life. If you're willing to work and believe in yourself, anything is possible.

CHAPTER 2

WHAT YOU NEED
TO KNOW FIRST

There isn't a person anywhere who isn't capable of doing more than
he thinks he can.

—Henry Ford

M ANY PEOPLE HOPE to achieve great success in the stock market,
but few actually do. Over time the average investor realizes only
mediocre or inconsistent results at best. The reason for this lack of success is
simply that most investors have not taken the time to study and understand
what really works in the stock market and what actually accounts for superperformance. The vast majority of investors operate from faulty assumptions that are based on personal opinion or theory, not unbiased facts. Only
a fraction of stock traders have made the effort to carefully study the characteristics and behavior patterns of superperformance stocks. Among those
who acquire the necessary knowledge, many fail to develop the emotional
discipline to execute a winning plan.

What is the underlying reason so many people fall short of achieving
their goals and fail to have big success in the stock market? Largely, it boils
down to the fact that few individuals truly believe they can achieve superperformance in stocks. They've been told that a big return entails big risks or
that if it sounds too good to be true, it probably is.

Let me assure you that you *can* achieve superperformance in stocks if you so desire and that it does not have to be a high-risk endeavor. It's not going to happen overnight, and you will most likely have to learn to do certain things that go against your natural instincts or perhaps relearn some ingrained investment beliefs. However, with the right tools and the right attitude, anyone can do it if he or she chooses.

No Luck Required

The more I practice, the luckier I get.

—*Gary Player*

Achieving superperformance in stocks is not a function of luck or even circumstance. Contrary to what many believe, it is not gambling either. As with any great achievement, superperformance is attained through knowledge, persistence, and skill, which is acquired over time through dedication and hard work. Most of all, long-term success in the stock market comes from discipline, the ability to consistently execute a sound plan and refrain from self-defeating behavior. If you have these traits, the odds are that you will succeed.

With gambling, in contrast, the odds are stacked against you. If you play enough, you will definitely lose. If you think stock trading is gambling, I suppose you could say the same thing about brain surgery (it certainly would be a gamble if I were performing the operation). To a trained surgeon with the necessary expertise, though, it is a job with risks that are offset by knowledge, training, and ultimately skill. Stock trading is no different.

Success in the stock market has little to do with luck. On the contrary, the more you work a sound plan, the luckier you will become.

You Can Start Small

A new idea is delicate. It can be killed by a sneer or a yawn; it can be stabbed to death by a quip and worried to death by a frown on the right man's brow.

—*Charles Brower*

With every new endeavor that you try, you will encounter naysayers. There are people out there who will tell you that you can't do it. If you don't have much money, they will say you don't have enough trading capital, so don't even bother trying. Nonsense! I'm here to tell you that you *can* get rich from the stock market even if you start small. Unless you've been successful in your professional life already, you may not have much money to devote to trading, and if you're a young person just starting out, it may seem impossible to bankroll a trading operation. Don't be discouraged. You can start out small, just as I did.

A friend of mine ran into the naysayer syndrome not too long ago when he wanted to learn how to trade. Since he is a close friend, I let him come to my office each day and sit next to me to gain some hands-on experience. Trading his relatively small account, he started to understand how to make consistent trades and manage his risk. After he got the hang of it, my friend decided to trade on his own from his home. One day I heard that he had quit trading. I was surprised because he'd gotten off to a pretty good start. When I asked him why he gave up, he told me that another friend had told him that he couldn't do it because his trading capital was too small and that he was wasting his time. Discouraged, my friend just gave up.

Michael Dell started by selling computers out of his college dorm. Then, in 1984, he founded what became Dell Computer Corporation with only $1,000. Dell went on to become the largest personal computer company in the world. I started with just a few thousand dollars, and within just few years it grew to more than $160,000. A year later it was at half a million. With a decent bankroll at last, I was able to parlay my winnings into my personal fortune. The rest is history.

I am certainly not the only one who has accomplished superperformance. David Ryan won three consecutive U.S. Investing Championships, posting triple-digit returns every year. Reading about David in the mid-1980s prompted me to embark on my own quest for superperformance and go on to win the U.S. Investing Championship myself.

There are many of us out there who started small and ended up rich. What we have in common is that we refused to let others convince us it couldn't be done. Remember, people who say something can't be done never did it themselves. Surround yourself with people who encourage you and don't let the naysayers knock you off track.

No! It's Not Different This Time

During every bull and bear market for the last three decades I have heard the words "It's different this time." Surely, during the 1920s, the legendary stock trader Jesse Livermore heard these same words. In *How to Trade in Stocks*, Livermore said, "All through time, people have basically acted and reacted the same way in the market as a result of: greed, fear, ignorance, and hope. Wall Street never changes, the pockets change, the stocks change, but Wall Street never changes, because human nature never changes."

Of course, there are technological advancements along the way, and some styles work better than others during certain periods. However, stocks today rise and fall for the same basic reasons as they did before: people drive stock prices, and people are basically the same emotionally. Trading can get very emotional, and emotions can easily lead investors to false conclusions. **On the basis of 30 years of personal experience and historical analysis of every market cycle going back to the early 1900s, I can assure you that nothing has changed very much. In fact, history repeats itself over and over.**

Let the pundits clamor that it's different this time. Meanwhile, new leaders in the stock market emerge, hit the new high list, and amaze all the so-called experts. Fortunes are made and lost time and time again for the same timeless reasons. One thing you can count on is that history will repeat itself. The only question is: How good a student are you?

Your Greatest Challenge Is Not the Market

The world is full of people looking for a secret formula for success. They do not want to think on their own; they just want a recipe to follow. They are attracted to the idea of strategy for that very reason.
—*Robert Greene*

The best computer with the fastest processor to crunch numbers won't do anything to improve your psychology or mental preparedness. The road to success in the stock market is not a system or strategy; it's within you, and it will be realized only to the extent that you are able to control and direct your emotions as you encounter challenges, of which I assure you there will be many. You might as well know that at the start. Otherwise, you'll only be chasing false hopes.

If you want a decent return, you can always put your money with a good mutual fund manager, in a hedge fund, or in an index fund. If you want super-performance, you are going to have to go the extra mile. But first you need to understand that your greatest challenge is not the stock market. It's you.

No One Is Going to Do It for You

My first experience investing in the stock market was with a full-service stockbroker in the early 1980s, and it wasn't pleasant. In a few short months my entire account was wiped out. Although this was painful and a major set-back financially, it turned out to be one of my most valuable lessons about investing.

My broker at the time persuaded me to buy stock in a biotech com-pany that supposedly had developed an AIDS cure. He said that he had a really good indication from some important industry "pros" that U.S. Food and Drug Administration (FDA) approval was coming and the stock would rocket on the news. Being a novice to the market, I bought that line of BS. I was blinded by the potential reward and did not even think about the risk.

Shortly after I purchased the stock, it sold off from $18 to around $12. I was extremely concerned, but when I called the broker, he assured me that this was "a once-in-a-lifetime opportunity" and that the stock was a "bar-gain." He recommended that I double up my position because that would lower my average cost and give me even more profit when the stock finally took off. (Does this sound familiar?) Long story short: the stock kept sink-ing, and eventually I lost all my money as I watched in horror while it fell to less than $1. Of course the broker still got his commissions.

In hindsight, this broker did me a very big favor. It was precisely at that point that I decided to do my own research and trading; I vowed I would never again surrender my investment decisions to someone else. **If you aren't prepared to invest a good portion of your time before you invest**

your money, you're just throwing darts. At some point, you will surely be taken to the cleaners.

Have confidence in your ability. Learn to do your own research and think for yourself. Your own resources are far superior to outside research, tips, and so-called expert opinions because they're yours and therefore you can keep tabs on them. No one cares about your money and your future as much as you do. Do the work, own your failures, and you will own your success. No one is going to make you rich except you.

DO YOU WANT TO BE RIGHT OR MAKE MONEY?

After my biotech fiasco with the full-service broker, I decided to take matters into my own hands. I opened a trading account at a discount house where I met a broker named Ron. Over the course of a couple of years, Ron and I became pretty close friends; we had certain things in common, but it certainly wasn't evident in our trading styles. He was sort of a value buyer who wasn't concerned about supply and demand or price trends. My style, in contrast, was to buy new, relatively unknown companies on the rise. I demanded that they be in a price uptrend, and if they went down much below my purchase price, I would sell them. At least that was the plan.

As Ron and I watched each other's trades, our favorite sport became giving the other guy a hard time when one of his stocks tanked. Sometimes I'd hit a few losers in row, and Ron would razz me: "Hey, genius, what happened? That one sure went down the toilet!" The verbal jabs really got to me. Sometimes I held on to losing stocks because I couldn't stand the thought of the ridicule awaiting me when I phoned in a sell order to Ron.

A stock would fall 5 percent and then 10 percent, and I knew I should sell. Then I'd think of Ron and hold on to that dog while it fell 15 percent and then 20 percent. The bigger the loss was, the harder it became to call Ron and place the sell order. Even if he didn't say a word to me, I felt humiliated. Meanwhile, the stock continued to suck money out of my account like a rupture in the hull of a ship.

Both opportunities and perils surface suddenly in the market. It takes swift, resolute action to exploit one and elude the other. Nothing can unravel a trader's courage more than a huge loss in a stock trade. **It wasn't until I suffered enough big losses that I made the decision that turned my performance from mediocre to stellar: I decided it was time to make money and stop stressing about my ego.** I began selling off losing stocks quickly, which meant taking small losses but preserving the lion's share of my hard-earned capital. Almost overnight, I regained a feeling of control.

That new approach also freed me to take an objective look at my performance. In the past, I'd tried to forget about my losing stocks. Now I was analyzing my losers and learning from them. I saw my portfolio with fresh eyes and finally began to understand that trading is not about picking highs and lows or proving how smart you are; trading is about making money. If you want to reap big gains in the market, make up your mind right now that you are going to separate trading from your ego. It's more important to make money than it is to be right.

PRACTICE DOES NOT MAKE PERFECT

I know people who have managed money on Wall Street for decades yet have only mediocre results to show for it. You would think that after all those years of practice their performance would be stellar or at least would improve over time. Not necessarily. Practice does not make perfect. In fact, practice can make performance worse if you are practicing the wrong things. When you repeat something over and over, your brain strengthens the neural pathways that reinforce the action. The problem is that these pathways will be reinforced for incorrect actions as well as correct actions. **Any pattern of action repeated continuously will eventually become habit. Therefore, practice does not make perfect; practice only makes habitual.** In other words, the fact that you've been doing something for a while doesn't mean you are guaranteed success. It could be that you're just reinforcing bad habits. I subscribe to the advice of the legendary football coach Vince Lombardi. As he said, "Practice does not make perfect. Only perfect practice makes perfect."

In the stock market, practicing wrong will bring you the occasional success even if you're using flawed principles. After all, you could throw darts at a list of stocks and hit a winner once in a while, but you will not generate consistent returns and eventually you will lose. The reason most investors practice incorrectly is that they refuse to objectively analyze their results to discover where their approach is going wrong. They try to forget the losses and keep doing what they've always done.

The proliferation of cheap brokerage commissions, Internet trading, and web-based stock market data may have provided everyone with the same technology, but it did not grant investors an equal ability to use those resources. Just as picking up a five-iron doesn't make you Tiger Woods, opening a brokerage account and sitting in front of a computer screen doesn't make you Peter Lynch or Warren Buffett. That's something you must work for, and it takes time and practice. What's important is that you learn how to practice correctly.

Why I Don't Like Paper Trading

Do the thing and you will have the power.

—Ralph Waldo Emerson

As new investors learn the ropes, often they engage in paper trading to practice before putting real money at risk. Although this sounds reasonable, I am not a fan of paper trading, and I don't recommend doing it any longer than absolutely necessary until you have some money to invest. To me, paper trading is the wrong type of practice. It's like preparing for a professional boxing match by only shadowboxing; you won't know what it's like to get hit until you enter the ring with a real opponent. Paper trading does little to prepare you for when you are trading for real and the market delivers a real punch. Because you are not used to feeling the emotional as well as the financial pressure, it will be unlikely that you will make the same decisions you did in your practice sessions. Although paper trading may help you learn your way around the market, it can also create a false sense of security and impede your performance and learning process.

The psychologist Henry L. Roediger III, who is the principal investigator for the department of psychology at Washington University in St. Louis, conducted an experiment in which students were divided into two groups to study a natural history text. Group A studied the text for four sessions. Group B studied only once but was tested on the subject three times. A week later the two groups were tested, and group B scored 50 percent higher than group A. This demonstrates the power of actually doing the thing you're trying to accomplish versus preparing for it in simulation.

If you're just starting out, you should trade with real money as soon as possible. If you're a novice trader, a good way to gain experience is to trade with an amount of money that is small enough to lose without changing your life but large enough that losses are at least somewhat painful. Don't fool yourself into a false sense of reality. Get accustomed to trading for real because that's what you're going to have to do to make real money.

Trading Is a Business

Many people have the misconception that stock trading is a mysterious endeavor that is governed by a set of laws different from those for an ordinary business. Trading stocks and running a business are virtually identical. In fact, to be successful, you must trade just as if you were running a business. As an investor, your merchandise is stocks. Your objective is to buy shares that are in strong demand and sell them at a higher price. How much of a profit margin you make will depend a lot on the type of business (portfolio) you are running. You may be like Walmart, which operates on very small margins but does a tremendous amount of volume with high inventory turnover. Or you may be like a boutique that offers unique and trendy merchandise and earns higher margins but does much lower volume. You may be making numerous trades for a small gain, but by sheer volume you turn in an impressive return at the end of the year. Or you may be a long-term investor with select merchandise that also produces a solid return.

In the end, it all comes down to having your gains on average be larger than your losses, nailing down a profit, and repeating the process. This is the basic objective of any business endeavor. Most investors treat trading as a hobby because they have a full-time job doing something else. However, if you treat trading like a business, it will pay you like a business. If you treat trading like a hobby, it will pay you like a hobby, and hobbies don't pay; they cost you.

Don't Invest Like a Fund Manager

> The amateur investor has many built in advantages that could result in outperforming the experts. Rule #1 is to stop listening to the professionals.
>
> —*Peter Lynch*

As a stock trader in search of superperformance, not only should you not listen to most professionals, you should not invest the way they do. If you're going to invest like a fund manager, why not just give your money to a fund manager? This will achieve essentially the same result without the work. Better yet, why not just invest in stock market index funds, which beat most fund managers? The fact is that to outpace their peers, most big fund managers need to learn how to invest less like fund managers and more like superperformance traders. Most big funds are doomed to mediocrity by design. Individuals, however, have a big advantage over these institutional investors.

Contrary to what many believe, a professional money manager has no advantage over an individual investor. Many big institutions utilize flawed principles that are based on personal opinion, tradition, and ego as well as, in many cases, pure ignorance. The biggest handicap facing virtually every big fund manager is size. First and foremost, institutional investors need liquidity to handle the large blocks of shares they must buy to add positions that will have a meaningful impact on their portfolios. This forces big players to pick companies with relatively large amounts of shares outstanding. This is the exact opposite of what we know to be a key factor for superperformance: a relatively small number of shares in the float.

Big institutions have a difficult time taking a position in a company with a small number of shares outstanding. Even if they can, the real problem comes later, when it's time to sell the stock in a falling market. When forced to liquidate a large position, an institution risks precipitating a further plunge in the stock's share price as a result of the fund's large block sell-ing activity. An individual investor, however, can move quickly and respond in an instant during both entry and exit, taking advantage of the best high-growth situations available early on and then stepping aside when necessary.

Another drawback is that many big fund managers can invest only in shares from a committee-approved list. Managers meet with these commit-tees to justify buy and sell decisions. A dreadful situation for a manager is having to explain a position gone disastrously wrong in a small, presumably risky situation even though the company showed great growth prospects. A safer bet with better job security is for that manager to buy larger, seemingly safe plays such as IBM and Apple. Then, if something goes wrong, the entire market most likely is suffering, and the losses can be attributed to the overall environment. At the very least, the manager's reputation is insulated by the fact that he or she bought "quality." As the old Wall Street saying goes, "You will never lose your job losing your clients' money in IBM."

Institutions generally need to stay invested in portfolios that are diversi-fied across many individual stocks and industries. This is primarily a result of their need for liquidity and the belief that spreading risk over many names will reduce the risk in any one name. The vast majority of funds must stay at least partially invested even during dreadful market conditions. Moving to the safety of cash is frowned on. Most mutual funds never raise more than 5 or 10 percent cash. Managers are always being compared to benchmarks such as the S&P 500. If fund managers fall behind their benchmark averages for any length of time, investors will jump ship, and the managers could lose their jobs.

Individuals, in contrast, can react to surprises that create new price trends almost instantly. There is no committee approval process and no diversification mandate. With today's technology, most traders—profes-sional and individual alike—have nearly identical tools at their disposal. However, individual traders have a tremendous advantage over profession-als mainly because they have greater liquidity and speed, enabling them to be more concentrated in a small list of well-selected names at even lower risk because an individual can utilize stop-loss protection with little or no slippage. An individual, with a faster response time, can be more patient and strike at only the most opportune moments, which is the best advantage of all.

Most big institutions would rather make what they regard as safe investments than pursue big capital gains. They will boast about success if the market is down 40 percent but their portfolio has lost *only*, say, 32 percent. That's an example of what they claim is beating the market! **If you think for a minute that the big institutional approach is safer or less risky, I suggest you take a look at your favorite mutual funds and study their performance during past major bear markets.**

For a big fund manager, size impairs precision: the ability to enter and exit stock positions without affecting price in a counterproductive way. This technical disadvantage forces the manager to seek informational superiority. Although tactics and techniques play a role for virtually every investor, the individual can utilize a tactical approach with far greater efficiency and effectiveness than can the large institutional player.

The bottom line is that if you want mutual fund–like results, invest like a fund manager. If you want superperformance results, you must invest like a superperformance investor.

CONVENTIONAL WISDOM PRODUCES CONVENTIONAL RESULTS

> A "sound" banker, alas! is not one who foresees danger, and avoids it, but one who, when he is ruined, is ruined in a conventional and orthodox way along with his fellows, so that no one can readily blame him.
>
> —*John Maynard Keynes*

Throughout this book you will read about findings and facts that debunk many widely accepted notions about how to succeed in the stock market. Many of these nostrums are taught by universities and fill weighty textbooks. Some of them hold up as standard references on investing. This should come as no surprise. Nothing in our society is more respectable than conventional wisdom.

In my experience, attaining superperformance in stocks comes from doing things that are different from what is obvious or popular. This is often misinterpreted as risky. Applying conventional wisdom produces conventional returns, not superperformance. If success were as easy as acting like everyone else, we could become rich by mimicking the crowd.

As you observe and analyze the market, be open-minded and willing to do things that most people won't do. Growth comes at the expense of comfort. Learn to venture outside your comfort zone and always question conventional wisdom. If you wish to be exceptional, you must by definition be unconventional.

THE UNAVOIDABLE COST OF SUCCESS

If you want to be the best, you have to do things that other people are unwilling to do.

—*Michael Phelps,*
winner of 17 Olympic medals

Ask yourself, What are my goals? Even if you haven't thought out a life plan, probably a few aspirations come to mind right away. Now ask yourself, What would I give up to achieve those goals? That's another story, isn't it? The choice to sacrifice is difficult, but it is one of the most important decisions you will make in the pursuit of success. Sacrifice means prioritizing, which could result in giving up certain activities to have the time to pursue trading. Admittedly, this is a tough step to take, but no champion has a completely balanced life when he or she is going for a gold medal. Champions are laser-focused on their goal; they understand the power of a narrow focus. This comes at a price; it's called sacrifice.

TO DEFINE IS TO SACRIFICE

I fear not the man that has practiced 10,000 kicks once, but I fear the man that has practiced one kick 10,000 times.

—*Bruce Lee*

Because you are reading this book, I assume that one of your goals is to become the best stock trader you can be or at least to improve your investment results. To have any chance of real success, you will have to make some choices about how you are going to pursue that goal. Odds are that you won't be the best value trader, the best growth trader, the best day trader, and the best long-term investor. If you try to do it all, you will most likely end up a mediocre jack-of-all-trades. You can't say that a trader is a trader any more than you can say that a doctor is a doctor. Can a physician be the best brain surgeon, the best heart surgeon, the best psychiatrist, the best pediatrician, the best rheumatologist, and the best bone specialist? Of course not.

Consequently, you will enjoy market cycles when your trading style outperforms other styles, and you will also learn to accept periods less conducive to your style. I doubt you will overcome these less favorable phases by adopting a different style each time you run into difficulty. When it comes to stock trading, I know no one who, for example, can successfully trade value in one cycle and then switch to growth the next or be a long-term investor one day and then a day trader to suit the market du jour. To become great at anything, you must be focused and must specialize.

TRADER OR INVESTOR?

The average trader spends the majority of his or her time vacillating between two emotions: indecisiveness and regret. This stems from not clearly defining one's style. The only way to combat paralyzing emotions is to have a set of rules that you operate from with clearly stated goals. You simply must make a decision: Are you a trader or an investor? Some people have a personality best suited for trading, and some prefer a longer-term investment approach. You will have to decide for yourself which is best for you. Keep in mind that if you fail to define your trading, you will almost certainly experience inner conflict at key decision-making moments.

INDECISIVENESS

- Should I buy?

- Should I sell?

- Should I hold?

REGRET

- I should have bought.

- I should have sold.

- I should have held.

If you are a short-term trader, recognize that selling a stock for a quick profit only to watch it go on to double in price is of no real concern to you. You operate in a particular zone of a stock's price continuum, and someone else may operate in a totally different area of the curve. However, if you're a longer-term investor, there will be many times when you make a decent short-term gain only to give it all back in the pursuit of a larger move. The key is to focus on a particular style, which means sacrificing other styles. Once you define your style and objectives, it becomes much easier to stick to a plan and attain success. In time, you will be rewarded for your sacrifice with your own specialty.

EXPECT SOME ROTTEN DAYS

> Many of life's failures are people who did not realize how close they were to success when they gave up.
>
> —*Thomas Edison*

The key to success is to become a successful thinker and then act on those thoughts. That doesn't mean that all your ideas and actions will always produce the desired results. At times you will feel that success is unattainable. You may even feel like giving up. I know. I've been there. I went six consecutive years without making a penny while pursuing stock trading. Along the way I had days when I felt so demoralized by my unsatisfactory results that I almost threw in the towel and gave up. However, I knew the power of persistence. Then, after more than a decade of trial and error, I was making more money in a single week than I dreamed of making in a year. I experienced what the English poet and playwright Robert Browning meant when he wrote, "A minute's success pays the failure of years."

Remember, if you choose not to take risks, to play it safe, you will never know what it feels like to accomplish your dreams. **Go boldly after what you want and expect some setbacks, some disappointments, and some rotten days. Embrace them all as a valuable part of the process and learn to say, "Thank you, teacher."** Be happy, feel appreciative, and celebrate when you win. Don't look back with regrets at failures. The past cannot be changed, only learned from. Most important, never let rotten days make you give up.

RECORDS ARE MADE TO BE BROKEN

For many years, it was widely believed to be impossible for a human to run a mile (1,609 meters) in under four minutes. In fact, for many years, the thinking was that the four-minute mile was a physical barrier that no human could break without causing significant damage to the runner's health. Then on May 6, 1954, during a meet between the British AAA and Oxford University, the English athlete Roger Bannister ran a mile in 3 minutes, 59.4 seconds. Suddenly, the impossible was possible. Fifty-six days after Bannister broke through the four-minute barrier, the Australian champion runner John Landy ran a mile in 3 minutes and 57.9 seconds in Finland. Within three years, 16 other runners also cracked the four-minute mile. What happened to the physical barrier that had prevented humans from running a mile in less than four minutes? Was there a sudden leap in human evolution? No; the *change in thinking* made the difference.

Often the barriers we perceive exist only in our minds. Beliefs influence what we attempt or choose not to attempt in life. In these pages, you will learn powerful lessons and proven techniques that will make an enormous difference in what you can attain with stock trading. Records are made to be broken, mine included. If you are willing to apply yourself and learn the lessons, how can you fail? Believe you *can* do it. That's the first thing you need to know.

CHAPTER 3

SPECIFIC ENTRY POINT®
ANALYSIS: THE SEPA®
STRATEGY

WHEN I BEGAN TRADING STOCKS in the early 1980s, my idea of a strategy consisted of nothing more than impulse buying of low-priced stocks that had been beaten up. When stocks were trading near their historical lows, I figured they had to be bargains. I didn't have much success with that approach. In fact, the results were downright dreadful. It wasn't long before I realized that many of these stocks were low-priced for good reason and in most cases were on their way to lower lows. I did, however, see many stocks hit the 52-week-high list and then skyrocket even higher in price. The question became, What differentiates the highfliers from the duds, and is there a way to identify the big winners before they become big winners?

Over the next five years, 1983–1988, I embarked on a comprehensive research process, reading every book I could get my hands on and devouring the daily financial news. I bought books when I could afford them. What I couldn't afford to buy and take home, I stood at the bookstore shelves reading, taking notes with a pad and pencil. I would even go to the local university libraries with a pocketful of change and photocopy entire books for a penny a page and then staple them together. Looking back, it must have been comical to see my collection of photocopied books held together by a few staples and me sitting at a fold-out card table that I used as a desk in the corner of mother's dining room. No one in my family had a clue about what I was doing with those makeshift books. It was a modest beginning, but in the long run, it got the job done.

THE BEGINNING OF A TURNING POINT

The knowledge I have amassed has come not only from three decades of hands-on experience but also from the study of those who arrived before me. Although I have taken the information in, refined it, and retooled it into my own Specific Entry Point Analysis, or SEPA, to suit my own trading, I am indebted to the market masters whose groundbreaking works go back many decades. An eye-opening book for me was Richard Love's *Superperformance Stocks*. Although much of the book was about the political cycle, I was intrigued by Chapter 7, which focused on the commonalities of big winning stocks. Love's studies from 1962 to 1976 focused on the characteristics of stocks that went up a minimum of 300 percent in a two-year period; he called them superperformance stocks.

Although Love's approach caught my attention, initially I wasn't sure exactly how to use it in my own trading, and so the information stayed tucked away in my mind unused while I continued my quest to learn more. In 1988, I read an article in the March–April issue of *Financial Analyst Journal* titled "The Anatomy of a Stock Market Winner." The article discussed the findings from a study of superior securities: stocks that went up a minimum of 100 percent in a calendar year. The author, Marc R. Reinganum, had explored the 222 stock market winners from 1970 to 1983 to determine what contributed to their superior performance.

As I read the article, the proverbial bell went off in my head and I recalled Love's book. For one thing, there was a partial overlap between the time frames studied by Love and Reinganum. Furthermore, the purposes of their studies were almost identical: focusing on stocks that had made the biggest gains to identify the characteristics that accounted for their stellar performance. Now all I needed was to get my hands on Love's book again, which was out of print and pretty rare. Luckily, a friend of mine found a copy in Canada at a book fair for only a dollar, which he bought and mailed to me. With Love's book and Reinganum's results in hand, I compared the findings of both studies and focused on the similarities between them. As I cross-referenced the two, my confidence increased that this approach (known as *reverse factor modeling*) had merit and that there was a possibility I could use it in a methodical fashion to find big stock winners. It made intuitive sense to me: studying the best to find the best.

Studying Love's work set me on a course to learn what makes a stock move up dramatically in price to join the elite circle of superperformers. This ultimately became my life's work. Love's findings convinced me of three empowering points:

1. There is a right time and a wrong time to buy stocks.

2. Stocks with superperformance potential are identifiable *before* they increase dramatically in price.

3. By correctly investing in these stocks, it is possible to build a small amount of capital into a fortune in a relatively short period.

THE MELTING POT

Over the course of my trading career, in addition to Richard Love's book, the works of others have inspired me. Among them was *The Relative Strength Concept of Common Stock Price Forecasting* by Robert A. Levy, which helped me banish the "buy weakness" mentality and was instrumental in my new approach of focusing on strength. Then there was Edward S. Jensen's *Stock Market Blueprints*, published in 1967. Jensen's book included his blueprints for each type of stock, which were based on criteria such as income, growth, cyclical growth, and dynamic growth. What I liked about Jensen was that he, like Love, proceeded from an objective study of stocks to create templates from factor models. This rigorous approach inspired me to create my own Leadership Profile®.

Another influence was Richard Donchian, who was born in Hartford, Connecticut; graduated from Yale with a degree in economics; and went to work on Wall Street in the 1930s. Donchian is considered the creator of the managed futures industry. He developed a rule-based trading approach that became known as *trend following*. Among his principles was the buying and selling of stocks when the 5-period moving average crossed above and below the 20-period moving average. It was Donchian's work that influenced me to add certain trend elements to my model for qualifying trades and timing entries.

Later I came across William L. Jiler, who did extensive work in chart patterns. In his book, Jiler acknowledged the contribution of Donchian, who at the time was director of commodity research at the securities firm Hayden Stone. These men became my professors as I meticulously studied the market. From Love, I learned historical precedent analysis and the commonalities of superperformance stocks; from Jensen, blueprinting and profiling; from Donchian, trend following; and from Jiler, chart patterns, including his famous saucer with platform, which is now known as the cup-and-handle pattern, popularized by William O'Neil, who also worked at Hayden Stone in the 1960s.

Of course, the master of them all was Jesse Livermore, the greatest trader ever. In 1907, he made $3 million in a single day. While most investors were devastated during the great crash of 1929, Livermore made a whopping $100 million shorting the market. For me, this was incredibly inspiring. Although most people associate Livermore with the book *Reminiscences of a Stock Operator*, I gravitated to his pragmatic work *How to Trade in Stocks*. Reading Livermore's book crystallized my thoughts. Many of the principles that were starting to work for me seemed no different from those that had worked for Livermore back in the first decades of the twentieth century.

From one market professor to the next, the lessons were consistent and clear. The basics of what made a superperformance stock in the past had not changed appreciably. No matter how the economy evolved or which industries emerged, the basic criteria for superperformance were constant. Many people before me had come to the same conclusion. Although the names differed and each had his or her own tactics for exploiting this phenomenon, a collective body of knowledge existed and waited for new explorers to build on that foundation.

At Last Technology

By the late 1980s I bought my first "powerful" computer; by that I mean a machine I could use for something other than playing Tennis Pong on a monochrome green screen. In addition to putting real-time quotes right on my desk, the computer allowed me to create a database and gave me access to more information. Now I could conduct quantitative analysis: tracking and studying more big winners and observing stocks in real time to confirm historical findings in a modern time frame. The computer also allowed me to screen thousands of potential companies on the basis of superperformance characteristics. Before this, I was finding and tracking stocks manually, which as you might guess placed a severe limitation on how many I could cover. Early on, I even created my stock charts by hand on graph paper daily. What a chore!

As I studied and traded stocks in real time, the data I collected and the results I produced agreed with Love and Reinganum's conclusions. Up to this point, I had not developed a specific formula for trading, but I was homing in on the characteristics of superperformance stocks and starting to have some meaningful success by trading on those insights for my own account.

Putting the Findings to Work

The boom in technology, consumer retailing, and healthcare in the early 1990s transformed obscure companies into household names. Utilizing what I had learned during the 1980s, I was able to catch some big movers as stocks transitioned from the 1990 bear market into a new bull market. US Surgical, Amgen, American Power Conversion, Ballard Medical Products, US Healthcare, Surgical Care Affiliates, Medco Containment, Microsoft, Home Depot, Dell Computer, International Game Technology, and Cisco Systems were at that time relatively unknown names that displayed strong fundamental and technical characteristics. Many investors missed these great companies during their phenomenal growth phases because of their relatively high price/earnings (P/E) ratios. In 1991, the 40 top-performing stocks (starting at above $12 a share) began the year with an average P/E of 29, and by year end their P/E ratios had expanded to 83.

THE LEADERSHIP PROFILE

By using almost three decades of actual trading and meticulous accumulation of historical data from as far back as the late 1800s, I've constructed a blueprint of the characteristics shared by superperformance stocks. I call this a Leadership Profile, which is an ongoing effort to identify in detail the qualities and attributes of the most successful stocks of the past to determine what makes a stock likely to dramatically outperform its peers in the future. The focus is not just on the magnitude of a price move—how much a stock goes up—but also on the time element of the equation: how fast it goes up and what accounts for the rapid rise. In the stock market, timing is crucial because time is money. When screening my database, I compare each stock candidate to how well it fits the optimal Leadership Profile and rank it accordingly. The result is a dramatic increase in the probability of finding the next superperformer.

SEPA: A STRATEGY OF PRECISION

Honing my timing for entries and exits has been a major focus for me. Over the years, my SEPA methodology evolved into a strategy that has been referred to by some as trading with surgical precision. The SEPA approach, which I will explain in detail, allows me to find those elite candidates that have the potential to become superperformers. The objective of SEPA is to take all the pertinent information available and pinpoint the precise spot at which to enter a high-probability trade in terms of risk versus reward. SEPA combines corporate fundamentals with the technical behavior of a stock. The underlying criteria of SEPA are derived from rigorous research, decades of application in the real world, and observed facts, not personal opinions or academic theories.

THE FIVE KEY ELEMENTS OF SEPA

The basic characteristics are broken down into five major categories, which make up the key foundational building blocks of the SEPA methodology:

1. **Trend.** Virtually every superperformance phase in big, winning stocks occurred while the stock price was in a definite price

uptrend. In almost every case, the trend was identifiable early in the superperformance advance.

2. **Fundamentals.** Most superperformance phases are driven by an improvement in earnings, revenue, and margins. This typically materializes *before* the start of the superperformance phase. In most cases, earnings and sales are on the table and measurable early on. During a stock's superperformance phase, a material improvement almost always occurs in the fundamental picture with regard to sales, margins, and, ultimately, earnings.

3. **Catalyst.** Every stock that makes a huge gain has a catalyst behind it. The catalyst may not always be apparent upon a casual glance, but a little detective work on the company's story could tip you off to a stock with superperformance potential. A new hot-selling product that accounts for a meaningful portion of a company's sales may provide the spark to ignite a superperformance phase in that company's stock price. Approval by the FDA, a newly awarded contract, or even a new CEO can bring life to a previously dormant stock. In dealing with small, lesser-known names, it often takes some event to attract attention to a stock. I like to see something that gets investors excited. Examples would include Apple (AAPL) reaching cult status with its Mac and "i" products, Research in Motion (RIMM) with its BlackBerry (so habit-forming for Internet and e-mail junkies that it's been nicknamed CrackBerry), and Google (GOOG), which became so synonymous with Internet search engines that it made it into the dictionary as a verb. Each situation may be somewhat different whether the stock is a classic growth company, a turnaround situation, a cyclical stock, or a biotech trading on the promise of a new drug. Whatever the reason, behind all superperformance there is always a catalyst driving institutional interest.

4. **Entry points.** Most superperformance stocks give you at least one opportunity and sometimes multiple opportunities to catch a meteoric rise at a low-risk entry point. Timing the entry point is

critical. Time your entry incorrectly and you will be stopped out unnecessarily or lose big if the stock turns around and you fail to sell. Time the entry correctly during a bull market and you could be at a profit right away and on your way to a big gain.

5. **Exit points.** Not all stocks that display superperformance characteristics will result in gains. Many will not work out even if you place your buys at the correct point. This is why you must establish stop-loss points to force you out of losing positions to protect your account. Conversely, at some point your stock must be sold to realize a profit. The end of what once was a superperformance phase needs to be identified to keep what you've made.

The SEPA ranking process can be summarized as follows:

1. Stocks must first meet my Trend Template (see Chapter 5) to be considered a potential SEPA candidate.

2. Stocks that meet the Trend Template are then screened through a series of filters that are based on earnings, sales and margin growth, relative strength, and price volatility. Approximately 95 percent of all stocks that qualify under the Trend Template fail to pass through this screen.

3. The remaining stocks are scrutinized for similarities to my Leadership Profile to determine whether they are in line with specific fundamental and technical factors exhibited by historical models of past superperformers. This stage removes most of the remaining companies, leaving a much narrower list of investment ideas for an even closer review and evaluation.

4. The final stage is a manual review. A narrowed list of candidates is examined individually and scored according to a "relative prioritizing" ranking process that takes into consideration the following characteristics:

- Reported earnings and sales

- Earnings and sales surprise history

- Earnings per share (EPS) growth and acceleration

- Revenue growth and acceleration

- Company-issued guidance

- Revisions of analysts' earnings estimates

- Profit margins

- Industry and market position

- Potential catalysts (new products and services or industry- or company-specific developments)

- Performance compared with other stocks in same sector

- Price and trading volume analysis

- Liquidity risk

The SEPA ranking process is focused on identifying the potential for the following:

1. Future earnings and sales surprises and positive estimate revisions

2. Institutional volume support (significant buying demand)

3. Rapid price appreciation based on a supply/demand imbalance (lack of selling versus buying)

PROBABILITY CONVERGENCE

I developed SEPA to identify precisely the point at which I can place a trade to have the lowest risk and the highest potential for reward. My goal is to purchase a stock and be at a profit immediately. To accomplish this, I take into account all the relevant fundamental, technical, and market factors and pinpoint the position at which there is a supportive convergence. **I execute a trade only at the point of alignment across the spectrum with regard to company fundamentals, stock price, and volume activity as well as overall market conditions.** I want to see these factors converge like four cars arriving at the same time at a four-way intersection. The SEPA method stacks supporting probabilities to produce that alignment.

Virtually every big winning stock exhibits very specific and measurable criteria before making its big moves. In their superperformance days, these stocks have distinguishing characteristics—whether a new product, an innovative service, or some kind of fundamental change—that enables the company to make money at a superior or accelerated rate and in some cases for an extended period. As a result, the shares of these companies experience significant price appreciation by attracting institutional buying. You don't have to know everything about a company or the market; however, you need to know the right things. By putting all these elements together—fundamental, technical, qualitative, and market tone—and demanding that stocks be able to cross multiple hurdles, you will be far more likely to identify something exceptional. The collective value of these parameters is greater than the sum of their parts.

Superperformance Traits

Over the years, I've concluded that most superperformance stocks have common identifiable characteristics. In the majority of cases, decent earnings were already on the table. In fact, the majority of superperformance stocks already had periods of outperformance in terms of fundamentals as well as technical action before they made their biggest gains. More than 90 percent of superperformance stocks began their phenomenal price surges as the general market came out of a correction or bear market. Interestingly, very few stocks had superperformance phases during a bear market.

Superperformers Are Youthful

Generally, a superperformance phase occurs when a stock is relatively young, for example, during the first 10 years after the initial public offering (IPO). Many superperformers were private companies for many years before going public, and when they finally did, they had a proven track record of earnings and growth. Some superperformance companies already established successful product lines and brands before coming public.

During the bear market correction of the early 1990s, I focused on stocks that were holding up well and then moved into new high ground first off the market's low. Most of the names I traded were relatively unknown at the time. These stocks were propelled by characteristics such as big earnings growth and strong product demand. One example was US Surgical, which pioneered products such as the surgical staple and laparoscopic surgery. Software, computer peripheral, and technology-related stocks also performed well during that period, fueled by the boom in personal computing. Most investors shy away from names they have never heard of. This is exactly the opposite of what you should do if your goal is to find big stock market winners.

Size Matters

Most companies have their high-growth phase when they're relatively small and nimble. As they grow older, larger, and more mature, their growth begins to slow, as does the rate at which their stock prices appreciate. Superperformance stocks are often small-cap companies, although occasionally a big-cap name could see a surge in price after a turnaround or a period of depressed stock prices resulting from a bear market. Most of the time, however, it is a small-cap or a mid-cap stock that hits a period of accelerated growth, which in turn creates a superperformance price phase. Investors interested in superperformance should keep a constant lookout for small to medium-size companies in the growth stage of their life cycle (accelerating earning and sales). On balance, the growth of earnings and sales and, more important, the stock price is usually more rapid for a small to medium-size company than for a larger, mature company. Large companies usually have proven track records of execution. With smaller companies it's important in most cases to confirm that they're already profitable and have proved that their business model can be scaled and duplicated.

Look for candidates with a relatively small total market capitalization and amount of shares outstanding. All things being equal, a small-cap company will have the potential to appreciate more than a large-cap, based on the supply of stock available. It will take far less demand to move the stock of a small company with a comparatively small share float than a large-cap candidate.

This realization can also help you develop realistic expectations about the profit side of the equation. Large-cap companies are not going to make large-scale price advances the way a younger, smaller company will. There are times when a big-cap stock will be depressed because of a bear market or a temporary economic hardship, which may provide the opportunity to buy a company such as Coca-Cola or American Express or Walmart at the beginning of a decent price move as it recovers. Generally speaking, though, if a large-cap company advances rapidly in a short period, I'm inclined to take profits on it more quickly than I would with a smaller, faster-growing company that may have the potential to double or even triple in a number of months.

STOCK SCREENING

Since the 1980s, I have been using computer assisted screening as a way to narrow down a tremendous amount of information—as many as 10,000 stocks daily—to produce a manageable list of candidates that meet some minimum criteria to be studied further. Today, there are many screening tools available for the investor. Here are a few suggestions on screening.

When you are conducting quantitative analysis (stock screening), keeping it simple will serve you better than using a complicated model. You must be careful not to put too much into each screen. Otherwise, you may inadvertently eliminate good candidates that meet all your criteria except for one. For example, let's say you want to select stocks that exhibit a certain level of earnings, market cap, estimate revisions, and so forth, until you have 12 lines of criteria. If a stock meets 11 but misses by a hair on the twelfth, you will never see that stock. Remember, if you have 100 items in your criteria, a stock needs to miss only 1 to be filtered out even though the other 99 are met.

A better approach is to run separate screens that are based on smaller lists of compatible criteria, for example, one screen for relative price strength and trend and a separate fundamental screen that is based on earnings and sales. Often, as you run isolated screens, you will see some of the same names recurring, whereas a few names will appear on only one list. Remember, computers are great for weeding out noise and pointing your research in the right direction; however, if you want consistent superperformance, you will need to roll up your sleeves and do some old-fashioned manual analysis. That's the interesting part of trading, and that's what makes it fun and rewarding.

Make a Commitment to an Approach

You don't need a PhD in math or physics to be successful in the stock market, just the right knowledge, a good work ethic, and discipline. The SEPA methodology was developed after decades of searching, testing, and going back to the drawing board countless times to uncover what actually works. It has been time-tested and proved effective in the real world with real results. You, too, will go through your own trial-and-error period: window-shopping and trying various concepts and approaches to the stock market, whether value, growth, fundamental, technical, or some combination. In the end, to succeed, you will need to settle on an approach that makes sense to you. Most important, you must commit to perfecting and refining your understanding of that methodology and its execution. A stock trading strategy is like a marriage; if you're not faithful, you probably won't have a good outcome. It takes time and dedication, but your objective should be to become a specialist in your approach to the market.

Although strategy is important, it's not as critical as knowledge and the discipline to apply and adhere to your rules. A trader who really knows the strengths and weaknesses of his or her strategy can do significantly better than someone who knows only a little about a superior strategy. Of course, the ideal situation would be to know a lot about a great strategy. That should be your ultimate goal.

CHAPTER 4

VALUE COMES AT A PRICE

It's far better to buy a wonderful company at a fair price than a fair
company at a wonderful price.

—*Warren Buffett*

WHEN YOU THINK OF VALUE in the traditional sense, bargains
immediately spring to mind: something once priced higher
now is priced lower. It seems logical. Growth stock investing, however, can
turn this definition on its head. In the stock market, what appears cheap
could actually be expensive and what looks expensive or too high may turn
out to be the next superperformance stock. The simple reality is that value
comes at a price.

THE P/E RATIO: OVERUSED AND MISUNDERSTOOD

Every day, armies of analysts and Wall Street pros churn out thousands of
opinions about stock values. This stock is overvalued; that one is a bargain. What is the basis of many of these valuation calls? Often it's the price/
earnings ratio (P/E), a stock's price expressed as a multiple of the company's earnings. A great amount of incorrect information has been written
about the P/E ratio. Many investors rely too heavily on this popular formula
because of a misunderstanding or a lack of knowledge. **Although it may
come as a surprise to you, historical analyses of superperformance stocks
suggest that by themselves P/E ratios rank among one of the most useless
statistics on Wall Street.**

The standard P/E ratio reflects historical results and does not take into account the most important element for stock price appreciation: the future. Sure, it's possible to use earnings estimates to calculate a forward-looking P/E ratio, but if you do, you're relying on estimates that are opinions and often turn out to be wrong. If a company reports disappointing earnings that fail to meet or beat the estimates, analysts will revise their earnings projections downward. As a result, the forward-looking denominator—the E in P/E—will shrink, and assuming the P remains constant, the ratio will rise. This is why it's important to concentrate on companies that are reporting strong earnings, which then trigger upward revisions in earnings estimates. Strong earnings growth will make a stock a better value.

BOTTOM FISHERS' BLISS

Some analysts will recommend that you buy a stock that has had a severe decline. The justification may be that the P/E is at or near the low end of its historical range. In many instances, however, such price adjustments antici-

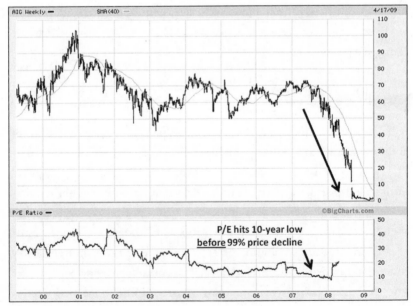

Figure 4.1   **American Intl Group (AIG) 1999–2000**

pate poor earnings reports. When quarterly results are finally released and a company misses analysts' estimates or reports a loss, the P/E moves back up (in some cases it skyrockets), which may cause the stock price to adjust downward even further. This was the case for Morgan Stanley (MS/NYSE) in late 2007. The stock price fell and drove the P/E to a 10-year low. Morgan later reported disappointing negative year-over-year earnings comparisons, and the P/E ratio promptly soared to more than *120* times earnings. With earnings deteriorating and the stock selling at a P/E of 120, the stock was suddenly severely overvalued. The share price plunged even further to under $7. The cause of Morgan Stanley's decline was an industrywide financial crisis, and by 2008 the P/E ratios of Bank America, Citigroup, and AIG all hit 10-year lows, along with those of many others in the banking and financial sector. Within 12 months, all three stocks plunged more than 90 percent.

The Cheap Trap

Buying a cheap stock is like a trap hand in poker; it's hard to get away from. When you buy a stock solely because it's cheap, it's difficult to sell if it moves against you because then it's even cheaper, which is the reason you bought it in the first place. The cheaper it gets, the more attractive it becomes based on the "it's cheap" rationale. This is the type of thinking that gets investors in big trouble. Most investors look for bargains instead of looking for leaders, and more often than not they get what they pay for.

Don't Pass on High P/E Stocks

It is normal for growth stocks to fetch a premium to the market; this is especially true if a company is increasing its earnings rapidly. Shares of fast-growing companies can trade at multiples of three or four times the overall market. In fact, high growth leaders can command even higher premiums in times when growth stocks are in favor relative to value stocks. Even during periods when growth is not in favor, they can sell at a significant premium to the market.

In many cases, stocks with superperformance potential will sell at what appears to be an unreasonably high P/E ratio. This scares away many amateur investors. When the growth rate of a company is extremely high, traditional valuation measures based on the P/E are of little help in determining overvaluation. However, stocks with high P/E ratios should be studied and considered as potential purchases, particularly if you find that something new and exciting is going on with the company and there's a catalyst that can lead to explosive earnings growth. It's even better if the company or its business is misunderstood or underfollowed by analysts.

Internet providers were a great example. When Yahoo! was at the forefront of one of the greatest technological changes since the telephone, I was asked in a television interview if I thought the Internet would survive. Can you imagine the Internet failing to exist? Not today. But in the early to middle 1990s you might have had a different view, as many did. That period was precisely when Internet technology stocks were making new 52-week highs and trading at what appeared to be absurd valuations.

Most of the best growth stocks seldom trade at a low P/E ratio. In fact, many of the biggest winning stocks in history traded at more than 30 or 40 times earnings *before* they experienced their largest advance. It only makes sense that faster-growing companies sell at higher multiples than slower-growing companies. If you avoid stocks just because the P/E or share price seems too high, you will miss out on many of the biggest market movers. The really exciting, fast-growing companies with big potential are *not* going to be found in the bargain bin. You don't find top-notch merchandise at the dollar store. As a matter of fact, the really great companies are almost always going to appear expensive, and that's precisely why most investors miss out.

HIGH GROWTH BAFFLES THE ANALYSTS

> You might recall when Mark [Minervini] was here last in mid-October [1998] he recommended Yahoo!, which is up 100 percent since then. . . .
>
> —*Ron Insana, CNBC interview, November 1998*

Wall Street has little idea what P/E ratio to put on companies growing at huge rates. It's extremely difficult, if not impossible, to predict how long a growth phase will last and what level of deceleration will occur over a particular time frame when one is dealing with a dynamic new leader or new industry. Many superperformance stocks tend to move to extreme valuations and leave analysts in awe as their prices continue to climb into the stratosphere in spite of what appears to be a ridiculous valuation. Missing out on these great companies is due to misunderstanding the way Wall Street works and therefore concentrating on the wrong price drivers.

In June 1997, I bought shares of Yahoo! when the stock was trading at *938* times earnings. Talk about a high P/E! Every institutional investor I mentioned the stock to said, "No way—Ya-WHO?" The company was virtually unknown at the time, but Yahoo! was leading a new technological revolution: the Internet. The potential for what was then a new industry was widely misunderstood at the time. Yahoo! shares advanced an amazing 7,800 percent in just 29 months, and the P/E expanded to more than 1,700 times earnings. Even if you got only a piece of that advance, you could have made a boatload.

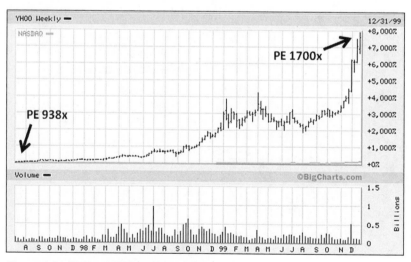

Figure 4.2   **Yahoo (YHOO) 1997–1999**

What's High? What's Low?

> Jan. 9 Minervini bought Taser (TASR/Nasdaq), a company that
> makes Taser guns—nonlethal weapons for police departments. He
> spotted its potential using his proprietary methodology, "Specific
> Entry Point Analysis" (SEPA). He then rode the stock up 121% in
> only six weeks.
>
> —BusinessWeek Online, *May 10, 2004*

Everybody knows the old adage "buy low and sell high." It makes sense—
like going to a store to find something on sale. However, buying low and
selling high has little to do with the current stock price. How high or low
the price is relative to where it was previously is *not* the determining factor
in whether a stock will go higher still. A stock trading at $60 can go to $260,
just as a stock trading at $2 can go to $1 or even to $0. Was Yahoo! too high
when it boasted a P/E ratio of 938? How about TASER (TASR/NASDAQ)
in January 2004, just before it advanced 300 percent in three months; was it

Figure 4.3   **TASER Intl. (TASR) 2004**

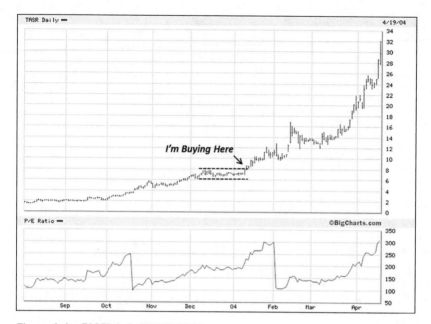

Figure 4.4   **TASER Intl. (TASR) 2004**

TASER emerged from a tight four-week consolidation.

too high trading at a P/E ratio of more than 200 times earnings? Conversely, AIG appeared to be a bargain when its P/E hit a 10-year low in early 2008; the stock fell 99 percent before the year was finished.

THERE'S A REASON A FERRARI COSTS MORE THAN A HYUNDAI

If you want to buy a high-performance car such as a Ferrari, you're going to pay a premium price. The same thing applies to high-performance stocks. The top 100 best-performing small- and mid-cap stocks of 1996 and 1997 had an average P/E of 40. Their P/Es grew further to an average of 87 and a median of 65. Relatively speaking, their initially "expensive" P/Es turned out to be extremely cheap. These top stocks averaged a gain of 421 percent from buy point to peak. The P/E of the S&P 500 ranged from 18 to 20 during that period.

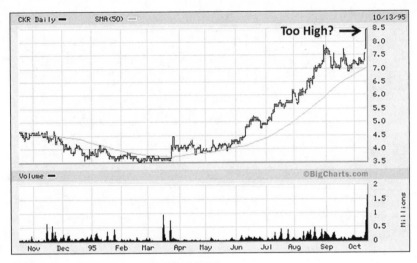

Figure 4.5   **CKE Restaurants (CKR) 1995**

On October 13, 1995, CKR emerged into new high ground trading at a 55x earnings.

Figure 4.6   **CKE Restaurants (CKR) 1998**

From the point CKR emerged into new high ground on October 13, 1995, the stock advanced more than 400% in 28 months, but the P/E ratio fell because earnings grew even faster.

Value investors often shy away from stocks with high price/earnings multiples. They won't touch a stock whose P/E is much higher than, say, that of the S&P 500 index. Savvy growth players know that you often have to pay more for the best goods in the market. Consider the example of CKE Restaurants, which sported a relatively high P/E just before the stock price took off. CKE Restaurants emerged into new high ground in extremely fast trading on October 13, 1995. Right before its breakout, the stock had a P/E of 55, or 2.9 times the S&P's P/E of 18.9. The company had scored triple-digit profit growth in the two most recent quarters. Analysts saw the operator of Carl's Jr. burger shops increasing profit by a whopping 700 percent from year-ago levels in the upcoming quarter. The stock climbed for 103 weeks. It finally peaked near $41 in October 1997 for a 412 percent gain. During its price advance, CKE averaged a spectacular 175 percent growth in earnings from 1995 to 1997. Its P/E fell to 47, or 1.8 times the P/E of the S&P.

Apollo Group (APOL)

Most of the time money in stocks is lost not because the P/E was too high but because earnings did not grow at a high enough rate to sustain expectations; the growth potential of the company was misjudged. The ideal situation is to find a company whose growth prospects warrant a high P/E: a company that can deliver the goods—and the longer it can maintain strong growth, the better.

Consider the example of Apollo Group. From mid-2001 through 2004, the P/E ratio for Apollo was virtually unchanged despite a 200 percent rally in the price of the stock. Why did the P/E remain at the same level as it was several years earlier even though the stock price soared? Because earnings kept pace with the stock's price appreciation. If a company can deliver strong earnings as fast as or even faster than its stock price appreciates, an initial high valuation may prove to be very cheap. Apollo Group went public in December 1994 with a market value of only $112 million. Apollo met or beat Wall Street estimates for 45 consecutive quarters. As you can probably imagine, this led the company's stock price to superperformance status.

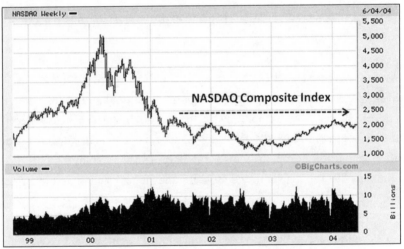

Figure 4.7   **Apollo Group (APOL) 1999–2004**
In 2001 APOL was trading at 60x earnings; by 2004 the price advanced 200 percent, but the P/E ratio remained at 60x due to earnings growth keeping pace.

From 2000 to 2004, Apollo Group's stock advanced more than 850 percent. During the same period, the Nasdaq Composite Index was down 60 percent.

CROCS MANIA

As the plastic clogs originally meant for gardeners and boaters became a fashion rage, everybody started wearing Crocs, and the popularity spilled over into the stock. Crocs (CROX/NASDAQ) shares boasted a P/E of more than 60 times earnings, *before* the price blasted higher. But fads come and fads go, and perhaps the world is finding that when it comes to Crocs, the shoe no longer fits. The P/E ratio for Crocs contracted from April 2006 to October 2007 as earnings grew faster than the stock's price appreciation. If you had bought Crocs when shares were trading at more than 60x earnings—the most expensive P/E in its history—you could have reaped a return of 700 percent on your money in only 20 months. If you had waited for the stock to trade at a more reasonable valuation and bought when the stock traded near its historical low P/E, you would have lost 99 percent of your capital in less than a year. Regardless of one's opinion, the market always has the last word.

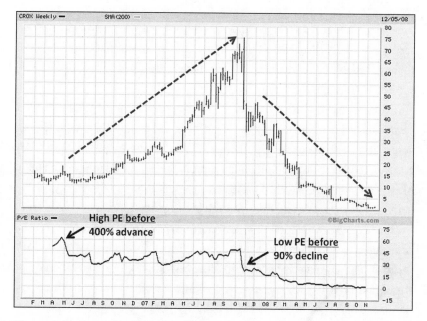

Figure 4.8   **Crocs (CROX) 2006–2008**

VALUE DOESN'T MOVE STOCK PRICES; PEOPLE DO

> Many people get confused: they think we are trading the actual companies themselves, that the pieces of paper we are trading, investing, owning, are some sort of redemptive right, a coupon that will give you certain cents off, or an ownership right that will allow you to have a chunk of the brick and mortar if not the cash in the treasury of the joint; untrue. These are, in the end, simply pieces of paper, to be bought, sold, or manipulated up and down by those with more capital than others . . . the fundamentals of the company play only a part in what moves the stock up or down.
>
> —*Jim Cramer*

Contrary to what many believe, the stock market doesn't trade on the basis of objective, mathematical measures of "intrinsic value" such as P/E ratios or a stock's price-to-book ratio. If that were the case, slavish devotion to computer models would consistently pump out winners and fund managers would regularly beat the market averages. If analyzing balance sheets were the Holy Grail for stock investing, accountants would be the world's greatest traders. Neither is the case. There is no magic formula or mechanistic model that can reliably generate excess returns in perpetuity. Everything is relative, subjective, and dynamic.

Valuation methods that work wonderfully during certain market conditions will fail miserably during others. Every stock carries a growth assumption, which constantly changes. These assumptions are in large part constructed and based on personal opinion. Stock prices move on the basis of what people think. Whether it's an opinion about a balance sheet, the company's assets, a hot new product, an exciting new industry, the P/E ratio, the book value, future growth prospects, or whatever, ultimately it's perception that motivates investors and creates price movement. **Value doesn't move stock prices; people do by placing buy orders. Value is only part of the equation. Ultimately, you need demand.**

Only the *perception* of value can influence people to buy, not the mere reading of a valuation metric. Without a willing buyer, stocks of even the highest-quality companies are worthless pieces of paper. The sooner you realize this, the better off you will be as a speculator.

In Search of Value

In 1987, *Irises*, a painting by Vincent van Gogh, sold for $49 million, a world record for a work of art. The painting changed hands at a price more than double what it had been expected to reach. The sale was also accomplished in what may have been record time in light of the figures involved; the bidding rose from a starting point of $15 million to reach the final sale price in less than two minutes.

Analysts and investors search continually for some intrinsic value that differs from a stock's current market price. Often that quest boils down to relating a stock's price to its earnings. **Concluding that a stock is overvalued because it sells for 65 times earnings is like saying that a van Gogh painting selling at $49 million at auction is overvalued because the paint and canvas cost only 40 bucks.** The price of a van Gogh has nothing to do with its intrinsic value; the painting sells on the basis of its perceived value, which is directly affected by the demand for a one-of-a-kind piece of art.

Wall Street commonly uses two measures for valuing stocks. One method involves comparing a stock's P/E ratio with that of its respective industry group or that of the overall market (S&P 500 Index, etc.). Often this leads to mistaken conclusions that laggard stocks are a value and market leaders are overpriced. More often than not, the market leader that appears expensive actually turns out to be cheaper in the long run than the lower-P/E, poorer-performing stocks in the group.

The other method is to compare a stock's P/E with its own historical range for a certain period. The argument goes that if the P/E is near the low end of its range or below the P/E of its industry group or the market in general, the stock must be cheap. The stock may look cheap, but the market may be marking down the merchandize for a good reason; indeed, that discount might presage wholesale write-offs.

If tomorrow the price of a stock you own fell 25 percent from your purchase price, would you feel better knowing that the P/E had fallen below its industry average? Of course not. You should be asking yourself: Do the sellers know something I don't? Stocks adjust to new circumstances every day, yet many investors keep holding their declining shares because they consider the stock to be a bargain. Some advisors will even tell you to buy more shares, throwing good money after bad. Meanwhile, your stock continues to get clobbered, and you keep losing money.

Some of the best value investors were down 60 percent or more in the bear market that started in 2007. Their experience of buying and holding "solid" companies, which had worked so well for so long, led to complacent behavior that resulted in large losses. In 2008, the overall market suffered heavy losses, with the Value Line (Geometric) Index finishing the year down 48.7 percent. The Dow was down 34 percent for the year. However, the worst-performing Value Line categories were low price to sales, down 66.9 percent; low price to book value, down 68.8 percent; and low P/E ratio, down 70.9 percent. **The bottom line: value investing does not protect you.**

No Magic Number

As history has shown, there is no common denominator or appropriate level when it comes to a P/E ratio and superperformance stocks. The P/E can start out relatively low or high. My suggestion is to forget this metric and seek out companies with the greatest potential for earnings growth. Most of the time, a true market leader is a much better value than a laggard despite its higher P/E multiple. Crossing a stock off your list because its P/E seems too high will result in your missing out on what could be the next great stock market winner.

The 25 top-performing stocks from 1995 to 2005 had an average P/E ratio of 33x, ranging from a low of 8.6x to a high of 223x. The three best performers in the group—American Eagle Outfitters, Penn National Gaming,

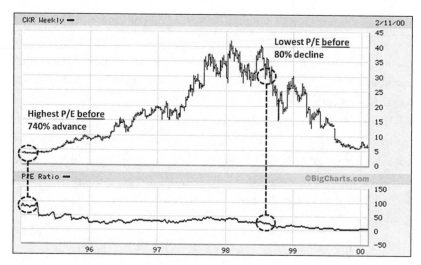

Figure 4.9   **CKE Restaurants (CKR) 1995–2000**

and Celgene—sported P/E ratios of 29x, 11x, and 223x, respectively, *before* they made their big price advances. All three saw their stock prices rise at a 40 percent or better compounded annual growth rate over the 10-year period. In early 1995, CKE Restaurants traded at a relatively high P/E ratio *before* staging a massive rally and then at a relatively low P/E before experiencing a major decline.

WARNING: THE SUPERLOW P/E

One of the worst trades I ever made was Bethlehem Steel trading at 2x earnings. I said "How low can it go?" It went to zero.

—*Jim Cramer*

Although I don't concern myself too much with the P/E ratio in my search for superperformance stocks, there is one situation that gets my attention. As a rule of thumb, I'm very reluctant to buy shares of a company trading at an excessively low P/E, especially if the stock is at or near a 52-week low in price. A stock with an exceptionally low P/E ratio can turn out to be real trouble. A stock trading at a multiple of three, four, or five times earnings or at a number far below the prevailing industry multiple could have a fundamental problem. The future prospects of the company may be questionable; earnings could be headed much lower. The company might even be headed toward bankruptcy.

Remember, the market is a discounting mechanism that trades on the future, not the past. Just as you can't drive a car by looking only in the rearview mirror, you shouldn't run a stock portfolio on backward-referencing valuation metrics. I would rather own a stock that's reporting strong earnings trading at a relatively high P/E ratio than a stock showing signs of trouble trading at a very low P/E.

P/E Deception

If you compare a stock's share price with its P/E ratio, often you will see that a depressed P/E coincides with a depressed stock price and vice versa. The same could be said about an overbought/oversold technical indicator such as the stochastic oscillator. On the surface, both of these popular metrics appear to have a degree of accuracy at turning points because the eye is drawn to peaks and troughs. However, this 20/20 vision is usually a gift of hindsight. In real time, the eye is not very good at filtering out all the noise and static between the upturns and downturns. In addition, what is mostly ignored or misunderstood is the varying time frames spent in the direction of the countertrend reading. For example, one stock can remain overvalued for months whereas another stock can remain at a similar valuation for years before a change in direction takes place.

Trying to buy oversold conditions and sell overbought conditions as a trading strategy is risky business. Trading with disregard for a strong directional trend will ultimately lead to buying into a precipitous decline. Similarly, buying stocks simply because the P/E is relatively low and selling because the P/E seems too high produces poor results time and time again. Although overbought and oversold conditions as well as high and low P/Es can exist at turning points, stocks can also have extreme high and low readings in a directional fashion just before major advances and declines. Major market declines always plunge to deeply oversold readings, and roaring bull markets storm through early overbought conditions while advancing much farther.

THE BROKEN LEADER SYNDROME

A common affliction among many investors, including some professionals, is what I call the *broken leader syndrome*. Here's how it works. Investors who refused to buy a dynamic new leader when it was emerging—*before* it skyrocketed—become interested after that stock has topped and broken down in price. Usually this occurs during a stage 4 decline. These people buy stocks that were previously expensive, thinking they will go back up.

The broken leader syndrome affects investors who weren't able to spot stocks such as Yahoo!, Amazon, and Apollo Group before their biggest price moves. They weren't on board when one of these incredible stocks made a huge run of several thousand percent. Then the stock gets slammed. Now these investors think they're on to something. With a former highflier well off its peak, these latecomers to the party think the stock looks good and is now a bargain.

They use all sorts of reasons, such as "it's trading near the low end of its historic range" and "it's trading at only 20 times earnings and has a growth rate of 40 percent." Worse yet, they'll say, "It's down 70 percent. How low can it go?"

With all their rationalizing, they ignore the supreme fundamental: the market's judgment. They stayed away when the stock was a market leader (probably because it looked expensive), and now they fail to recognize a broken leader. When a leader tops, more often than not the stock price is discounting a future slowdown in growth, which makes it no bargain at all.

Sun Microsystems is a good example of a broken leader play. The stock had an incredible price advance during the 1990s and then topped out in late 2000. Investors who were waiting for this powerhouse to correct, or "come in," so that they could buy it may have been elated to see the stock off 75 percent from its high in 2001. Unfortunately, the party was over, and a year later Sun's stock fell a further 80 percent. Eight years later, investors

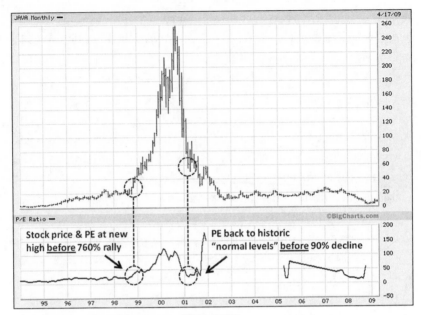

Figure 4.10   **Sun Microsystems 1994–2009**

who bought the stock at the discounted 75 percent off price not only didn't make money, they actually lost 99 percent of their capital.

Here's a common misperception when a stock has a precipitous drop. A stock that falls from $100 to $25 has declined by 75 percent. Since a stock can drop only 100 percent, the thinking is that the risk is only an additional 25 percent, right? Wrong! If you buy the stock at $25, you could lose another 75 percent if it falls to $6.26. And if you buy it at $6.26, you could lose yet another 75 percent if it falls to $1.56. After all, your money in the stock is always 100 percent.

P/E Ratio Is a Barometer of Sentiment

By themselves, P/E ratios aren't very helpful in determining the potential direction of a stock's price. The P/E ratio tells you what the market is willing to pay for a company's earnings at the current time. Think of the P/E as a barometer that measures the level of expectation. This is why many growth stocks experience P/E expansion during the growth phase; expectations keep getting higher as the company's performance expands.

Of course, there comes a time when the stock's prospects darken and business conditions change. The company may then be considered overvalued. At that point, perceptions change and the stock price will adjust to reflect the new set of circumstances. **I use the P/E ratio as a sentiment gauge that gives me some perspective about investor expectation. Generally speaking, a high P/E means there are high expectations and a low P/E means there are lower expectations.**

Seek out companies with the greatest potential for earnings growth. Companies growing revenues at a rapid pace are your best choice. Look for new emerging trends that can translate into mass expansion: trends that are scalable. Concentrate on entrepreneurially managed companies with exciting things going on (a catalyst), and you'll eventually latch on to some big winners. The current P/E ratio at which a company trades is only a minor consideration compared with the potential for earnings growth. Growth stocks are driven by *growth*.

THE PEG RATIO

The price/earnings to growth (PEG) ratio is calculated by dividing the P/E multiple by a company's projected earnings per share growth rate over the next year. For example, if a stock is trading at 20 times earnings and has a growth rate of 40 percent, the PEG ratio will be 0.5 (20 ÷ 40). The company is trading at half its growth rate.

The theory is that if the resulting value is less than 1, the stock may be undervalued; if the PEG ratio is over 1, the stock may be overvalued. The farther the value is from 1, the stronger the signal is. In general, if a company's earnings growth rate matches or exceeds its P/E multiple, investors using the PEG ratio for valuation may consider the stock fairly valued or even undervalued. If the P/E multiple significantly exceeds its growth rate, however, the stock will be considered risky and overvalued according to this school of thought. Many analysts intent on buying growth at a reasonable price (GARP) use PEG ratios in various forms.

The point at which a stock is deemed undervalued or overvalued can vary, depending on the analyst. Some investors look to pare their holdings in a stock as soon as its price multiple exceeds its growth rate by any margin.

Like its P/E cousin, the PEG ratio can exclude some of the most dynamic and profitable companies from a candidate buy list. The PEG ratio is limiting on the two sides of the equation that are most valuable: when a stock has an exceptionally high or low P/E. Should a stock with a growth rate of 2 percent trade at two times earnings? Probably not. However, valuing a high-technology stock such as Yahoo!, which traded at 938 times earnings, was nearly impossible using traditional valuation measures. Another drawback of the PEG ratio as I see it is that many of the broken leader plays are attractive with this method. This can entice you to buy into a stock that has put in a major top and headed for negative surprises.

GAUGING P/E EXPANSION

Because P/E is a ratio, its value will be affected if either the numerator or the denominator changes. For example, the P/E will expand if a stock's price (numerator) rises faster than the company's earnings (denominator). Both numbers, however, can be moving targets, particularly when a company has good potential for increasing its earnings and also is attracting buyers who are accumulating the stock, which pushes the price higher.

To illustrate, let's say Company A is trading at 25 times its earnings for a P/E of 25. If it reports earnings that are 20 percent higher and the stock price remains essentially unchanged, the P/E will drop to 20.83 times earnings. If the stock price jumps 20 percent on the earnings news, the P/E will remain the same at 25 times earnings. Over time, as a stock grows more and more popular and the price rises consistently, its P/E ratio can expand as the stock's price appreciates at a faster rate than its earnings growth. If the stock rises significantly over 12 to 24 months and the P/E expands by 100 to 200 percent, doubling or tripling from where it started near the beginning or from the bottom of the major price move, it's possible that the price move is in its later stage and is getting too widely recognized.

Historical study of superperformance stocks shows that the average P/E increased between 100 and 200 percent on average (or two to three times) from the beginning until the end of major price moves. This information can be used in two ways. First, you can get an idea of a stock's potential. You can estimate what it might sell for as an average best-case scenario within a year or two down the road from your initial purchase price, that is, if you're buying a dynamic leader in a bull market. You could estimate future earnings and apply the expanded P/E number to get a rough idea of the stock's theoretical potential.

Second, you can gain some perspective on how much of the company's good fortune has already been discounted by gauging how much P/E expansion has taken place already. Let's say you buy a stock with a P/E of 20 at its initial breakout from a sound base. Multiply 20 by 2 to 3 to see what the ratio could rise to. That gives you 40 to 60. You hope that the stock continues to rally. Though it's always prudent to look for sell signals, pay extra attention once the P/E nears 2x and especially around 2.5x to 3x or greater. It could top soon afterward. If this occurs, look for signs of decelerating growth and signs of weakness in the stock price as your signal to reduce your position or sell it out.

In the 1990s, as Home Depot stock became an institutional favorite, rampant enthusiasm ran the stock price up well ahead of its earnings growth. Home Depot's P/E expanded from the mid-20s to 70x earnings in just two years after the stock bottomed from its 1990 bear market low. A period of sideways consolidation took place for the next four years while the

Figure 4.11   **Home Depot (HD) 1988–2008**

earnings played catch-up with the stock price. Then, in 2000, Home Depot's P/E ratio expanded from 25x in 1997 to 75x. The stock topped shortly afterward.

What Does All This Mean?

As we've seen, what constitutes a high or low P/E is far less clear—or important—than you might have thought. What should you take away from this discussion? Should you ignore stocks that trade at relatively low P/Es and buy only those with high ratios? Not necessarily. The bigger point is that the P/E ratio doesn't have much predictive value for finding elite superperformance stocks. There is no magic number when it comes to the P/E. In fact, the P/E is far less important than a company's potential for earnings growth.

Stop worrying about the P/E ratio. If you have a company delivering the goods as Apollo Group did, earning 40 percent per annum for four or five consecutive years, whatever the initial P/E was is irrelevant; the P/E takes care of itself. Leave the overintellectualizing and complex theories to the professors and academicians and the valuation tactics to the Wall Street analysts. An oceanographer may be able to explain all the complexities of waves, tides, water currents, and undertows. When it comes to riding a wave, however, I'll put my money on a 13-year-old kid from Malibu, California, who knows none of those facts but has surfed all his life and has an intuitive feel for the water. As a superperformance trader, you learn to spot and ride trends to big profits and learn to detect when once-advantageous trends appear to be breaking down. Often, once the why becomes known, profits taken or losses incurred will already be a matter of history. Valuing a company on intrinsic value is not trading stocks; it's buying assets. Your goal is to make money consistently, not accumulate a lockbox of assets that you really don't own—just pieces of paper that were made for trade.

CHAPTER 5

TRADING WITH THE TREND

I don't set trends. I just find out what they are and exploit them.

—*Dick Clark*

Y SUCCESS AS A STOCK TRADER relies on a combination of science and art. Mechanical signals backed by scientific research and intuitive feel are both important tools. In the stock market, few things are purely black or white. To succeed, an astute stock trader must learn to read between the lines and decipher and make decisions often on the basis of incomplete information. There are, however, certain characteristics that are not ambiguous or even open for interpretation. I call them *nonnegotiable criteria*.

When I am screening for superperformance stocks, my initial filter is rooted in strict qualifying criteria that are based purely on a stock's technical action and is designed to align my purchase with the prevailing primary trend. Once this initial criterion is met, I run "overlay screens" and look at the company's fundamentals to narrow the remaining universe of candidates. Simply put, no matter how good a company looks fundamentally, certain technical standards must be met for it to qualify as a buy candidate. For example, I will never go long a stock that is trading below its declining 200-day moving average (assuming 200 days of trading exist). No matter how attractive the earnings per share, revenue growth, cash flow, or return on equity may be, I won't consider buying a stock that is in a long-term downtrend. Why? I want to see some interest in the stock, preferably from big institutional investors. I'm not interested in being the first one to the party, but I do want to make sure there's a party going on. The goal is to eliminate stocks that are not worth my time so that I can focus on contenders that have the best chance of being the next superperformers. Buying stocks in long-term downtrends will significantly lower your odds of owning a big winner. However, if you want to increase the odds, you should focus on stocks that are in a confirmed uptrend.

Making Friends with the Trend

Newton's first law states that an object in motion continues in motion. Things in motion possess inertia. An analogous property characterizes the stock market: a trend in force tends to remain in force until something occurs to change it. In other words, the trend is your friend. Although this adage is familiar, some investors may not fully appreciate its wisdom. I remember when I first grasped this concept in a meaningful way.

In 1990, I attended an investment conference in New York City. On the roster of market gurus and prognosticators were Ned Davis, founder of the well-known institutional research firm Ned Davis Research, and Marty Zweig, publisher of the popular market newsletter *The Zweig Forecast*; Marty coined the phrase "the trend is your friend." One of the speakers who caught my attention not only for his colorful personality but also for his approach to the stock market was Stan Weinstein, who at the time published the stock market newsletter *The Professional Tape Reader*. Over lunch we had a chance to chat, and as Stan explained his method, he left me with a core concept that has stayed with me ever since.

Stan's approach was based on a timeless principle of the four stages that stocks go through, placing importance on knowing what stage a stock is in at any specific time. The ideal scenario, as Stan saw it, was to buy stocks when they are coming out of the first stage and beginning to make a run higher, which is the second stage. Then the objective is to sell them as they approach the peak of the cycle, which is the beginning of the third stage. The fourth stage, as you might guess, is a full-fledged decline that you want to avoid or during which you go short. I had previously read about Stan's approach in his book *Secrets for Profiting in Bull and Bear Markets* (McGraw-Hill, 1988). Although Stan wasn't the only one to use this type of four-stage approach, he was the first I heard speak about it. I went on to adopt this concept as part of my stock analysis.

SUPERPERFORMANCE AND STAGE ANALYSIS

Like all stocks, superperformance stocks go through stages. Over the course of my trading career, I've taken a keen interest in studying the cyclical and secular life cycles of stock prices. In particular, in examining the historical price performance of the most powerful market leaders over many market cycles, I could clearly see how they go through various stages. A stock would trade sideways for a while and then move up rapidly. Eventually, the rate of upward momentum would slow and become more erratic as the stock was under distribution and topping out. After a top came the decline. Sometimes, after the decline, the stock returned to a basing stage before eventually making another run upward. The succession of one stage to the next, through all four, could take several years. **What I found through my study of the biggest price performers was that virtually every superperformance stock made its big gain while in stage 2 of its price cycle.**

As interesting as it was to study the stages of stocks' price maturation in hindsight, that didn't help me determine in real time when stocks on my radar were in the optimal stage 2 phase. Moreover, I asked, What created the profitable stage 2 advance? Hunting for a key to identifying the advent of second stages, I plotted and overlaid the underlying fundamentals of superperformance stocks to see how they correlated with price movement. My objective was to see whether there was any cause and effect in the movement from stage to stage and, if so, what it was.

STOCK PRICE MATURATION: THE FOUR STAGES

My studies of big market winners gave me an in-depth view of each of the four stages of a stock's life cycle: from dormancy into growth to peak and then into decline. In addition to focusing on stock prices, I asked what was happening to trigger each of these phases. From a fundamental perspective, the cause almost always was linked to earnings: from lackluster performance to upside surprise and accelerating growth, eventually followed by decelerating growth and then disappointment. These underlying fundamental changes drove big institutional players into and out of stocks, phases that could readily be identified by the huge volume spikes that occurred during both the advancing stage and the subsequent decline. I identify these four stages on the basis of what is happening with the stock in terms of price action:

1. Stage 1—Neglect phase: consolidation

2. Stage 2—Advancing phase: accumulation

3. Stage 3—Topping phase: distribution

4. Stage 4—Declining phase: capitulation

STAGE 1—THE NEGLECT PHASE: CONSOLIDATION

Stage 1 is when nothing noteworthy is happening. The stock is in a period of neglect; few big players are paying attention to the stock, or at the very least, the market has not yet paid up for the company's shares. During stage 1, a company's earnings, sales, and margins may be lackluster or erratic along with its share price. There may also be an uncertain outlook for the company or its industry. Nothing electrifying is happening to push the stock out of its doldrums and attract the needed institutional volume support to move it decisively into a stage 2 uptrend.

Stage 1 can last for an extended period, from months to years. Stage 1 can also be caused by a poor overall market environment. During a bear market decline, even stocks with good fundamentals can mark time and do nothing or even decline along with the overall market. **You should avoid buying during stage 1 no matter how tempting it may be; even if the company's fundamentals look appealing, wait and buy only in stage 2.** Remember Newton's first law, the law of inertia. An object in motion tends to stay in motion, and one at rest continues at rest. If your stock is dead in the water, guess where it's most likely to stay until something significant changes. You're not going to achieve superperformance by sitting with dead merchandise. To compound capital at a rapid rate and achieve superperformance, it is vital that you avoid stage 1 and learn to spot where momentum is strong during stage 2.

STAGE 1 CHARACTERISTICS

- During stage 1, the stock price will move in a sideways fashion with a lack of any sustained price movement up or down.

- The stock price will oscillate around its 200-day (or 40-week) moving average. During that oscillation, it lacks any real trend, upward or downward. This dead in the water phase can last for months or even years.

- Often, this basing stage takes place after the stock price has declined during stage 4 for several months or more.

Figure 5.1   **Amgen (AMGN) in stage 1: 1987–1989**

- Volume will generally contract and be relatively light compared with the previous volume during the stage 4 decline.

No Bottom Picking Required

I can tell you from experience that attempting to bottom fish—trying to buy a stock at or near its bottom—will prove to be a frustrating and fruitless endeavor. Even if you are fortunate enough to pick the exact bottom, making significant headway usually requires sitting without much progress for months and in some cases years, because when you buy a stock near its bottom, it is in stage 4 or stage 1 and therefore by definition lacks upside momentum.

My goal is not to buy at the lowest or cheapest price but at the "right" price, just as the stock is ready to move significantly higher. Trying to pick a bottom is unnecessary and a waste of time; it misses the whole point. To achieve superperformance, you need to maximize the effects of compounding; thus, it's important to concentrate on stocks that move quickly after you buy them. You want to focus on stocks that are already moving in the direction of your trade. To accomplish this, you should wait for a stage 2 uptrend to develop *before* you invest.

Transition from Stage 1 to Stage 2

A stage 2 advance may begin with little or no warning; there are no major announcements or news. One thing is certain, however: a proper stage 2 will show significant volume as the stock is in strong demand on big up days and up weeks, and volume will be relatively light during pullbacks. There should *always* be a previous rally with an escalation in price of at least 25 to 30 percent off the 52-week low *before* you conclude that a stage 2 advance is under way and consider buying.

In the following figure, note that the 200-day moving average for Amgen has turned up and is in a definite uptrend. The 150-day moving average is above the 200-day moving average, and the stock is trading above both the 150-day and 200-day moving average during the markup phase. Note, too, the surging volume on the rallies, contrasted with lighter volume on pullbacks. For Amgen, by the time stage 2 was clearly under way, the

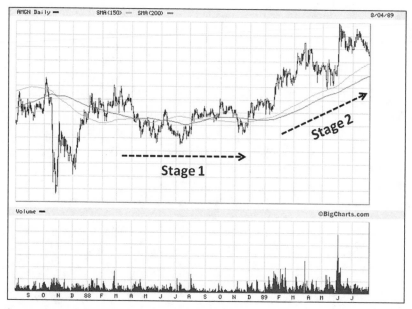

Figure 5.2a   **Daily price bars of Amgen (AMGN) transitioning from stage 1 to stage 2: 1987–1989**

stock price had already advanced more than 80 percent from its 52-week low. This would be the point at which I would *start* to consider a new purchase; any earlier lacks confirmation and is premature, meaning you run the risk of being stuck in dead money. Most amateurs would think the stock is too high and wish they had bought it when it was lower, using hindsight as a guide. That's why most amateurs don't make big money in stocks.

Transition Criteria

1. The stock price is above both the 150-day and the 200-day moving average.

2. The 150-day moving average is above the 200-day.

3. The 200-day moving average has turned up.

4. A series of higher highs and higher lows has occurred.

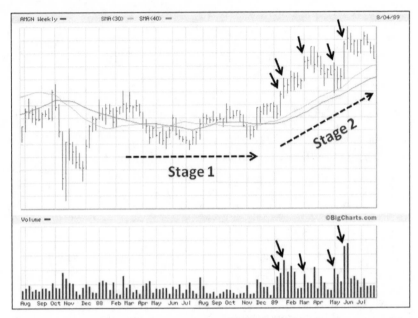

Figure 5.2b   **Weekly price bars of Amgen (AMGN) transitioning from stage 1 to stage 2: 1987–1989**

5. Large up weeks on volume spikes are contrasted by low-volume pullbacks.

6. There are more up weeks on volume than down weeks on volume.

Stage 2—The Advancing Phase: Accumulation

Although it may come without warning, a stage 2 advance can also be ignited by surprise news such as a beneficial regulatory change, a promising business outlook, or a new CEO whose vision could improve the company's prospects. Or perhaps it's a new company that suddenly attracts notice with a big earnings surprise that beat estimates.

As the proverbial wind shifts and is now clearly at your back, the stage 2 advance signals the potential for clear sailing ahead. With a buildup in earnings momentum (or in some instances earnings expectations), the stock price starts to escalate because of a surge in demand for shares as big institutions buy the stock in size. **A daily and weekly price and volume chart will show big up bars representing abnormally large volume on rallies, contrasted with lower volume on price pullbacks. These signs of accumulation should appear during every stage 2 advance.**

By the time stage 2 is under way, the stock has been moving upward in a stair-step pattern of higher highs and higher lows. The share price may have doubled or even tripled at this point; however, this may be only the beginning. The stock could still move substantially higher. If the company continues to deliver strong earnings, the growth rate will soon attract widespread attention and subsequent buying, especially if the company has reported several quarters of impressive earnings gains.

STAGE 2 CHARACTERISTICS

- The stock price is above its 200-day (40-week) moving average.

- The 200-day moving average itself is in an uptrend.

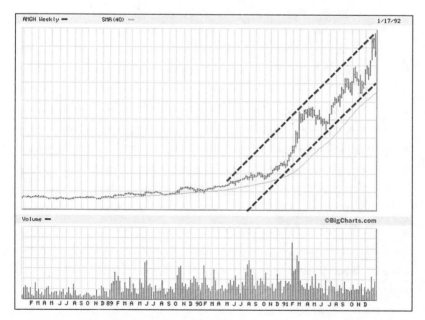

Figure 5.3   **Amgen (AMGN) in stage 2: 1992**

- The 150-day (30-week) moving average is above the 200-day (40-week) moving average.

- The stock price is in a clear uptrend, defined by higher highs and higher lows in a staircase pattern.

- Short-term moving averages are above long-term moving averages (e.g., the 50-day moving average is above the 150-day moving average).

- Volume spikes on big up days and big up weeks are contrasted by volume contractions during normal price pullbacks.

- There are more up days and up weeks on above-average volume than down days and down weeks on above-average volume.

STAGE 3—THE TOPPING PHASE: DISTRIBUTION

As the saying goes, all good things eventually come to an end. In the market, stocks cannot keep up the momentum indefinitely, churning out ever-increasing percentages of earnings growth. At some point, earnings, though still increasing, are going to rise by a smaller percentage. The stock price may still be edging its way higher, although it may be experiencing more high volume pullbacks and increasing volatility.

During stage 3, the stock is no longer under extreme accumulation; instead, it is changing hands from strong buyers to weaker ones. Smart money that bought early when the stock emerged onto the scene is now taking profits, selling into final signs of price strength. As that occurs, buyers on the other side of the transaction are weaker players who know about the stock because it has made such a dramatic run and captured headlines. In other words, the long trade in the stock has become crowded and too obvious. This distribution phase exhibits a topping pattern. Volatility increases markedly, and the stock becomes visibly more erratic relative to its previous stage 2 trading pattern.

Earnings estimates that have been continually ratcheted up on continued upside surprises will be too high to beat at some point. A company cannot keep beating estimates forever. At some point earnings per share (EPS) momentum will start to slow. Either the stock price will anticipate that change, trading lower than it did before the actual earnings event, or there will be several quarters of slowing earnings growth (deceleration) and then a breakdown in the stock price.

STAGE 3 CHARACTERISTICS

- Volatility increases, with the stock moving back and forth in wider, looser swings. Although the overall price pattern may look similar to stage 2, with the stock moving higher, the price movement is much more erratic.

- There is usually a major price break in the stock on an increase in volume. Often, it's the largest one-day decline since the beginning of the stage 2 advance. On a weekly chart, the stock may put in the

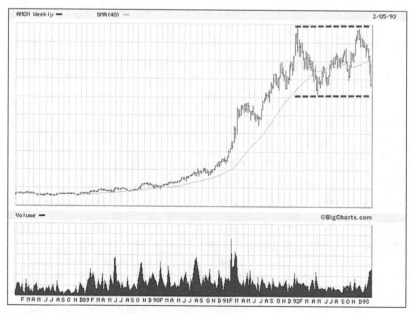

Figure 5.4   **Amgen (AMGN) in stage 3: 1993**

largest weekly decline since the beginning of the move. These price breaks almost always occur on overwhelming volume.

- The stock price may undercut its 200-day moving average. Price volatility around the 200-day (40-week) moving average line is common as many stocks in stage 3 bounce below and above the 200-day average several times while topping out.

- The 200-day moving average will lose upside momentum, flatten out, and then roll over into a downtrend.

Stage 4—The Declining Phase: Capitulation

As the company starts to lose its EPS momentum and earnings slow down, at some point there will be a negative surprise. The company will miss an earnings estimate or preannounce earnings and guide Wall Street analysts lower. For some stocks in certain industries, this may be foretold by inventories, with a buildup of finished product or retail goods that reflects declining demand or greater competition in the marketplace, which hurts the company's growth prospects. What was once an uptrend that then transitioned into a topping phase has turned into a full-blown stage 4 downtrend.

During stage 4, earnings models are generally revised downward, which puts more selling pressure on the stock. The stage 4 selling may continue for an extended period until it's finally exhausted, and the stock enters another period of neglect. As a stock languishes, it's back to stage 1. It may take a while for the company to get back on the growth track and return to strong earnings, or the company may remain in stage 1 for many years. In some cases the company may go bankrupt.

Stage 4 is essentially the opposite of stage 2 in terms of price and volume characteristics, with higher volume on down days and lower volume on up days. You should definitely avoid buying while a stock is in stage 4.

STAGE 4 CHARACTERISTICS

- The vast majority of the price action is *below* the 200-day (40-week) moving average.

- The 200-day moving average, which was flat or turning downward in stage 3, is now in a definite downtrend.

- The stock price is near or hitting 52-week new lows

- The stock price pattern is characterized as a series of lower lows and lower highs, stair-stepping downward.

- Short-term moving averages are below long-term moving averages.

- Volume spikes on big down days and big down weeks are contrasted by low-volume rallies.

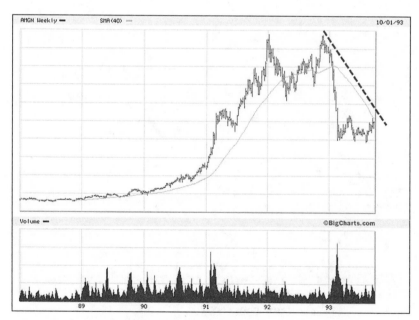

Figure 5.5   **Amgen (AMGN) in stage 4: 1993**

- There are more down days and weeks on above-average volume than up days and up weeks on above-average volume

The Price Maturation Cycle

Now that we have broken down the four stages individually, it's important to understand that the study of the four stages of a stock's life cycle is not meant for pinpoint timing purposes, which requires a more precise approach and tactics that I will discuss below. Rather, the four stages are most useful for gaining perspective on where a stock is in its life cycle price-wise and then to compare that with where the company is in its earnings cycle. A stock can go through the cycle many times. By studying the four stages, you will see clearly that you want to be involved in stage 2. I'm not at all interested in getting in early when a stock is still in stage 1, and I definitely don't want to hang around for stage 3, let alone stage 4.

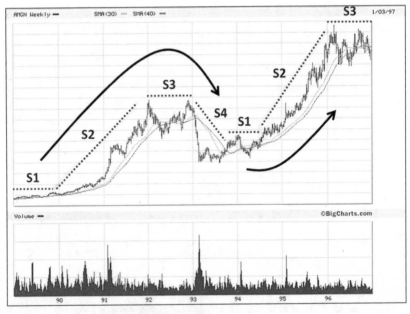

Figure 5.6   **Amgen (AMGN) 1989–1997**

Using Amgen as an example of a stock cycling through the various stages, you can clearly see why you would want to be long during stage 2 and avoid the other stages.

Figure 5.7   **F5 Networks 2007–2011**

F5 Networks transitioned quickly from stage 3 to stage 4 and declined more than 50 percent in only eight months.

Figure 5.8   **Weight Watchers (WTW) 2009–2012**

Weight Watchers topped in May 2011 but took a year to build a stage 3 top before transitioning to stage 4.

Figure 5.9   **Novell (NOVL) 1989–1998**

Novell topped in 1993. With the exception of a bear trap rally in 1995, the stock price spent the next five years in a stage 4 decline, falling more than 80 percent.

Figure 5.10   **Novell (NOVL) 1994–1996**

Novell was unable to transition into stage 2 and set up constructively.

How to Pinpoint Stage 2

As I've stated, history clearly shows that virtually every superperformance stock was in a definite uptrend *before* experiencing its big advances. In fact, 99 percent of superperformance stocks traded above their 200-day moving averages *before* their huge advance, and 96 percent traded above their 50-day moving averages.

I apply the Trend Template criteria (see below) to every single stock I'm considering. The Trend Template is a qualifier. If a stock doesn't meet the Trend Template criteria, I don't consider it. Even if the fundamentals are compelling, the stock must be in a long-term uptrend—as defined by the Trend Template—for me to consider it as a candidate. Without identifying a stock's trend, investors are at risk of going long when a stock is in a dangerous downtrend, going short during an explosive uptrend, or tying up capital in a stock lost in a sideways neglect phase. It's important to point out that a stock must meet all eight of the Trend Template criteria to be considered in a confirmed stage 2 uptrend.

Trend Template
1. The current stock price is above both the 150-day (30-week) and the 200-day (40-week) moving average price lines.
2. The 150-day moving average is above the 200-day moving average.
3. The 200-day moving average line is trending up for at least 1 month (preferably 4–5 months minimum in most cases).
4. The 50-day (10-week) moving average is above both the 150-day and 200-day moving averages.
5. The current stock price is trading above the 50-day moving average.
6. The current stock price is *at least* 30 percent above its 52-week low. (Many of the best selections will be 100 percent, 300 percent, or greater above their 52-week low *before* they emerge from a solid consolidation period and mount a large scale advance.)
7. The current stock price is within at least 25 percent of its 52-week high (the closer to a new high the better).
8. The relative strength ranking (as reported in *Investor's Business Daily*) is no less than 70, and preferably in the 80s or 90s, which will generally be the case with the better selections.

RIDING THE TIDE; TIMING THE WAVES

By using the Trend Template criteria, you will be able to immediately identify companies that are in a stage 2 uptrend; there will be no guesswork
involved. However, we are not buying a stock just because it happens to be in
a stage 2 uptrend. Therefore, it's important to consider what happens within
the stage 2 acceleration. To illustrate, think of the upward movement during
stage 2 as high tide coming in. As you know, the tide doesn't come in all at
once; it arrives on successive waves that take the water level steadily higher.
The overall direction of the trend is upward, but within it there are pulses, or
waves, of movement.

Within an overall long-term uptrend (the tide) there will be short- or
intermediate-term price action (the waves) that consist of pullbacks and
basing. These shorter-term moves may last from four or five weeks up to a
year or more in many cases. Most commonly, base patterns forming within
a stage 2 uptrend last anywhere from 5 to 26 weeks. During these basing
periods, the stock will basically go sideways for a while, as if it's catching its
breath before making the next push higher. This sideways price is not to be
confused with a stage 1 phase. The stock is now in a stage 2 uptrend, stair-
stepping higher from base to base. This will continue all along the stage 2
advance.

WHERE ARE WE ON THIS MOUNTAIN?
THE BASE COUNT

Switching metaphors, think of the movement of a stock's price through the
four stages of its life cycle as the outline of a mountain, from the flatlands to
the summit and back to the flatlands again. As the mountain rises up the left
side (stage 2), there are areas where the path or ascent plateaus for a bit. This
is where mountain climbers would build a base camp, rest, and recharge,
getting ready for the next phase of the climb to the summit. That's exactly
what happens with a stock. After a run upward, there is profit taking, causing a temporary pullback, during which the stock builds a base. If the stock
is truly in the middle of something significant, the longer-term trend will

resume. The short-term pauses allow the stock to digest its previous run-up so that it can move even higher as it emerges from a constructive consolidation period.

At some point, the upward momentum ceases; the stock tires, and the top is put in. This is like reaching the summit, and there is no more mountain left to climb; now comes the descent. Generally, this occurs after three to five bases have formed along the way in a stage 2 uptrend. The later-stage bases coincide with the point at which the stock's accumulation phase has become too obvious, tapping out the last of the heavy institutional demand.

Bases 1 and 2 generally come off a market correction, which is the best time for jumping on board a new trend. As the stock makes a series of bases along the stage 2 uptrend, base 3 is a little more obvious but usually still tradable. By the time a fourth or fifth base occurs (if it gets that far), the trend is becoming extremely obvious and is definitely in its late stages. By this point, abrupt base failures occur more frequently. Some stocks, how-

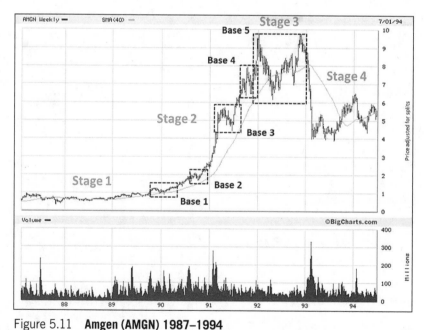

Figure 5.11 **Amgen (AMGN) 1987–1994**
In 1992, Amgen formed a double top before completing stage 3 and transitioning into a sharp stage 4 decline.

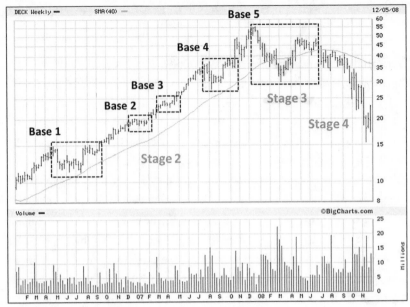

Figure 5.12 **Deckers Outdoor (DECK) 2006–2008**
In 2008, Deckers Outdoor formed a stage 3 top marked by a relatively wide fifth base.

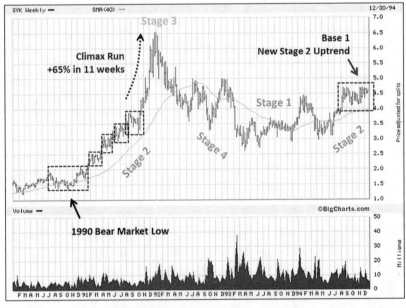

Figure 5.13 **Stryker Corp. (SYK) 1990–1995**
In 1991, Stryker topped after a climax run. Five years later a new base developed during a renewed stage 2 uptrend.

ever, can turn up in a parabolic fashion and end in a climax run or blow-off top. By itself, base counting will not tell you if a stock has topped or is about to move substantially higher. It does, however, provide a great way to gain perspective on where you are within the stage 2 advance. Combined with specific price and volume analysis along with fundamental analysis, it can be a very powerful tool. Base counting was introduced to me by Bill O'Neil and David Ryan many years ago; it is a valuable way to ascertain where a stock is within its price maturation cycle.

Trust but Verify

I never place much faith in my fundamental ideas about a particular company without confirmation from the market, namely, the price of the stock. The way I see it is simple: if a company's management is so great and its products are so great, the stock should at some point reflect those fundamentals. If strong fundamentals are not confirmed by the stock's price action, the future may not be as bright as it appears. Or perhaps investor perception of the company has not changed or has not materialized yet. **You want to get on board when institutional money is pouring into a stock and lifting it significantly higher. To do that, you need confirmation that this inflow is starting to happen** *before* **you invest.**

Why is price action so important? Even if you're correct in your fundamental analysis of the company, investor perception is what creates buy orders, and you are going to need big buy orders in your stock to move it up significantly. Keep in mind that if the institutional investment community doesn't see what you see, your stock could sit dormant for an extended period. Why sit and wait when you can put your money in another stock that is already on the move higher and has attracted big institutional volume support?

To compound your capital rapidly, you must be where the action is; you can't afford to have your money tied up in a stock waiting for what you think is a great fundamental story to get noticed by the rest of the world. I'm willing to give the first leg up in a stock to someone else in exchange for confirmation that the trend is definitely in stage 2 with some momentum building. **The goal is not to buy at the cheapest price but to sell your stock for significantly more than the price you paid in the shortest period. That's how superperformance is achieved.**

HEED A TREND REVERSAL

At some point your stock will reach its highest price and top out. This can occur with or without warning. Regardless of your fondness for or attachment to a particular security, it's important that you learn to detect and, more important, respect a change in trend. Stocks very often top out while earnings still look good. Investors who wait for the earnings picture to dim before hitting the bid in the face of a stage 3 top or stage 4 decline often end up with a huge loss or at the very least give back much if not all of

Figure 5.14   **Netflix (NFLX) 2008–2012**
In July 2011, Netflix plummeted through its 40-week moving average on enormous volume as institutions ran for the exits.

what they made on the upside. When topping signs start to appear after a long, extended price run, it's time to take your profit and head for the exit. Companies will announce record earnings and try to create hype to keep their stocks up. Carefully watch the stock's price action for valuable clues to which way institutional investors are leaning and, like a tree, bend with them. If you are inflexible and fight the powerful force of institutional money flow, you risk being snapped like a brittle twig.

FINANCIAL STOCKS WARN OF IMPENDING TROUBLE

The news media would have you believe that the troubles in financials in 2008 came out of nowhere. The truth, however, is that the stock prices of financial companies were falling in a stage 4 decline for many months, warning of trouble ahead. All you had to do to avert a major disaster was heed the stage 4 decline and sell. Even if you bought near the all-time high price,

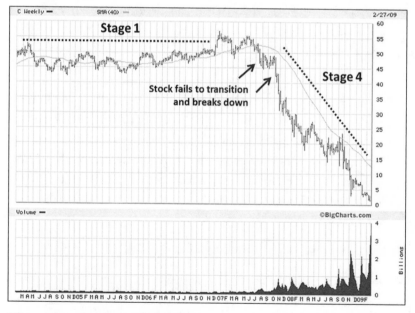

Figure 5.15   **Citigroup (C) 2004–2009**

Warning signs were abundant in Citigroup (C) with a stage 4 decline under way in late 2007 and early 2008, long before the worst of the financial crisis hit.

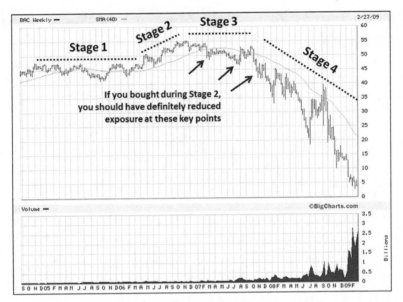

Figure 5.16   **Bank of America (BAC) 2004–2009**

In 2001, stage 3 warning signs should have caused you to sell Bank America stock. Even if you reduced your exposure gradually, you would have avoided the carnage that came in 2008.

you could have taken a relatively small loss on many of the bank stocks that ended up being a total disaster, that is, if you had paid attention to the danger signs. For many of the financial stocks, such as Citigroup and Bank of America, there were clear-cut warnings. At the time, if you held those names, you should have sold or at least reduced your position progressively until you were in cash.

TRUST YOUR EYES, NOT YOUR EARS

When a stock shows signs of topping or, even worse, enters a stage 4 decline, you should trust what you see, not what you hear. Tune out the analyst and discount company hype. The chart of Vicor shows that by the time the flat earnings were reported (which was a dramatic deceleration from the previ-

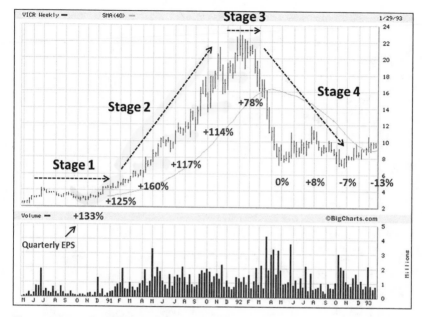

Figure 5.17   **Vicor (VICR) 1990–1993**

By the time a material change in earnings was reported, Vicor's stock price had already declined by almost 70 percent.

ous trend of triple-digit growth), the stock had already suffered a vicious decline. This was the result of large institutional investors anticipating a loss of earnings momentum going forward and exiting the stock in anticipation. By the time a material change in earnings was reported, Vicor's stock price had already declined by almost 70 percent.

As you look at Crocs (next), note how the negative quarter (−71 percent) was reported long *after* the stock topped and not until the price was already down 73 percent from its high. This demonstrates clearly why you cannot wait for a fundamental change when the price action of a stock turns volatile or hostile into stage 3 or, even worse, stage 4. To be successful, you must respect the trend and the wisdom of the market. Crocs' weekly chart shows the mass exit taking place as big institutions unwind positions as the stock quickly transitions from stage 2 to stage 4.

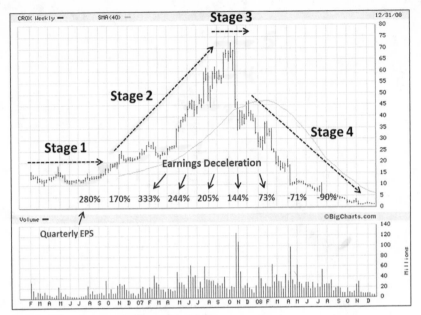

Figure 5.18   **Crocs (CROX) 2006–2009**

Crocs weekly chart shows the mass exit that took place as big institutions unwound positions and the stock quickly transitions from stage 2 to stage 4.

Figure 5.19   **Green Mountain Coffee, Inc. (GMCR) 2010–2012**

GMCR's earnings didn't show material earnings deceleration until *after* the stock price was already down close to 80 percent.

BROKERAGE HOUSE OPINIONS

Should you buy a stock on the basis of a brokerage house's recommendation? If the stock is in a stage 4 downtrend, definitely not. Big brokerage houses love to recommend stocks that are down in price. Often these upgrades are based on valuation and completely ignore the fact that the stock price suffered a major price break. Often, stocks that are upgraded on the basis of valuation after a large price decline turn out to be good short candidates. Learn to do your own analysis and base your purchases on sound criteria, not because someone else says a broken stock is a good value.

We put CMG on our short alert list eight days before Citigroup raised its rating to buy. Three months later the stock was down 40 percent.

Figure 5.20 **Chipotle Mexican Grill (CMG) 2011–2012**

A MATERIAL CHANGE IN BEHAVIOR IS A MAJOR WARNING

Institutional investors can become wary of what had been a strong performer; they can suddenly send a stock plummeting as they get out. When that happens, take heed. Before it becomes apparent that the fundamentals have changed, a major break in the stock price often will occur on overwhelming volume. If your stock experiences its largest daily and/or weekly price decline since the beginning of the stage 2 advance, this is a sell signal in most cases even if it comes on the heels of a seemingly great earnings report. Don't listen to the company or the media; listen to the stock. I have seen companies report earnings that were only a few cents better than expected on in-line revenues and skyrocket, and I have also seen companies report

Figure 5.21   **Crocs (CROX) 2007**

Crocs' (CROX) stock price sold off an overwhelming volume after a "better than expected" earnings report. This was just the beginning of what turned out to be a 99 percent decline in the stock price over the next 12 months.

earnings and sales much better than expected but the stocks sold off hard and could not recover.

After the market close on October 31, 2007, Crocs reported quarterly earnings per share of $0.66 versus a consensus of $0.63. Although this report was 144 percent ahead of the previous year and even beat Street estimates, the stock's reaction was less than enthusiastic, falling 36 percent in just one day on overwhelming volume after the earnings release. Notwithstanding a one-day 5 percent dead cat bounce (a short-term recovery from a selloff that did not resume the uptrend), the share price dropped another 29 percent over the next six trading days. On November 13, 2008, Crocs stock traded as a penny stock at $0.79 per share, down 99 percent off a high of $75 just a year earlier.

Many times before a fundamental problem is evident, there will be a hint in the form of a material change in price behavior. That change should always be respected even if you don't see any reason for the sud-

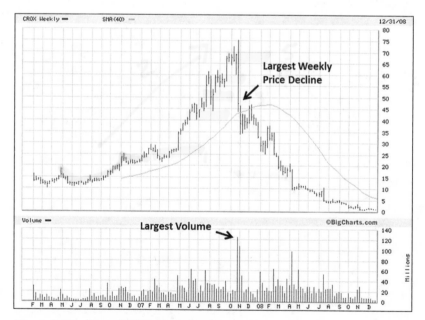

Figure 5.22 **Crocs (CROX) 2006–2009**

The largest daily decline for Crocs also came on the largest weekly decline on huge volume.

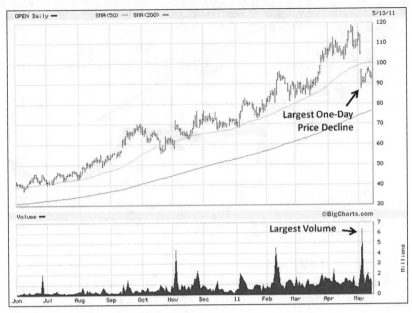

Figure 5.23   **Opentable (OPEN) 2011**

Opentable breaks down on huge volume after an earnings report.

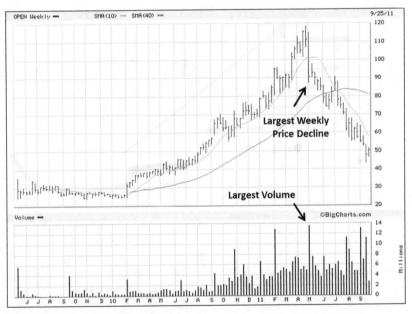

Figure 5.24   **Opentable (OPEN) 2011**

The largest weekly price decline on the largest swell in volume indicated institutions were dumping the shares.

den change in sentiment. Earnings may still look good. The story may still be intact. However, in most cases, you'll be far better off getting out—shooting first and asking questions later—than waiting to learn the reason why. When a stock that had been in a strong stage 2 suddenly goes into a stage 3 topping pattern or transitions quickly into stage 4, don't sit there and assume that everything is fine. There is a reason for the adverse price move; you just don't know it yet. Whatever you do, don't think that a big break in the stock is now a buying opportunity. Many investors get caught in this trap: A stock they own suddenly declines sharply. Believing that the marketplace must be wrong and that the stock is still a good performer, they decide it's time to buy more. They don't realize that the stock price is down because the big players know (or at least suspect) something is wrong and are getting out. When you see that happen in the price action, regardless of what the fundamentals are saying, it's time to exit.

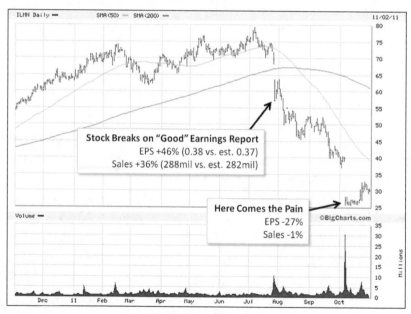

Figure 5.25   **Illumina Inc. (ILMN) 2011**

Illumina sold off big on what appeared to be a decent earnings report. The stock declined 50 percent leading up to its next earnings report, which was negative in terms of both earnings and sales.

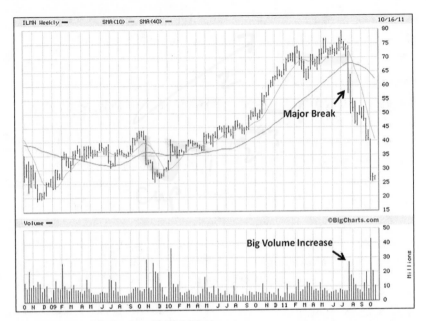

Figure 5.26   **Illimina Inc. (ILMN) 2011**

A major trend break occurred after Illumina reported earnings.

LET THE WIND FILL YOUR SAILS

As we've discussed in this chapter, to achieve superperformance, you need the powerful force of institutional buyers on your side to propel your stock's price sharply higher. A proper stage 2 uptrend provides evidence that institutions are indeed stepping up to the plate, just as a stage 4 decline clearly demonstrates the opposite. Having the long-term trend on your side is like sailing with the wind at your back. If there's no wind, you're dead in the water (stage 1), and if the wind is against you, you have little chance of moving forward (stage 4). The proverbial wind in your sails is the long-term trend of big money that's buying in sync with you. You should look to align yourself with this powerful force. Stick with stocks that are in a solid uptrend and you will be much more likely to own a stock that has the potential to skyrocket and become a superperformer.

CHAPTER 6

CATEGORIES, INDUSTRY GROUPS, AND CATALYSTS

W HEN I'M CONSIDERING a stock for purchase, the first thing I do is determine the type of situation I'm dealing with. In the context of the nature of the business and the industry in which a company operates, I want to develop an expectation of its prospective earnings growth and find out whether those prospects are widely recognized and therefore discounted in the current stock price. Categorizing companies is a good way to gain perspective and organize your thoughts about a particular stock. It will help you establish the type of company you're considering relative to others in the market so that you can make a judgment about where the stock is in its maturation cycle or curve. Companies don't stay in the same part of the curve forever, and some spend more time than others in certain phases of the cycle; however, nearly all companies undergo a natural maturation. Over the years I have analyzed tens of thousands of publicly traded companies. What I've discovered is that they generally tend to fall into one of six categories:

1. Market leaders

2. Top competitors

3. Institutional favorites

4. Turnaround situations

5. Cyclical stocks

6. Past leaders and laggards

THE MARKET LEADER

My favorite type of stock to invest in—the area where I have made most of my money trading—is the market leader. These companies are able to grow their earnings the fastest. An industry's strongest players are usually number one, two, or three in sales and earnings and are gaining market share. Market leaders are easy to spot, but most investors have psychological difficulty deciding to buy them. The share prices of market leaders power up the most percentagewise in the initial stages of a market rally. They move into new high ground first. That unbelievable price strength causes most investors to think these stocks have run up too far; hence, most investors are afraid to buy the very best stocks capable of superperformance.

What propels them even higher? Institutions that know enough about a company and its future prospects provide the buying power. They are not concerned about how far the stock has already advanced but about where it's going and what the prospects are for future growth. The best type of growth situation is scalable growth: a company gaining market share in a rapidly growing industry. The market for the company's products or services is extremely large in relation to the company's size, and those products and services are in high enough demand that the company can grow at a high rate for an extended period. These companies have superior products and services, and they are often part of a growing industry; although it is not necessary that a market leader be in a fast-growing industry or sector, it is certainly an additional plus if it is.

A company that is taking market share in a slow-growth industry can also grow its earnings quite nicely. What's most important is that the company can make substantial profits. A good balance sheet, expanding margins, high return on equity, and reasonable debt are all signs of good management. Some market leaders grow earnings at a very healthy rate for extended periods in industries with percentage growth rates in the low to mid-single digits. However, a company that is taking market share or has a large portion of market share in a fast-growing industry can increase its earnings at a meteoric pace.

The main questions should be: What is the company's competitive advantage? and Is the business model scalable? Then it's a matter of whether management is executing successfully and delivering the goods, namely, earnings.

Market leaders are capable of producing huge price appreciation during their high-growth phase. They generally grow earnings at a rate of 20 percent or higher. Many average 35 to 45 percent during their best 5- or 10-year stretch. During their greatest growth period, some increase their earnings at triple-digit rates. From March 1989 through May 1993, Cisco Systems averaged over 100 percent quarterly earnings growth. Cisco's stock price advanced more than 13-fold in that period. During the early 1980s, when Walmart was a little-known company trading as few as 20,000 shares a day, earnings growth averaged 38 percent for 14 consecutive quarters. Walmart's stock price appreciated 1,000 percent in that period. Today, Walmart trades more than 7 million shares a day on average.

WHEN EXPENSIVE IS ACTUALLY CHEAP

Market leaders in the high-growth stage are almost always going to appear expensive. It only makes sense to value a rapidly growing company higher than a slower-growing one. **Here's the beauty about ultrafast growers: these companies grow so fast that Wall Street can't value them very accurately. This can leave a stock inefficiently priced, providing a big opportunity.** As long as a company can sustain significantly expanding sales and earnings, the stock price will follow—maybe not immediately, but stock prices do follow earnings growth over time. The faster a company can grow earnings, the more likely it is that its stock price will follow.

Don't be misled; there's plenty of risk in high-growth companies. Wall Street can punish a fast-growing company if earnings slow down even by the smallest amount in relation to expectations. High-growth companies live and die by earnings expectations. These companies have to constantly beat consensus forecasts. As a company reports better than expected earnings, the bar moves up for that company to beat them the next time. Eventually, the bar is too high and the company misses. However, as long as the company can deliver strong earnings and manage expectations well, the stock price can soar and experience P/E multiple expansion. The goal is to identify and invest in market leaders relatively early in the growth phase when profits are accelerating.

THE CATEGORY KILLER

Every so often a company comes along and totally dominates a category; the company has such a clear and sustainable competitive advantage that other firms in the same market or niche find it nearly impossible to compete. These market leaders are known as *category killers*. **A category killer is a company whose brand and market position are so strong that it would be difficult to compete against it even if you had unlimited capital.** A good example is eBay, with an online auction site that gives it an overwhelming advantage since buyers and sellers want to participate in the biggest market with the most players. Therefore, they come to eBay, which gobbles up the opportunity, leaving everybody else with the crumbs. Consider Apple, which dominates its space, setting the prevailing trend with innovative technologies and truly unique products. Disney's theme parks certainly rank as a category killer with little formidable competition. So does a company such as Walmart, which has taken a toll on the retail sector, in which many stores find it hard to compete against the giant.

THE COOKIE CUTTER CONCEPT

When a firm produces a successful formula in one store and then replicates it over and over—in malls and in locations around the country or around the world—it's a cookie cutter. Think of McDonald's, Walmart, Starbucks, Taco Bell, The Gap, Home Depot, Chili's, Cracker Barrel, The Limited, Dick's Sporting Goods, Wendy's, Outback Steakhouse, and Costco Wholesale, which are great examples of successful rollouts of the cookie cutter concept.

As you can see, many of the names that achieve success with the cookie cutter business model are in the retail area. With this concept, when a company expands into new markets, bringing on new stores rapidly (especially if same-store sales are brisk as well), earnings can accelerate at a healthy sustained pace. These types of companies are some of the easiest to spot, monitor, and invest in during their high-growth phase. Their earnings up cycles last for a long enough time for you to identify earnings growth "on the table" while they still have plenty of growth in the future.

Points to Consider When Investing in the Cookie Cutter Model

Same-store sales, or what is also referred to as comparable store sales (comps), are a very important statistic used for analysis of the retail industry. This statistic compares sales of stores that have been open for a year or more. This allows investors to determine which portion of new sales has come from sales growth and which portion from the opening of new stores. This analysis is important because although new stores are a major part of a company's expansion and earnings growth, a saturation point in which future sales growth is determined by same-store sales growth eventually occurs. With these comparisons, analysts can measure sales performance against other retailers that may not be as aggressive in opening new locations during the evaluated period. **You want to see same-store sales increasing each quarter. High-single-digit to moderate-double-digit same-store sales growth is high enough to be considered robust but not so high that it's unsustainable (25 to 30 percent or more same-store sales growth is definitely unsustainable over the long term).** In general, same-store sales growth of 10 percent or more is considered healthy.

What factors affect same-store sales? The two main factors are prices and customer volume. By measuring the sales increase or decrease in stores that have been open a year or more, you can get a better feel for how a company is really performing, because this measure—same-store sales—takes store closings and chain expansions out of the mix. Rising same-store sales means that more customers are buying product at the stores or are spending more than they did a year ago or some combination of the two. This is a sign that management's marketing efforts are paying off and that the brand is popular with consumers.

Falling same-store sales obviously represents a problem. Weakening comps could mean one of a few things:

- The brand is losing strength, and people aren't shopping at the company's stores.

- The economy is worsening, and people aren't interested in shopping anywhere.

- The company has too many items at discount prices, and dollar volume per customer is less than usual.

Some companies grow by franchising their business or through a combination of company-owned and franchised stores. Although franchise fees can lead to big profits for the franchisor, the earnings are considered lesser quality than a company-owned base with less earnings stability. If the company franchises a relatively high percentage of new store openings, the risk of store failures and an earnings disappointment is heightened. In 2007, McDonald's, one of the best-run franchise cookie cutter models in history, had about 60 percent of its restaurants operated by franchisees.

Another important consideration for the cookie cutter model (particularly if the business concept is relatively new) is a past track record of success in diverse geographic locations (Northeast, South, Midwest, international, etc.). You want to get evidence that the model is scalable. In addition, too much, too fast can be a red flag. For most companies, opening more than 100 stores per year is a number that is difficult to maintain. In 2006, Starbucks opened 1,102 more stores than it had the previous year; Starbucks' stock price peaked and fell 82 percent over the next 24 months. By 2011, Starbucks had fewer stores open than it did in 2008. Other key metrics to consider include comparing sales per square foot and sales per dollar of capital invested per unit with other companies in the same business.

THE TOP COMPETITOR: KEEP YOUR EYE ON THE COMPETITION

Usually only one, two, or possibly three companies truly lead an industry group. If I asked you to name the number one and number two soft drink companies, you would almost surely say Coca-Cola and Pepsi. If I asked you who was number three, could you give as quick an answer? How about coffee—Starbucks and Dunkin' Donuts perhaps? Or home improvement—Home Depot and Lowe's? Keep in mind that we're looking for the next superperformers, the Starbucks, the Apple, the Google of tomorrow. In 1981, MCI Communications challenged the dominant market leader AT&T. MCI reported strong earnings as the stock price emerged from a 17-week consolidation and made a new high on April 2, 1981, but that was only the beginning. Over the ensuing 22 months MCI's stock advanced 500 percent.

A top competitor may not be the superior company in an industry group or even have superior products compared with the true market leader; rather, it's in the right place at the right time. Even though it may be in the same rapidly growing industry as the market leader, the company's products or stores may be less popular or in some way inferior to those of the leader. These "competitor" companies can also produce high rates of earnings growth and enjoy large-scale price advances, albeit inferior to that of the leader. Even so, the number two company in an industry can eventually take market share from the leader and in some cases take over the number one spot. The stock prices of top competitors can reflect this phenomenon, performing relatively well while the market leader digests its previous stock gains.

From 1990 through 2000, Home Depot's stock price advanced 3,700 percent, more than a 40 percent compounded annual rate of return. During that period, Lowe's stock advanced only 1,000 percent, amassing only about a quarter of Home Depot's price advance. Then, from January 2000 through January 2004, Lowe's stock price ran up more than 100 percent while Home Depot's stock price actually fell, giving back more than 40 percent from its all-time high. This put the 14-year track record for Lowe's up 2,900 percent and for Home Depot up only 1,800 percent. Home Depot had been the leader for more than a decade, and for investors who saw its potential, it was just a matter of when they got on board.

Always track the top two or three stocks in an industry group. The online access provider America Online was the clear leader in the Internet market until the search engine Yahoo! moved into the top slot. Google, a direct competitor to Yahoo!, then went public and is now considered the number one powerhouse in search engines. A competitor of the market leader can offer a great investment opportunity, especially if it's in a strong industry group. Like a NASCAR racer who follows in the leader's draft, waiting to make a pass at the right moment, a top competitor can ride the heels of a market leader and eventually win market share. You should concentrate on the top two or three stocks in a group: the leaders in terms of earnings, sales, margins, and relative price strength. This is especially true if the industry group is a leading sector during a bull market.

Netflix Goes Public; Blockbuster Tops

It's no coincidence that within only 15 trading days of Netflix going public, Blockbuster Video's stock permanently topped out. It makes sense; competition rears its head, providing a more convenient solution to the movie rental business. Blockbuster's stock price topped at the same time Netflix came on the scene, almost as if the dollars from its shares were rotating directly out and into its new competitor. I could see this story unfolding in my own neighborhood as the mom-and-pop video rental stores went out of business one by one. Then the small regional chains started closing their doors, and the writing on the wall was beginning to look crystal clear; brick-and-mortar video rental was on its way out.

Coming off the market bottom in 2009, Blockbuster was plagued with declining sales as the stock traded as low as $0.13. This was off a high of $18.00! Meanwhile, on March 18, 2009, just seven days after the Nasdaq Composite traded at its bear market low and only 10 days after the Dow traded at its bear market low of 6,469, Netflix hit an all-time high. Just 17 trading days later Netflix's stock price was up an additional 20 percent. Sales had been brisk and accelerating over the previous three quarters from 11 percent to 16 percent and 19 percent, respectively. Earnings were even more impressive, up 36 percent, 38 percent, and 58 percent, respectively. In October 2009, I was buying Netflix shares. Netflix's earnings, sales, margins, return on equity, and debt levels all were superior to those metrics at Blockbuster. Netflix was trading at 32x earnings while Blockbuster traded at just 2x earnings. Which stock was really the "cheap" stock? From the

Figure 6.1   **Netflix (NFLX) vs. Blockbuster Video (BLOAQ) 2002–2011**

Top competitor Netflix takes market share and claims the number one spot in video rental with a new business model as Blockbuster fails to evolve.

point at which Netflix went public, the stock increased more than 3,400 percent. During the same period Blockbuster's stock price lost 99 percent of its value.

The Institutional Favorite

Institutional favorites are also referred to as quality companies or official growth stocks, but don't let those titles impress you too much. These are mature companies, and they're certainly no secret. They generally have a good track record of consistent sales and dividend growth, and they often attract conservative institutional capital because of their proven history of management's ability to increase earnings, expand margins, and create shareholder value. Their earnings growth is generally in the low to middle teens. These companies are regarded as the ones that most likely won't go out of business. Often they are referred to as blue chips or stalwarts. Examples include Coca-Cola, Johnson & Johnson, and General Electric, to name a few. Although all that sounds good, there's one problem: they're usually big and sluggish by the time they reach institutional favorite status. Although their earnings are deemed to be consistent and of high quality, usually the growth is slow, and the companies are so widely followed that there's little room for rapid price appreciation.

In certain markets these stocks can come into favor and do quite well. However, you're not likely to get a superperformance move out of General Electric or Procter & Gamble. Sometimes mismanagement, some other misfortune, or a severe bear market correction will drive some of these companies down precipitously. As the stocks recover, they can make a nice advance coming out of the correction phase.

The Turnaround Situation

Big profits can be made in troubled companies that turn around. In purchasing a turnaround situation, you should look for companies that have very strong results in the most recent two or three quarters. You should see at least two quarters of strong earnings increases or one quarter that is up enough to move the trailing 12-month earnings per share to near or above its old peak. In looking at turnarounds, ask yourself: Are profit margins recovering, and are they at or close to the peak? Are the results based only on cost cutting? What is the company doing to increase earnings beyond cost cutting, productivity enhancements, and shedding losing operations? How much cash does the company have? Although a company can burn its cash, you can try to assess the burn rate and debt load to get an idea of how long it can last while running in the red. How much debt does the company have? Bank debt is the worst kind and is less favorable than bond debt. How long can the company operate while it works out its problems?

It's important to follow the story and ascertain whether the turnaround is running better than, worse than, or as expected. Worse than expected is usually a reason to consider selling. I look for acceleration in the growth rate in the most recent couple of quarters compared with the three- and five-year growth rate, which often is negative or reflects very slow growth. The most important questions to ask in purchasing a turnaround are: Is the stock acting well in market? and Are the fundamentals coming in strong? You want to see both. Turnaround stocks are up against relatively easy comparisons from earlier quarters, and so it's important to see the most recent results up significantly: generally 100 percent growth or more in the most recent two or three quarters and a dramatic acceleration versus the past growth rate.

Remember, stocks don't necessarily stay in one category forever. This is why it's important to understand the dynamics that are taking place with regard to a company's products and services and the potential for sales growth. Apple Computer was a turnaround situation that morphed into a growth stock and since then has reached institutional favorite status. From 2001 to 2003, revenue and margins were under severe pressure, which in turn led to lackluster earnings and a falling stock; the price of Apple's shares was down more than 80 percent from its high. Things were so bleak that when Michael Dell, founder of rival computer maker Dell Inc., was asked

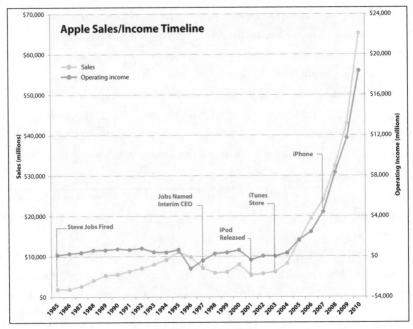

Figure 6.2   **Apple Computer (AAPL) 1985-2010**

Apple Computer experiences a phenomenal turnaround on the heels of newly released products including the iPod, iTunes, and the iPhone.

Created by Max Olson/Max Capital Corporation.

what he would do if he ran Apple, he said he would "shut it down and give the money back to the shareholders."

However, a new product can bring new life to a dormant company, and the release of the iPod in 2001 and iTunes stores in 2003 was about to fuel what has been called the greatest turnaround in corporate history. From 2003 to 2011, Apple's net profit margins increased every year from just 1.2 percent to an impressive 23.9 percent. During that period, revenue growth averaged 39 percent per year. With the rapid expansion of margins and strong sales, earnings soared, averaging 114 percent per year. **From its 2003 low, Apple's stock price increased in value by more than 10,000 percent; 73 percent of that phenomenal growth came from newly launched products.**

CYCLICAL STOCKS

> Buying a cyclical after several years of record earnings and when the P/E ratio has hit a low point is a proven method for losing half your money in a short period of time.
>
> —*Peter Lynch*

A cyclical company is one that is sensitive to the economy or to commodity prices. Examples include auto manufacturers, steel producers, paper stocks, and chemical companies. Interestingly, cyclical stocks have an inverse P/E cycle, meaning they generally have a high P/E ratio when they are poised to rally and a low P/E near the end of their cycle. This is due to the fact that Wall Street analysts try to anticipate the earnings-cycle dynamics of these companies, which are dependent on the business cycle. Growth investors may become confused when they attempt to apply an earnings model to the selection process for cyclical stocks, and their stock picks do not respond like a cookie cutter retailer or a high-growth technology company poised for many continued quarters or even years of growth after earnings are already on the table. This is the reason I put them into their own category and apply a slightly different approach from what I do with stock categories that have sustainable growth prospects.

With cyclical stocks, the trick is to figure out whether the next cycle turn is going to happen earlier or later than usual. Inventories and supply and demand are important variables in analyzing the dynamics of cyclical stocks. When the P/E ratios of cyclical stocks are very low after earnings have been on the rise for many months or several years, it's often a sign that they're near the end of their up cycle. When P/Es are superhigh and you've heard nothing but doom and gloom about the company or industry for an extended period, the bottom may be near.

At the bottom of a cyclical swing, the following things happen:

1. Earnings are falling.

2. Dividends may be cut or omitted.

3. The P/E ratio is high.

4. News is generally bad.

At the top of a cyclical swing:

1. Earnings are moving up.

2. Dividends are being raised.

3. The P/E ratio is low.

4. News is generally good.

Stay Away from the Laggards

A laggard is a stock that belongs to the same group as the market leader but has inferior price performance and in most cases inferior earnings and sales growth. These stocks can have periods of decent performance, usually brief ones, as they try to catch up with the true leaders near the end of a cycle or during times when a sector is red hot and the real leader has run up rapidly. The price moves in laggard stocks, however, usually pale in comparison to those of the true market leader.

Laggards usually appear to be relatively cheaper than market leaders, and that attracts unskilled investors. Don't be tempted by a stock with a relatively low P/E or one that hasn't appreciated as much as has the leader in its industry. There's always a reason why one stock trades at a high multiple and another trades at a low multiple. More times than not, the expensive market leader is actually cheap and the laggard is really the more expensive choice.

Over the years, many people thought buying Wild Oats, the smaller rival to Whole Foods, was a better way to play the healthy food trend because of its lower P/E. There was a good reason for the low P/E: Wild Oats failed to generate much in the way of earnings growth. Investors who concentrated on earnings growth made a lot more money by owning Whole Foods even though it was popularly perceived to be more expensive than Wild Oats.

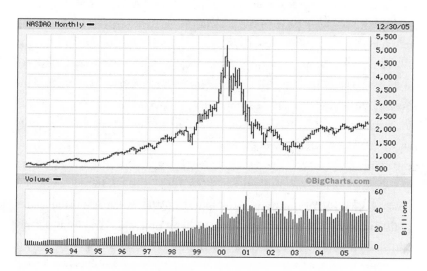

Figure 6.3   **Whole Foods (WFMI) vs. Nasdaq Composite Index 1993–2005**

From 2000 through 2005, the stock price for Whole Foods increased eightfold.
In the same period, the Nasdaq Composite fell more than 50 percent.

Whole Foods rarely traded below 30 times earnings during its dramatic growth phase. On the surface, it's not surprising that many investors passed on a grocer with such a high P/E, but if they had understood the growth opportunity, the high P/E wouldn't have mattered much. The key for Whole Foods was its ability to expand earnings at a high rate, growing by more than 20 percent on average. By doing that, the stock paid off big for its investors.

Specific Industry Groups Lead New Bull Markets

The formation of a bear market bottom typically begins with signs of accumulation in certain market sectors or segments. In general, 3 or 4 to as many as 8 to 10 industry groups or subgroups lead a new bull market. The market can also have a broader theme such as growth, value, small-cap, large-cap, and so on. The leadership groups or categories can start to stage their bull market rallies before the broad benchmark's bottom. For example, at the 1974 market bottom, mid-cap and small-cap stocks began to show noticeable signs of accumulation during September and October even though the major market indexes did not bottom until December. When a new bull market began in March 2003, it was already apparent that investors had been accumulating financial, energy, and basic materials stocks, as well as mid-caps and small-caps, for several months. How do you find which groups are leading? Follow the individual stocks. I like to track the 52-week new high list. **The industry groups with a healthy number of stocks hitting new highs early in a bull market will often be the leaders. Your portfolio should consist of the best companies in the top four or five sectors.** In a bull market, some sectors advance several hundred percent and others barely beat the average or even underperform. There are broad sectors that include a wide range of companies and subgroups. Healthcare/medical, technology, services, basic materials, consumer cyclical, consumer noncyclical, financial, transportation, capital goods, energy, and utilities are all broad sectors.

In each sector there are subsectors or industry groups. For example, in the healthcare/medical sector, subsectors include drugs, generic drugs, ethical drugs, biotechnology/genetics, HMOs, hospitals, nursing homes, outpatient/home care, medical equipment, medical services, and medical supplies.

Buying into the leading areas early in a bull market can lead to significant capital gains. Some groups start emerging late in a bull cycle and can lead during the next upturn after a bear market. It's definitely worth investigating the industry groups in which the most stocks were resisting the decline and then subsequently broke into new highs while the market was coming off its lows or during the market's initial few rallies.

The top relative strength leaders in these groups typically lead their group's advance from the beginning and are likely to show the greatest appreciation. When you see a growing number of names in a particular industry making new 52-week highs (especially coming off a market low), this could be an indication that a group advance is under way.

I tend to let individual stocks lead me into an industry group or sector, taking more of a bottom-up approach as opposed to top-down. **I have found that more often than not, the best stocks in the leading groups advance before it's obvious that the group or sector is hot. Therefore, I focus on stocks and let them point me to the group.** Not always, though. I still stay in touch with what is happening on an industrywide level, and if I see something that attracts my interest, I look at the stocks that make up the industry and sort them according to my criteria. I look at the strongest stocks first: the ones that have the best earnings and sales, are closest to a new high, and show the greatest relative price strength versus the market. This is where you find the real market leaders.

History shows that big winning stocks tend to favor certain industry groups. The groups that have produced the largest number of superperformance stocks include the following:

- Consumer/retail

- Technology, computer, software, and related

- Drugs, medical, and biotech

- Leisure/entertainment

NEW INNOVATIONS CREATE
NEW OPPORTUNITIES

Material changes in underlying conditions can have a dramatic effect on group performance. This doesn't mean that a stock must belong to a strong group to make a big advance or imply that a strong tide will lift all the proverbial boats higher. Be on the lookout for new industries and companies with market niches, specialized expertise, proprietary technology, or a positive sector change such as deregulation. Look for new technologies or adaptations of old technologies that promise to help people work better, live longer, and enjoy life more or that help companies cut costs and improve productivity and efficiencies. Look for opportunities in companies undergoing positive changes. You can read industry trade magazines. You can call company representatives and ask which publications they recommend for keeping up with new industry events and happenings in their field.

When a new category is established or a company creates a new industry, often it's an extension of a broader group category. For example, US Surgical was a medical products company. After it pioneered the surgical staple in 1987, a whole new medical approach became its own niche. In the early 1990s, US Surgical introduced the Endo Clip, which allowed laparoscopic gallbladder removal, and the market for those devices began to grow rapidly. Soon, laparoscopy was also being used for hernia operations, appendectomies, hysterectomies, and other types of abdominal surgery. With a virtual monopoly on sales of the equipment for these operations, US Surgical saw its sales grow by 50 percent in 1990 and 75 percent in the first half of 1991. Earnings during that time grew by 78 percent, and by the end of the year they had nearly doubled. US Surgical sold more than $300 million worth of laparoscopic equipment in 1991 to become one of the fastest-growing companies in the United States, with profits of $91 million. Just a few years earlier US Surgical had sold only $10 million worth of laparoscopic tools; by 1992 the company's revenues for the year surpassed $1 billion.

GROUP CYCLE DYNAMICS

Events in one industry group can have an effect on other industry groups. For instance, the Iraq war and the 9/11 terrorist attacks had a dramatic effect on military and defense companies. This in turn had an effect on electronic parts manufacturers, in particular, companies that manufactured delicate measuring devices. In the 1990s, healthcare reform boosted HMOs, and that produced a need for cost-containment companies and software to help those companies deal with patients and logistics. The advent of the personal computer had a direct effect on semiconductors. The proliferation of small handheld devices produced demand for one-inch hard drives. High energy prices in the period 2006–2008 and ever-increasing worldwide energy use, as well as increased levels of pollution, have led to the proliferation of solar and alternative energy technology. Personal computing created the need for software and peripherals, which in turn led to the widespread use of the Internet, creating the need for faster speed and broadband access. Now we see social media and cloud computing as new frontiers. You can be assured that future growth areas will show up in leading stocks of leading industry groups.

WHEN THE LEADER SNEEZES, THE GROUP CAN GET A COLD

Just as leading stocks can at times foretell a powerful group advance, keeping an eye on the top two or three companies in an industry group could provide a tip-off to when the group may be headed for trouble. It's important to keep your eye on important leading names in the top-performing sectors. Often you'll see an important stock in a group break badly, and the whole group will suffer. If one or more important stocks in an industry group top, that could be a warning that the whole group will soon run into trouble. Even stocks that are outside the group, such as suppliers and customers, may share in the suffering. Historically, more than 60 percent of superperformance stocks were part of an industry group advance. It pays to keep an eye on an industry's top stocks to get a feel for that group's potential strength. However, if a key leader breaks down after a big advance, beware. This is often the initial symptom that the entire group is about to get sick.

New Technologies Become Old Technologies

Every innovation eventually ceases to be an innovation; in doing so, it follows a path of market penetration and eventual saturation. This is a timeless truth. Initially, every new innovation (railroads, automobiles, radios, televisions, computers, the Internet, etc.) begins at a relatively high price point that only a small market segment can afford. Progress in technology and manufacturing gradually reduces the relative price of the new product. This leads to market penetration in which more and more potential users can acquire the new product or service. At some point market saturation is reached: all firms or households that will buy and use the new product have access to it; good examples are the automobile and the television. The market becomes largely a replacement market with overall unit growth bounded by the slow growth of the economy overall.

Once a market reaches saturation, little room remains for further penetration. Relative price declines have less and less of a positive impact on unit sales. The industry ceases to be a growth industry. In some cases, tech-

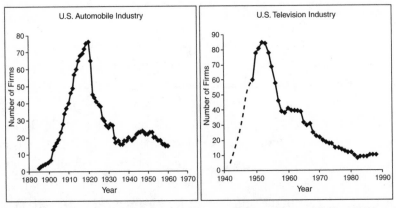

Figure 6.4   **Number of companies in the automobile industry (1890–1970) and television industry (1940–1990).**

Source: James M. Utterback, "Mastering the Dynamics of Innovation."

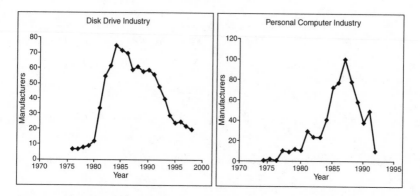

Figure 6.5   **Number of manufacturers of disk drives (1976–1998) and personal computers (1974–1992).**
Source: DISK/TREND reports, Management Science, and CSFB estimates.

nological and manufacturing progress may lead to price declines that exceed consequent increases in unit sales. During such periods of market saturation, competitive pressures usually lead to severe declines in profit margins. A former growth industry geared to rapid sales expansion enters a period of consolidation in which competition becomes unusually intense. Such periods of consolidation are usually characterized by profit rates well below the prior industry average, a decline in the number of companies in an industry, and bankruptcies. In the 1980s and 1990s, the PC-based high-tech industry underwent such a process of market penetration. This was no different from the experience of the automobile industry in the 1920s and the television industry in the 1950s; however, the cycle moved at a faster pace, probably as a result of the increase in information flow and access to world markets.

CHAPTER 7

FUNDAMENTALS
TO FOCUS ON

HEN A STOCK SUFFERS A MAJOR BREAK in price, there's a
reason, and very often it's the beginning of lower prices to
come. In almost every case, something is fundamentally wrong with the
company's business or industry. Entering 2008, many of the big banks,
including Citigroup, along with their broker-dealer and investing bank-
ing cousins such as Lehman Brothers and Bear Stearns, were overlever-
aged and held deteriorating balance sheets. This toxic cocktail would set
up the financial sector for collapse as the overall economy was stunned into
a severe recession. From 2007 to 2009, former Dow component American
International Group (AIG) crashed from a high of $103 down to a minus-
cule $0.33. On September 22, 2008, AIG was removed from the Dow Jones
Industrial Index. Citigroup was removed from the Dow on June 8, 2009.

You've heard the old adage about buying low and selling high, so maybe
you figure this is a once-in-a-lifetime opportunity—that is, to buy GE,
Citigroup, or some other familiar company while it's down in price. I bet
those who bought the blue chip carmaker General Motors in 2008 felt they
were getting a bargain, too. However, in just one year GM stock dropped to
a level not seen since 1933, shedding almost 95 percent of its value. On June
8, 2009, General Motors was also removed from the Dow Jones Industrials
Index. The fact is, no matter how big or prestigious a company is, when
fundamentals deteriorate—namely, earnings—you never know how far the
stock will fall.

Figure 7.1   **Citigroup (C) 2006–2011**

WHAT DRIVES SUPERPERFORMANCE?

The stock market cares little about the past, including the status of a company. What it cares about is the future, namely, growth. Keep in mind that our goal is to uncover superperformance stocks: shares that will far outpace the rest of the pack. These stocks are the ones with the strongest potential, and they seldom are found in the bargain bin. They are going strong because of a powerful force behind them: growth—real growth—in earnings and sales. Why buy damaged merchandise?

If your goal is to achieve superperformance in stocks, each company must earn its place in your portfolio by being an outstanding business. Superperformance stocks show their strength through their ability to improve and grow earnings, sales, and margins. These powerhouse companies report quarterly results that are better than Wall Street anticipates, with upside surprises that propel the stock higher. Don't become enamored with a stock selling down in price because it has a well-known name. Many winning stocks may be companies that you never heard of before. Their best days lie ahead, not in the past. **Regardless of a company's size, status, or reputation, there is no intelligent reason for an investor to settle for an inferior track record in a marketplace filled with companies with outstanding fundamentals.**

Each quarter, earnings and sales reports provide a refreshed set of statistics with new names, as those with poorer prospects are often replaced with those with greater potential. The same release of quarterly results also brings fresh data with which to evaluate the companies already in one's portfolio. In this way, the portfolio naturally evolves to achieve its performance goal through forced displacement. Stocks that continue to deliver the goods can remain in the portfolio, and the ones that fail to perform must go.

WHY EARNINGS?

In real estate, the mantra goes "location, location, location." In the stock market, it's earnings, earnings, earnings; after all, it's the bottom line that counts. How much money can a company earn and for how long? This leads to three basic questions every investor should ask when it comes to earnings: How much? How long? and How certain? Profitability, sustainability, and visibility represent the most influential factors that move stock prices.

To understand the impact of earnings on stock prices, let's go behind the scenes and examine how Wall Street operates. Who moves stock prices? Big institutional investors such as mutual funds, hedge funds, pension funds, and insurance companies. Many institutional investors, encompassing a relatively large number of investment professionals, use investment models that identify earnings surprises, that is, reported earnings that beat analysts' expectations. As soon as an earnings surprise is reported, these opportunists will jump onboard or at least put the stock on their radar screens as a potential buy candidate.

Most of the big institutional investors utilize valuation models that are based on earnings estimates to determine a stock's current worth or value. **When a company reports quarterly results that are meaningfully better than expected, analysts who follow the stock must reexamine and revise**

their earnings estimates upward. This increases the attention paid to a stock. The upward estimate revision is going to raise institutional investors' projected value of the company. When earnings estimates for a stock head up, shares, of course, become more attractive—and invite buying.

ANTICIPATION AND SURPRISE

Stocks move for two basic reasons: anticipation and surprise. Every price movement is rooted in one of these two elements: anticipation of news, an event, an important business change, or reaction to an unexpected event and a surprise, whether positive or negative.

Anticipation means expectation, for example, rumors that a large contract may be awarded to a contractor. In anticipation of an announcement, the stock price may advance. Once the deal is on the table and the contract is officially awarded, the stock could sell off. The same thing can happen with earnings that are in line with expectations; once the announcement is made, the stock declines because that event had already been priced into or discounted in the stock price. Stocks often move in anticipation of good and bad news and then after the fact may move in the opposite direction (i.e., rallying in anticipation of a favorable development and selling off when the announcement is made). This market phenomenon may baffle newbie investors. The reason for it is that the stock market prices in future events. That is what is meant when people say the stock market is a discounting mechanism. Although anticipation moves prices, once the expected event occurs, the market sells on the news. Hence the old adage "Buy the rumor; sell the fact."

Surprises can take many forms, from earnings that were far above or below estimates to a sudden development that significantly changes a company's business outlook. What surprises have in common, by definition, is that they are unexpected. Suddenly, the idea of deregulating an industry catches on in Congress or a drug that seemed unlikely to win U.S. Food and Drug Administration (FDA) approval unexpectedly gets the green light. With earnings, results come in well above expectations for a positive surprise or well below for a negative surprise.

The Earnings Surprise

Let's define what Wall Street means by an earnings surprise: simply stated, a company's earnings are better (or worse) than the consensus of analysts' estimates. You can find out what the estimates are for a company's earnings through news sources such as Yahoo! Finance, Zacks, and Briefing.com. If a dozen analysts follow XYZ Corp. and the consensus (average) for quarterly earnings is $0.53 per share, if the company reports results of $0.60 a share, that will be a $0.07 positive surprise. If the company reports $0.48 a share, that will be a $0.05 negative surprise.

A surprise could set off a flurry of activity, including a wave of buying that, in the case of a positive surprise, raises the stock price. Studies have shown that the effects of the surprise and the postnews drift (movement in the direction of the surprise reaction) can last for months. Efficient market theory holds that the market reacts instantaneously and fully prices in new information completely. Experienced traders know that this theory is false for several reasons. For one thing, it's impossible for everybody to respond at the exact same time. Liquidity is also a factor; only so many shares are available to be bought and sold. Large buyers must buy over time to avoid running a stock up too quickly, and if they sell too fast, they can crush the stock. This is what accounts for postearnings drift, a persistent bias in the direction of the surprise. **Be on the lookout for companies that are beating earnings estimates; the bigger the earnings surprise, the better.**

The Cockroach Effect

They call it the cockroach effect because as with cockroaches, if you see one, you can bet there are others. The same thinking applies to companies reporting earnings surprises. If a company has posted very good quarterly results that are much better than were anticipated by analysts, there are probably more good quarters ahead. If a company is performing well with earnings surprises, other companies in the same industry or sector may post some upside surprises as well.

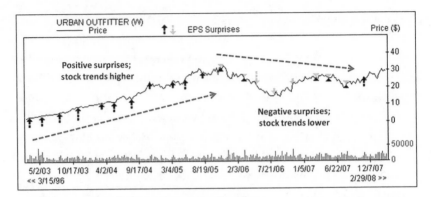

Figure 7.2   **Urban Outfitter (URBN) 2003–2007**
Fueled by persistent positive earnings surprises, the price of Urban Outfitter rose dramatically from 2003–2005. In contrast, from 2006–2007, a period dominated by negative surprises, the stock was essentially unchanged.
Chart courtesy of Zacks Research Wizard.

The prospect of further surprises may lead to speculation by institutional investors in some stocks even before the earnings come out. Such a strategy can be profitable. An authentic earnings surprise for the quarter probably portends higher earnings in the next quarter as well. The mirror effect often holds true for negative surprises. Companies that miss earnings estimates often disappoint again in subsequent quarters. **Because earnings surprises have a lingering effect, we want to focus on companies that beat estimates and avoid firms that have negative earnings surprises.** One way to find candidates is to check to see if earnings reported in the last couple of quarters were better than expected.

Not All Surprises Are Created Equal

Not all surprises are really surprises. Sometimes a company will beat the published consensus number; for example, Company XYZ reports earnings of $1.23 a share versus the Street estimate of $1.20. Although that's a $0.03 upside surprise, don't be unduly impressed with companies that beat analysts' estimates. News reports often emphasize that companies' announced earnings beat analysts' estimates by a penny or two a share; this isn't anything new. Companies more often than not beat their estimates. This happens because they're careful to guide expectations in their public statements during the quarter, ensuring that analysts' estimates converge around a number slightly below what management knows the company will deliver. It's also partly due to a herd effect among analysts who don't want their quarterly forecasts to be too far above or below the average of their peers.

Analysts are typically conservative in making earnings estimates. Since the market likes upside surprises and Wall Street firms are in the business of selling stocks to consumers, you can see how this happens. When it comes to estimates, there is no benefit to being aggressive. If the majority of analysts are between, say, $0.25 and $0.30 a share in their earnings estimates and the consensus is $0.27, who would want to crank up the earnings model to project $0.40 a share? Even a better than expected earnings report could look like an earnings disappointment; the stock could get clobbered, and as a result, the analyst could be out of a job. Being conservative and safe within a reasonable range of the consensus number makes everybody happy, especially if the company beats the estimates. Although it may look good on the surface, don't be fooled into thinking this is a true upside surprise. You are looking for a significant event with results that beat estimates by a meaningful margin.

Years ago, it was popular to discern the *whisper number* on the Street, a shadowy figure that was more realistic than the published estimate or consensus. The whisper number existed because company management once could legally share information within a closed circle of certain analysts; those analysts in turn would share that information with their biggest clients.

The Sarbanes-Oxley Act of 2002 silenced the whisper number with stricter rules that required companies to disseminate information in a more restricted fashion, with stiff penalties for violations. Even earlier, the Securities and Exchange Commission in August 2000 adopted Regulation FD (Fair Disclosure) to address "non-public information" (information that had not yet been announced) that could be disclosed by publicly traded companies. In general, the rule states that if a company releases certain information to certain individuals, such as analysts, it also has to make a public disclosure of that information. The purpose of the rule is to promote "full and fair disclosure," according to the SEC.

ANALYSTS' REVISIONS OF ESTIMATES

When a company reports a meaningful earnings surprise, analysts who follow that stock are likely to revise their earnings estimates. I like to see estimates raised not only for the current quarter but also for the current fiscal year. Studies have shown that when estimates are revised upward by 5 percent or more, stocks tend to show better-than-average performance. Conversely, with downward revisions of 5 percent or more, stocks exhibit lower than average performance.

Generally, adjustments to estimates following an earnings surprise are made shortly after the announcement. Sometimes, however, estimates are raised *before* an earnings report, for example, in the middle of the quarter. This reflects the expectation of good results. It may be that a product is selling better than expected or business conditions have improved. Analysts who follow companies very carefully revise their estimates not only based on historical data but also because of what they learn by talking with customers and suppliers.

As the reporting period approaches, estimates probably will start to converge around the consensus estimate. It's your job to watch a stock to get an idea of whether the price is already anticipating these expected results. Also note that when analysts raise their earnings estimates on the basis of the latest results, this lowers the price/earnings (P/E) ratio of a stock because the denominator—earnings—is larger.

To calculate future earnings, analysts start with a revenue projection, such as all the contracts that a company has or says it will have. Then they apply the company's expected profit margin and subtract a certain percentage for taxes. The result is the earnings per share for the quarter or the year. Most of the inputs for an estimate come from company guidance in the form of press releases, conference calls, and personal one-on-one discussions with executives. The analyst may adjust the numbers in the earnings forecast on the basis of conversations with customers who may indicate that

Consensus EPS Earnings Trends
Estimates Trending Higher 30-Days Earlier

	This Quarter	Next Quarter	This Year	Next Year
Current	0.34	0.66	1.32	1.94
7 Days Ago	0.32	0.65	1.28	1.94
30 Days Ago	0.29	0.65	1.18	1.92
60 Days Ago	0.29	0.65	1.18	1.92
90 Days Ago	0.29	0.63	1.09	1.88

Figure 7.3   **Earnings estimate revisions**

sales are not as good as projected or, conversely, better than the company has stated. Or the analyst may determine that the company is going to qualify for a lower tax rate. A competitor may be about to announce lower pricing, which will lead to a price war that will grind down profit margins.

Look for companies for which analysts are raising estimates. Quarterly as well as current fiscal year estimates should be trending higher; the bigger the estimate revisions, the better. At the very least, I like to see the current fiscal year or the next year's estimates trending higher from 30 days earlier; if both are trending higher, that is even better. Although I won't necessarily disqualify a stock as a buy candidate if it lacks upward earnings revisions, large downward estimate revisions are definitely a red flag.

BIG EARNINGS ATTRACT BIG ATTENTION

When a company delivers several quarters of strong earnings, this not only prompts more upward revisions of analysts' earnings estimates and brokerage upgrades but also results in more coverage of the stock as additional investment houses assign analysts to follow the company. More upbeat analysis can lead to more buying. The stock, which was hardly noticed just a few quarters ago, is starting to attract attention and bask in the limelight.

If earnings accelerate quarter by quarter at a strengthening pace, earnings per share (EPS) momentum can propel the share price even higher. As

EPS momentum builds—for example, 10 percent earnings growth, then 30 percent, 50 percent, and so on—the earnings momentum buyers will jump on the bandwagon. A feeding frenzy is now under way, all of it fueled by EPS growth and expectations of future growth.

As the stock's price rises quickly because of the prospects of improving fundamentals from institutional buying, additional quantitative models kick in and price momentum players start to buy the stock purely on the basis of a strong price trend and price momentum. Some of these investors will buy stocks that show strong price action regardless of the fundamentals. They believe that a stock that is rising strongly will continue to rise over the short to intermediate term purely as a result of momentum.

At some point, the growth becomes obvious and essentially everybody knows about it. The stock is officially termed a growth stock. The smart money that got in early is getting out with a hefty profit, and naive investors step in to buy what they've been reading about in the financial pages or hearing about on TV. Then the momentum stalls. What follows is the loss of EPS momentum, an eventual negative earnings surprise, and downward revisions, all of which puts considerable pressure on the stock price. This earnings maturation cycle happens time and time again, market cycle after

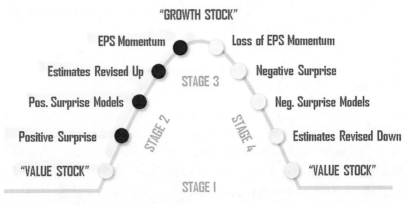

Figure 7.4   **Earnings maturation cycle**

In order to find your next superperformer, look for stocks that are in stage 2 with strong earnings, positive surprises, and upward revised estimates.

market cycle. The key is to understand where you are in the cycle and take advantage of its effect.

Get It on the Table

Big earnings will eventually attract the big players and create the conditions for big price performance. The length of time a stock remains in stage 2 depends on the company's fundamentals, specifically, how long it's able to continue its pattern of strong earnings growth. Some companies can keep this up for quite a stretch. To take advantage of this phenomenon, you don't need to guess or predict, and you don't have to settle for less than stellar performance in terms of fundamentals. Look for stage 2 uptrends supported by strong earnings growth, and you will dramatically increase your chances for attaining big success in stocks.

Sometimes a company with a rocketing stock price may not be making much money, but the rising price means that investors are hoping that it will be profitable in the future. However, three out of four times, the very best performers will show meaningful earnings increases in the most recent quarter from the same quarter a year earlier. **You should demand not only that the most recent quarter be up by a meaningful amount but that the past two or three quarters also show good gains.**

In fact, it's even better if the earnings are getting stronger sequentially each quarter. In our study of past superperformance stocks, as well as in the Love and Reinganum studies, current quarterly earnings showed the highest correlation with big stock price performance.

To ensure that your stock is attractive to institutional investors, demand that a minimum level of current quarterly earnings performance be met before investing. Many successful growth managers require a minimum of 20 to 25 percent year-over-year increases in the most recent one, two, or three quarters. The greater the percentage increases, the better. **Really successful companies generally report earnings increases of 30 to 40 percent or more during their superperformance phase.** In a bull market you can set your minimum even higher; look to find companies delivering increases in earnings of 40 to 100 percent or more in the most recent two to three quarters. Companies that report four, five, or six strong quarters in a row provide even more assurance that they are on the right track.

It's important to know when the companies in your portfolio and the ones on your watch list will report quarterly earnings. It's not uncommon for a company to issue a preannouncement about its results before the actual earnings date. You should, in addition, be aware of earnings reports and news from companies that are in the same industry group as the stocks you hold.

The following are some examples of big winners that had their earnings on the table when they made a large-scale advance in price:

- March 1989 through May 1993: Cisco Systems (CSCO) reported 15 out of 17 quarters of earnings increases of 100 percent or more, with the other two quarters at 92 percent and 71 percent, respectively. Cisco's stock price advanced more than 13-fold during this period.

- September 1989 through December 1992: Home Depot (HD) reported 14 consecutive quarters of earnings in excess of 29 percent; Home Depot's stock price advanced more than 500 percent.

- From 1987 through 1991, Microsoft (MSFT) reported only one quarter below 36 percent for 16 straight quarters. The stock price advanced more than 1,200 percent.

- Apollo Group (APOL) reported 45 consecutive quarters at or above Wall Street's estimates. Apollo's stellar price performance qualifies it as one of the greatest stock market winners of all time.

- From 2009 through 2011, Green Mountain Coffee Roasters (GMCR) averaged quarterly earnings increases of 112 percent and quarterly sales increases of 67 percent. The stock price advanced more than 650 percent in 24 months.

- Amgen (AMGN) averaged quarterly earnings increases of 288 percent during its phenomenal run in the early 1990s.

CROCS: GETTING IN AND GETTING OUT AT THE RIGHT TIME

Crocs Inc. (CROX) was a flash-in-the-pan retail fad, similar to a sneaker company I traded in the 1980s called LA Gear. Both had meteoric price surges in a relatively short period because of rapid sales of their trendy shoes. Initially priced at $9.90, Crocs opened up 200 percent at $30 per share on February 8, 2006. Crocs boasted triple-digit earnings per share every quarter from June 2006 until September 2007. From its initial public offering through October 2007, quarterly earnings per share averaged 229 percent. The stock advanced a whopping 400 percent during that period.

Hot one-product stocks that go from unknown to all the rage overnight can be great investments if you get in and get out at the right time. Crocs skyrocketed while business was booming, albeit briefly. There are countless examples of companies that produced huge earnings growth as a result of a cyclical fad. While a product is selling rapidly, there can be a great deal

Figure 7.5   **Crocs 2006–2009**
Crocs Inc. (CROX) benefited from rapid sales of its trendy shoes, which translated into six consecutive quarters of triple-digit earnings growth and a very profitable stage 2 price advance.

of enthusiasm over the company's shares. Whatever the reason, some sort of positive development in the company is accelerating the growth rate and the share price. Although this rate of growth is not sustainable forever—no company can do it indefinitely—it may last for 6, 9, or 12 quarters or even longer with strong EPS momentum. If you get onboard during this period of strong earnings growth, the stock can rally 100 percent or even rise by 300, 500, or in some rare instances 1,000 percent over a year or two.

VICOR: TRIPLE-DIGIT EARNINGS PROPELS STOCK

The earnings cycle phenomenon is *not* a one-time event or something unusual. It happens time and time again, market cycle after market cycle. The only thing that changes are the names. In 1991, I purchased shares of the electronic equipment manufacturer Vicor Corporation (VICR), which advanced more than 400 percent in less than a year. This was due to a rapid

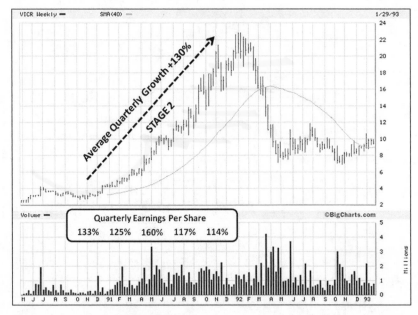

Figure 7.6   **Vicor (VICR) 1990–1993**

Vicor (VICR) sported five quarters of triple-digit EPS growth, which fueled a 460 percent share price advance in 14 months.

earnings spurt from sales of a patented approach to providing the electricity used for sensitive electronic equipment called a zero current switch. From September 1990 through September 1991, Vicor reported triple-digit percentage growth in its quarterly earnings. This was a tremendous performance that accelerated the stock price 460 percent, from a split-adjusted $4 a share to over $22.

As you can see, big profits can be made while earnings growth is strong; some price moves are meteoric. The key is to focus on the stage 2 portion of the cycle while the company is delivering strong quarterly EPS growth.

EARNINGS ACCELERATION

In addition to large earnings increases that are better than analysts expect, I'm looking for earnings acceleration, meaning that the growth in earnings is larger than it was in a previous period. **More than 90 percent of the biggest stock market winners showed some form of earnings acceleration before or during their huge price moves.**

For instance, let's say that four quarters ago the company reported a $0.05 decline year over year in quarterly earnings. Three quarters ago, earnings were up 10 percent year over year. Then, two quarters ago, earnings were up 28 percent, and in the most recent quarter, results are up 56 percent. That's three quarters of earnings accelerations. Year-over-year earnings are growing by an increased rate sequentially, quarter to quarter. This characteristic is very positive and has been shown to exist in most of the best performing stocks.

	Q4	Q1	Q2	Q3	Q4 (EST.)
EPS	-34%	+12%	+44%	+83%	+244%
EPS ($)	0.14	0.29	0.39	0.50	
ESTIMATE	0.16	0.23	0.30	0.36	0.48
+/-	-0.02	0.06	0.09	0.14	

Figure 7.7 **Example of quarterly earnings acceleration**

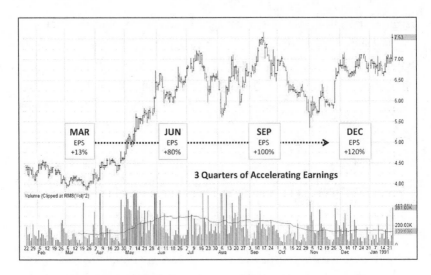

Figure 7.8   **Elan PLC (ELN) 1990**

In 1990, earnings accelerated for three consecutive quarters prior to emerging as a market leader. Elan rose 152 percent in 12 months.

Chart courtesy of Interactive Data © 2009.

Look for Earnings Supported by Revenue

In addition to strong, accelerating earnings per share growth, you want to see sales exhibit the same characteristics: strong quarterly growth and acceleration. **It's not uncommon for new market leaders to show triple-digit sales growth in the most recent two, three, or more quarters. In fact, some great stock market successes deliver large quarterly sales increases consistently for several years.** For example, from March 2009 through December 2010, Netflix reported eight consecutive quarters of sales increases that accelerated from 21 percent to 34 percent; during that period, quarterly earnings averaged 45 percent. Netflix's stock price advanced more than 500 percent. Home Depot made a 698 percent move from June 1982 to June 1983. Its sales grew 104 percent, 158 percent, 191 percent, and 220 percent, respectively, over the four quarters leading up to this major stock-price

Figure 7.9   **F5 Networks (FFIV) 2007–2011**

F5 Networks displayed both accelerating earnings and sales during its powerful stage 2 advance.

jump. In 2010, accelerating sales bolstered earnings and propelled shares of F5 Networks more than 500 percent. This is what really accounts for superior stock performance: strong earnings growth backed by brisk sales, not accounting gimmickry. If you demand that your stock selections not only show strong earnings but also show strong sales, you will increase your chances of latching on to a superperformer.

Check the Trend

Generally, I look back one to two years to see if there has been some form of earnings and sales acceleration. Life is not perfect, and so if one quarter here or there doesn't accelerate, it may not be a big deal. You can smooth out quarterly results by using a two-quarter rolling average over the past four, six, or eight quarters. Ideally, you want to see a steadily improving trend.

	Q1	Q2	Q3	Q4	Q1	Q2	Q3	Q4
EPS	-14%	17%	43%	23%	52%	36%	65%	59%
2Q AVG.		2%	30%	33%	39%	44%	51%	62%
SALES	0%	2%	2%	7%	13%	15%	15%	14%
2Q AVG.		1%	2%	5%	10%	14%	15%	14%

Figure 7.10   **Example of smoothing earnings and sales using a two-quarter rolling average**

In contrast, a trend of a material deceleration, with results trending sharply lower for several quarters or longer, should raise suspicion.

Annual Earnings

If a company is truly doing well, its success is unlikely to end overnight. A surprisingly good earnings report could be the beginning of a string of successful quarters. **Strong quarterly results should translate into strong annual results. Just one or two quarters of good earnings isn't going to be enough to drive a stock's price significantly higher for an extended period.**

One of the most successful stocks of the last several decades was Apollo Group. From 2000 to 2004, Apollo's stock price accelerated from $10 a share to $96. During that period, annual EPS growth averaged almost 40 percent, accelerating from 28 percent in 2000 to 55 percent in 2003. This is the type of growth that fuels superperformance. In addition to quarterly growth, look for strong annual growth.

Figure 7.11   **Apollo Group (APOL) vs. Nasdaq with annual earnings per share percent change: 1999–2004**

From 2000 through 2003 Apollo's earnings accelerated annually.

Look for a Breakout Year

You can go back two to four years or more to a record year and see if current earnings are breaking out above the previous trend. It can be a fairly significant event if earnings suddenly break out to the upside from a range that was established over several years. Finally, check the upcoming one or two quarters as well as the next fiscal year to see if earnings acceleration is expected to continue.

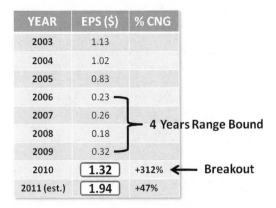

YEAR	EPS ($)	% CNG
2003	1.13	
2004	1.02	
2005	0.83	
2006	0.23	
2007	0.26	
2008	0.18	
2009	0.32	
2010	1.32	+312%
2011 (est.)	1.94	+47%

4 Years Range Bound

Breakout

Figure 7.12　**Example of an earnings breakout**
In this example, 2010 earnings not only break above the previous four-year trend, but also take out the high set in 2003. This is a significant development.

How to Spot a Turnaround Situation

Another form of earnings acceleration to look for is a turnaround situation. A stock had been doing well but then fell on hard times. During the difficult period, the company probably had some negative earnings surprises, for example, growing at a slower rate than expected, growing by only a single-digit percentage, or perhaps reporting negative results. In some quarters, earnings may have declined compared with the year-ago period. Then, all of a sudden, earnings growth explodes. The company reports quarterly earnings that are up 50 percent from the prior-year period, and the next quarter it shows a greater than 100 percent year-over-year gain; in the subsequent quarter, results are up 150 percent. Amplifying this performance are the easy comparisons from the prior year when the company was struggling. Now, as things start to turn around, not only is the company able to post higher earnings, the gains on a percentage basis look dramatically better.

With turnaround situations, investors should insist that the current earnings be very strong (+100 percent or better in the most recent one or two quarters). If the previous results were dismal, the company should be doing significantly better percentagewise in light of easy comparisons. You could also insist that earnings and margins be at or close to a new high for added confirmation that the company is back on track.

In some cases, you can spot turnarounds and earnings acceleration by comparing the current annual growth rate or current quarterly results with the three- or five-year growth rate. **A company that has been growing 12 percent a year and suddenly starts to show growth of 40 percent and then 100 percent could be a hot prospect.**

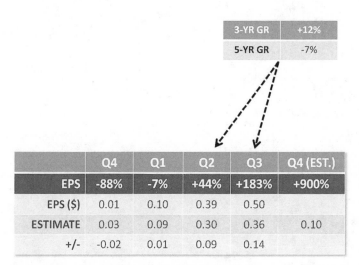

3-YR GR	+12%
5-YR GR	-7%

	Q4	Q1	Q2	Q3	Q4 (EST.)
EPS	-88%	-7%	+44%	+183%	+900%
EPS ($)	0.01	0.10	0.39	0.50	
ESTIMATE	0.03	0.09	0.30	0.36	0.10
+/-	-0.02	0.01	0.09	0.14	

Figure 7.13 **Example of earnings acceleration versus the three- and five-year growth rate**
Q2 and Q3 show significant acceleration compared with the three- and five-year growth rates with a triple-digit gain in Q3.

DECELERATION IS A RED FLAG

A company can be doing great with high-double-digit percentage growth and then "deteriorate" to mid-double-digit growth. For another company, growing by 20 or 30 percent may be a big improvement. However, for a company that had been growing at upward of 50 to 60 percent or more, a growth rate of 20 to 30 percent would be a material deterioration. Consider what happened with Dell Computer, which from 1995 to 1997 had grown its earnings per share at 80 percent annually and then declined to around 65 percent in 1998 and 28 percent in 1999. Although this was still decent growth, it was a material change and marked the end of the tremendous move in Dell's stock price. The stock peaked in 2000. Ten years later Dell's stock price was considerably lower, down more than 80 percent from its high.

Figure 7.14 **Dell Computer 1995–2009**

HOME DEPOT

After a five-year period of stagnation that began in 1994, when Home Depot was clearly in a sideways stage 1 pattern, the stock entered an acceleration phase in 1997. Earnings (shown on an annual basis) rose by 21 percent that year, followed by an increase of 37 percent in 1998 and 41 percent in 1999. This demonstrates how a stock performs best when earnings have the strongest rate of growth. Home Depot's stock advanced from $10 a share to a peak of over $70 a share. What fueled Home Depot's price growth was an average annual EPS growth rate of 27 percent, which accelerated in 1998 and 1999.

The peak for Home Depot's stock was in 2000. After a strong earnings performance in 1999 with a 41 percent growth rate, EPS momentum slowed dramatically. In 2000, EPS growth was only 11 percent. The deceleration

Figure 7.15   **Home Depot (HD) 1992–2008**
Chart of Home Depot (HD) shows that strong, accelerating annual earnings triggered a rapid rise in the stock price, followed by a long, precipitous decline as the earnings growth rate slowed considerably.

brought the stock down from its lofty levels as average annual EPS growth from 2000 to 2007 was 15 percent, almost half of what it had been during the upward momentum phase. Home Depot shares performed poorly during the slower-growth period. This was due to the stock price running up ahead of its earnings and then eventually falling victim to earnings deceleration, which can happen when a growth stock becomes too popular.

In summary, institutions like to see the following:

- Earnings surprises

- Accelerating earnings per share (EPS) and revenues

- Expanding margins

- EPS breakout

- Strong annual EPS change

- Signs that acceleration will continue

CHAPTER 8

ASSESSING EARNINGS QUALITY

COMPANY CAN GENERATE EARNINGS in various ways, some not so trustworthy; I prefer high-quality earnings. In other words, where did the earnings come from? Did the company post better results because of stronger sales? If sales were strong, was it only because of a single product or one major customer? In that case, the growth is vulnerable. Or are the surprisingly strong results due to an industrywide phenomenon or an influx of orders from numerous buyers? Maybe the company is slashing costs and cutting back. **Earnings improvement from cost cutting, plant closures, and other so-called productivity enhancements walks on short legs. Such improvements can show up from time to time, but sustainable earnings growth requires revenue growth.** Examining earnings quality gives you perspective and rationale before you commit your hard-earned money to a stock.

NONOPERATING OR NONRECURRING INCOME

Depending on how you examine a company's quarterly report, it can look like a roaring success or a sagging sloth; it's all a matter of perspective. Here's how this can happen. XYZ Corp. reports $3.01 per share versus $2.40 the year before. This shows a hefty earnings gain of 25 percent. Looks great, right? On closer examination you notice that XYZ Corp. reported an "unusual gain" related to the sale of nonstrategic assets. This one-time event accounted for $0.84 per share of income and is considered nonrecurring. Therefore, this gain should be excluded from XYZ Corp's earnings. Doing this will result in an adjusted number of $2.17 a share, which is down 7 percent from the year before. Big difference!

I'm looking for earnings that come from core operations, not from a one-time gain or an extraordinary event. Most of the time the difference between operating income and nonoperating income is clear-cut. Consider a company that sells coffee; some of its stores are on company-owned real estate, and management decides to divest some of the properties in the belief that commercial real estate prices are high. These property transactions and the profits they generate are clearly outside of selling coffee. Therefore, any gain on the property sale would be a nonrecurring event or extraordinary gain that should be stripped away so that earnings reflect income from operations derived for the company's core business.

Beware Massaged Numbers

Management has become adept at managing expectations and massaging numbers in an effort to underpromise and overdeliver. The game players may even underdeliver by dropping an earnings bomb in an effort to have the estimate bar temporarily lowered for easy comparisons in the future.

One gimmick is to warn the public of a potential earnings problem, which will cause analysts to lower their earnings estimates. Then the company reports earnings that are better than the lowered estimate. This will result in an earnings surprise; however, it will be a surprise in the context of a lower consensus comparison. If you see that estimate revisions were recently lowered due to downside guidance, and then the company beat expectations, this should raise a red flag; the report may not be as good as it looks on the surface.

One-Time Charge

Another smoke-and-mirrors trick is to utilize a one-time charge or a nonrecurring charge. A company that would otherwise report weak earnings may in fact report a nonrecurring one-time charge that will account for a portion of the earnings. It's just a one-time expense, and business will be back to usual, right? Wrong! Not if this practice forms a pattern. Some companies are habitual abusers of the one-time charge. If the one-time charge is showing up over and over, you should seriously question the earnings quality of even the largest and most respected corporations engaging in this practice.

Write-Downs and Revenue Shifting

Inventories write-downs and ongoing expenses are also items to look out for. Some companies will bottle up and store write-downs for a later date when they'll need them. They may choose to recognize or shift revenues or expenses into the future or a different accounting period, which allows them to control in which quarter they will realize charges or recognize sales. Some companies will record revenues and accounts receivable at the time they ship product and estimate losses only for returned merchandise. If returns run higher than is accounted for, it could affect future earnings.

Management may also choose to shift earnings so that a hit can be absorbed in a single disappointing quarter. By shifting earnings to have one big down quarter, the company can beat estimates in the next quarter because the previous report prompted analysts to lower their estimates, making it easier for the company to beat the Street. You want to see earnings coming from robust top-line sales, not from accounting tricks and gimmicks.

Beware Profitability via Cost Cutting

With an understanding of the three major drivers of earnings (higher volume, higher prices, and lower costs), it pays to be cautious if a company is delivering only on cutting costs. **A company can increase profits by cutting jobs, closing plants, or shedding its losing operations. However, these measures have a limited life span.** Eventually, a company will have to do something else to grow its business and increase its top line. Therefore, check the story behind earnings growth. Make sure that it's not because of a

Figure 8.1   **Three ways a company can increase profits**
Higher sales and expanding margins can lead to higher earnings and P/E multiple expansion.

one-time event, because sales jumped as a result of some extraordinary gain, or because profits improved only as a result of cost cutting.

Companies with good potential for stock price appreciation show evidence that earnings growth is sustainable and will continue over some length of time. **The ideal situation is when a company has higher sales volume with new and current products in new and existing markets as well as higher prices and reduced costs. That's a winning combination.**

In general, the best growth candidates have the ability to expand, introduce new products and services, and enter new markets. They have the power to raise prices, and they can improve productivity and cut costs. The combination of revenue acceleration and margin expansion will have a dramatic effect on the bottom line.

The worst situation is when a company has limited pricing power, its business is capital-intensive, margins are low or under pressure, and it's faced with heavy regulation, intense competition, or both. An example would be the airline industry, which doesn't have much pricing power, faces government regulatory pressures, is very capital intensive, and is highly commodity-sensitive because of fuel costs.

When strong earnings are reported, check the story behind the results to make sure the good news is not due to a one-time event but is the product of conditions that probably will continue. Your questions should include the following:

•   Are there any new products or services or positive industry changes?

- Is the company gaining market share? A market is ultimately dominated by just a few companies.

- What is the company doing to increase revenue and expand margins?

- What is the company doing to decrease costs and increase productivity?

MEASURING MARGINS

The objective for any company is to retain as much money as it can from the revenue it generates, meaning that it has the highest profit margin possible. When margins expand, the company is getting a higher price for its products or has found a way to improve productivity or cut expenses, sometimes both. Increasing margins show that more profits are being made for each dollar of sales the company makes.

Margin metrics come in different varieties. Gross margin reflects how much more customers pay for a product compared with the company's costs. It shows investors how well a company is doing in keeping its costs in line and pricing its products. Gross margins depend on quite a few variables, some of which may be beyond the company's control, for example, if raw material costs were lower one quarter or if a competitor had a delivery problem that gave the company an unexpected advantage that could be a short-lived phenomenon. The best kind of margin improvement comes from pricing power because of strong demand for a company's products.

Net margin is based on a company's net income divided by sales and reflects all the variables that influence profitability. A falling net margin indicates that the company is making a smaller profit on its sales. This could be due to rising costs, inefficiencies, or taxation. Margin pressure can cause serious profit erosion. The cause of a decline in net margins could be temporary in nature, such as a short-term rise in raw material costs or temporary inefficiency in the production system. Far more worrisome is when the net margin declines because prices are dropping as a result of declining customer interest.

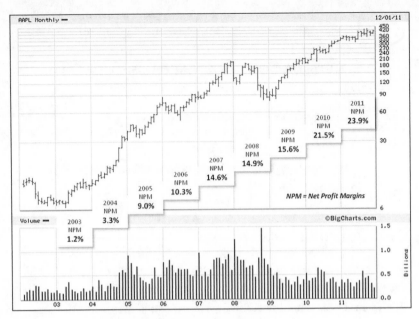

Figure 8.2 **Apple Computer (AAPL) 2003–2011**

From 2003 to 2011 Apple Computer's stock price advanced more than 6,000 percent. During that period, net profit margins expanded from just 1.2 percent in 2003 to 23.9 percent in 2011.

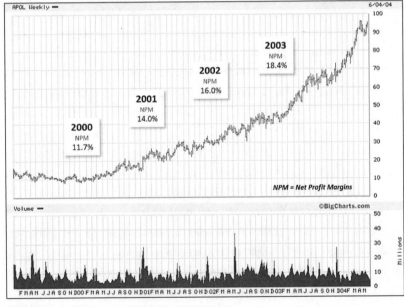

Figure 8.3 **Apollo Group (APOL) 1999–2004**

Apollo Group expanded net profit margins from 11.7 percent in 2000 to 18.4 percent in 2003.

A company with a strong net margin compared with the average in the industry has a competitive advantage. A comparison of net margin across companies in an industry can be used to gauge the quality of management. A well-run growth company should show consistent improvement in operating margins and net profit margins.

WHERE THE RUBBER MEETS THE ROAD

No matter how good an earnings report appears to be on the surface, you want to pay close attention to the stock's price reaction to determine how good the report really was or was perceived to be. One way to do this is simply to watch how the stock trades initially and over subsequent days after the earnings release. If the report really was great, you should see a strong stock price reaction that holds up and is supported by additional buying on reasonable pullbacks. I like to see the stock price react strongly to the report and hold its gains.

To determine whether the market is looking favorably on a company's earnings, I watch for three specific reactions:

1. **Initial response.** Did the stock rally or experience a sell-off? If it sold off, does it resume its slide after a dead cat bounce? Or, does the stock price come roaring back?

2. **Subsequent resistance.** How well did it hold its gains and resist profit taking?

3. **Resilience.** Did the stock recover quickly and powerfully? Or did it fail to rally after a pullback or, worse, sell off?

As an investor, you won't know for sure what Wall Street is looking for in an earnings report until you see the stock's reaction to the report. When an upside surprise is announced, I expect the stock price to do pretty well.

If that doesn't happen—say, the stock goes up briefly but then sells off and is down 15 percent and can't rally—that's a big problem. This type of reaction tells me that something may be wrong. Although it's not uncommon for stocks to sell off on profit taking after a big rally and decline on news, a superperformance stock will come back and resume its advance. **For a true superperformer, there should definitely not be a huge sell-off that breaks the whole leg of the stock's upward move.**

After a company reports its earnings, my focus turns to the postearnings drift (PED), which suggests that it may not be too late to buy a stock after it has reported better than expected earnings. Even if you miss the first upward reaction after results are reported, the postearnings drift after a significant surprise can last for some time. Stock price movements from significant earnings surprises not only are felt right way but can have a longer-term effect beyond the immediate price adjustments. Many studies have shown that the effect can persist for months after an earnings announcement.

Sometimes earnings are largely discounted, meaning that expectations for an earnings surprise were already priced in. Because such high expecta-

Figure 8.4   **Lululemon Athletica Inc. (LULU) 2011–2011**
Lululemon experienced post earnings drift (PED) after reporting earnings in September and December 2010.

tions had been discounted in the stock price, even an earnings surprise will not satisfy the market. If earnings came in at, say, $0.05 a share over expectations but that level of outperformance was already anticipated, this will be a disappointment to the market, which had hoped for an even bigger surprise, say, $0.07 or $0.10 a share. Even if the consensus was $0.50 and the company reported $0.55 a share, the stock could sell off because earnings did not come in even higher.

How do you know what the market wants other than the published estimates? Study how the stock price responds. Was the stock rewarded or punished when the results came in? Was an upside surprise big enough to move share prices higher, or did the stock sell off? Even if an earnings report appears to be a surprise, you can judge the true perception only from the response of the share price. Unexpected surprises can have a dramatic effect.

Figure 8.5 **Netflix (NFLX) 2009–2010**
In January 2010, Netflix shares gapped up big on its earnings report. After a brief and shallow pullback, the stock was back in new high ground.

COMPANY-ISSUED GUIDANCE

Company-issued guidance is simply comments that management provides publicly about what it expects in the future. These comments are also known as forward-looking statements and generally focus on earnings, sales, and margin expectations. Company guidance is given so that investors can evaluate the company's growth potential. Under current regulations, it is the only legal way a company can communicate its expectations to the market. Analysts use this information in combination with their own research to develop earnings forecasts.

Company-issued guidance plays an important role in the investment decision process because management knows its business better than anyone else and has firsthand information on which to base its expectations. Be aware, however, that management can use guidance to sway investors. For example, in a bull market some companies have given optimistic forecasts because the market wants momentum stocks with fast-growing earnings per share. In bear markets, companies have tried to guide expectations lower so that they can beat the earnings projections.

Companies generally issue guidance at or near the time a quarterly earnings report is released. Let's say that along with reporting stronger than expected earnings, the company issues guidance for the upcoming quarter and the rest of the year, projecting much better earnings ahead. For example, the company may say that for the next quarter it expects to earn $0.10 to $0.12 a share more than it previously predicted, and it also increases the expectation for year-end results by $0.30 to $0.35 a share. Not only has the company beaten the expectations for this quarter, it feels confident enough that it will have good results the next quarter to go public with a statement to that effect. Because companies are conservative about their earnings guidance, we know that a statement like this won't be issued unless management thinks the results will not only meet these higher expectations but also beat them. This is exactly what I'm looking for: better than expected earnings along with positive earnings guidance. A company should not only be doing well but be doing better than analysts anticipate.

Depending on what a company says about its business prospects going forward, positive or negative, the response of the stock price could be dramatic. **In some cases, the reaction to earnings guidance is stronger than the reaction to the actual earnings report when it is announced.** By tracking what a company says and then what develops later on, you can ascertain the quality and tendencies of the company's guidance.

If you think earnings expectations don't drive stock prices, watch what happens when a company announces earnings that fall short of expectations even by just a few pennies or when it issues downside guidance. Rosetta Stone Inc. (RST) raised its guidance for third-quarter and fiscal 2009 results in July 2009. After a brief pullback, four days after guidance was raised, the stock sold off and could not rally and recover. This was abnormal considering the rosy guidance. Just days later the company flip-flopped and issued lower guidance, and the stock got blasted. It simply did not make sense that the stock broke down and couldn't rally after what should have been perceived as great news. This was telling of the future. The fact that the com-

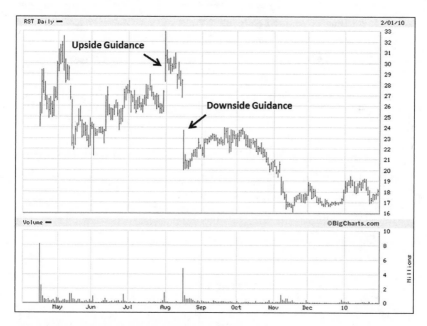

Figure 8.6   **Rosetta Stone (RST) 2009–2010**
Rosetta Stone shares were propelled higher when the company raised its earnings outlook. Eleven trading days later, the stock sold off sharply when the company unexpectedly lowered its guidance.

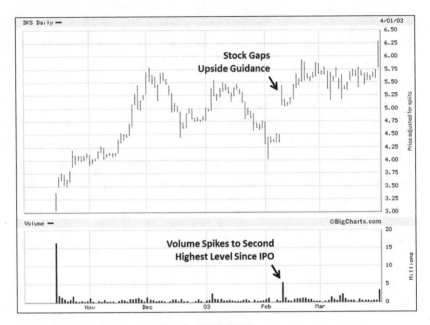

Figure 8.7   Dick's Sporting Goods (DKS) 2003
On the heels of positive company issued guidance Dick's Sporting Goods
exploded off its lows on the second highest volume since going public.

pany lowered guidance just 11 trading days after it had raised guidance was
a bewildering red flag.

As you can see from the previous Rosetta Stone example, company
issued guidance can send a stock soaring or plummeting depending on
how it is perceived by investors. In February of 2003, Dick's Sporting Goods
(DKS) gapped up big after the company issued positive forward guidance.
The overwhelming volume was revealing; a telltale sign that institutions
took comfort from the news.

LONG-TERM PROJECTIONS

When obliged to fess up to bad news, a publicly traded company will often
try to spin the message. It may announce a stock buyback or some other
"positive" news at the same time it reports a disappointing quarter in an
effort to soften the blow and offset any potential negative effects. This gener-

ally doesn't work. One feeble tactic is to issue an upbeat long-term projection at the same time they deliver bad news about an upcoming or current quarter. In dealing with future earnings, it's important not to look too far out. Growth investors tend to have a "what have you done for me lately" mentality. Therefore, focus on what the company is saying about the upcoming quarter and the current fiscal year. My rule of thumb is to take long-term forecasts with a grain of salt. **No one, not even management, can accurately forecast what a company will earn or what its rate of growth will be a year or two down the road.** If they say, "Business conditions will be tough this year, but we see improvement coming next year," that's *not* positive guidance. That's spin.

Analyzing Inventories

Back when I first started trading stocks in the early 1980s, public companies were not required to report inventory figures; now those figures are readily available. Inventory figures can be found in the published balance sheets of a corporation, which are available in 10-Q (quarterly) and 10-K (annual) filings to the Securities and Exchange Commission (SEC). Companies post the filings on their websites; corporate filings also are available on the SEC's EDGAR database.

With a manufacturer or retailer, inventory and accounts receivable analyses can provide a heads-up as to whether business conditions are likely to improve or if the good times are coming to an end. In late 2003–2004, the price of copper was going through the roof. This rapid escalation in the price of a raw material, I knew, would enable manufacturers of copper products to pass along a price increase to customers.

By examining the inventory figures in the quarterly reports of several manufacturers, I found my candidate: Encore Wire (WIRE). Encore possessed significant copper inventories and met the criteria of my SEPA stock analysis. I knew I had a potential big winner in sight. Encore had a stockpile of copper it had bought at lower prices. With the price of copper significantly higher, Encore could charge its customers significantly higher prices than it paid, which accounted for expanding profit margins.

Figure 8.8   **Price of copper and Encore Wire (WIRE) 2003–2006**
A stockpile of copper bought at lower prices allowed Encore Wire significant
margin expansion.

Compare Inventory with Sales

For certain industries, such as manufacturing, the comparison of inventory
and sales is crucial. Specifically, I look at the breakdown of inventory (i.e.,
finished goods, work in progress, and raw materials) and how each segment
relates to the others. The inventory breakdown also helps put sales in perspective. For example, a strong gain in sales may look impressive; however,
the company could be pushing on a string if in fact inventories are growing
much faster than sales. If the finished goods portion of inventories is rising
much more rapidly than the raw materials or work-in-progress segments,
this could mean that product is piling up. Therefore, production will slow
because the company already has a stockpile of finished goods.

If that inventory of finished products is highly depreciable—such as computers and certain retail goods—this could spell trouble ahead. A company sitting on a large stock of depreciating merchandise will have to slash prices to get rid of it. Also, that aging inventory will compete in the marketplace with newer product lines. Higher-trending inventories can lead to markdowns and write-offs, a scenario ripe for a hit on future earnings, causing the company to report a disappointing quarter.

Keep in mind that the amount of inventory by itself is not that meaningful to your analysis. It's the trend in inventories versus sales and the percentage increase or decrease within the inventory chain that yield valuable information.

Think of inventory as merchandise waiting to be sold. Under most conditions, inventories should rise and fall in a pattern similar to that for sales. Management tries to anticipate future sales and stocks inventory to meet demand or expected demand. **When inventory grows much faster than sales, it can indicate weakening sales, misjudgment by management of future demand, or both.** These scenarios are likely to undermine earnings. The more rapidly inventory depreciates, the more excess inventory will be detrimental.

DELL'S SOLUTION FOR INVENTORY BUILDUP

Companies that control their inventory the best in an environment of falling prices have the potential to hold up best and outperform the others, especially during an economic downturn. Dell Computer responded to this problem with its revolutionary "build-to-order" business model. The model transformed the manufacturing business by lowering inventory stockpiles and decreasing the risk of holding depreciating computers. Other companies have since adopted this simple concept even in industries outside the computer business. Dell's model is based on orders taken over the phone and on its website. Computers are not put into production until an order is placed. This dramatically reduced the number of days inventory was held and increased the company's inventory turnover ratio to more than three times that of its rivals.

This unique new business model allowed Dell to capture higher profit margins than its competitors, gain market share, and dominate the computer market during the 1990s. The reason this concept worked so well in the computer business is that the product was highly depreciable. Virtually all of Dell's competitors relied on a business model that involved stocking retail stores with merchandise. When business turned down, Dell's competitors were holding large inventories of merchandise, the value of which was eroding with time and advances in computer performance and capabilities. To keep their merchandise from spoiling like fruit in the sun, Compaq, Hewlett-Packard, and Gateway were forced to cut prices to unload their stockpiles. This condition will often show up in inventories, with finished goods usually rising and trending upward faster than sales and raw materials.

Not all inventory buildups are bad. Maybe a company has to fill the shelves of 20 new stores it just opened. The real red flag arises when an inventory buildup is unexplained or the explanation isn't a good one. If you spot an unexplained inventory buildup, you can call the company or go on an investor conference call to ask for an explanation.

On the flip side, if raw materials are suddenly building up, this could be an indication that the company believes business will be picking up. If that's the case, sales should show signs of acceleration shortly afterward to confirm that the raw material buildup was indeed in anticipation of stronger demand.

Analyzing Receivables

In addition to inventories, a part of a company's balance sheet that merits attention is receivables. Accounts receivable are what the company is owed for sales it has already made. Some receivables are to be expected in the course of doing business; it's normal to have a reasonable delay between delivery of products or services and receipt of payment. However, if receivables are increasing at a far greater rate than sales or if the trend is accelerating, this could be a warning that the company is having trouble collecting from its customers.

If receivables and inventories are both increasing at a greater rate than sales (twice or more without explanation), this could be double trouble.

Think about it. We know from the previous discussion that when inventories—particularly of finished goods—rise faster than sales, that means product is building up. The company has made more than it can sell in current market conditions, assuming that there isn't a good reason for the buildup, such as the need to stock new retail outlets. This is even a bigger problem if the inventory stockpile is of highly depreciable goods. When receivables are also rising, the company hasn't been paid for what it has sold to its customers. This is a double whammy that often forecasts trouble ahead: Consumers aren't buying, and retailers aren't selling and therefore aren't able to pay for the product they've got. The manufacturer isn't collecting on what it sold, and its warehouses are full of more product than it can ship.

There could be a reasonable explanation for the rising receivables, such as a new product line or new customers in a different industry that have been given longer credit terms. Maybe orders have not shipped as expected because of a production delay. Whatever the reason, it's worth investigating to see if this is a red flag or a situation that's easily explained.

In the example below, the rate of increase in total inventories is four times that of sales and receivables are up three times the rate of sales. More troubling is the fact that finished goods and work in progress are up big relative to raw materials. This could indicate an unusually large stockpile of goods. To the extent that those goods are depreciable, the product on hand will be worth less and less as time goes by, eroding margins and ultimately earnings. This type of scenario should raise a red flag.

Figure 8.9 **Red flag scenario**
Example of an inventory buildup with finished goods and receivables growing at a rate faster than sales.

Differential Disclosure

When a company says one thing in one document and something quite different in another, you have *differential disclosure.* This happens far more often than most people think. The reason is simple. Guidelines for reports to shareholders are far less restricted than those for reports submitted to the SEC. An example is shareholder reporting versus tax reporting. Make a point to compare footnotes and other disclosures related to taxes under the cash-basis accounting rules required for the Internal Revenue Service (IRS) with the earnings reported to shareholders under accrual accounting. If you spot a big difference, this is a red flag. In a similar vein, if a company is reporting great earnings but is not paying much in taxes, be skeptical.

Hitting on All Cylinders: The Code 33

When a company grows its sales at an accelerating rate (25 percent, then 35 percent, then 45 percent, and so on), this is great. Better still, though, is a company that accelerates its sales and expands its profit margins at the same time. This powerful combination can ignite earnings and fuel explosive stock price appreciation. The result is a condition in which the company can grow its earnings at a much faster rate than it could if sales or margins were accelerating only by themselves or if neither were accelerating. The best situation for rapid earnings growth is to be hitting on all cylinders as sales accelerate and profit margins expand simultaneously.

Look for what I call a Code 33 situation, three quarters of acceleration in earnings, sales, and profit margins. That's a potent recipe. If a company has

	Q4	Q3	Q2	Q1
EPS	-34%	+12%	+44%	+83%
REVENUE	-22%	+3%	+16%	+38%
NET PROFIT MARGINS	4.5%	4.9%	5.8%	6.6%

Figure 8.10 **The Code 33**
Earnings per share, sales, and margins accelerating for three consecutive quarters.

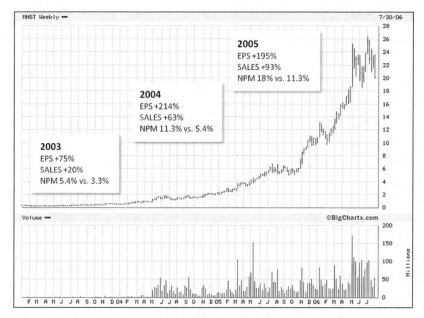

Figure 8.11   **Monster Beverage (MNST) 2003–2006**
Monster Beverage (MNST) (previously Hansen Natural Beverage) displayed classic Code 33 annual acceleration. From 2003 to 2005, earnings, sales, and margins accelerated dramatically, creating the condition necessary for superperformance.

hot-selling products or services and a management team that's on the ball, the proof should show up in the sales and margins. Profit margins should improve as the company improves productivity. Sales should increase as the company expands into new markets. If these things aren't happening, it may not be the optimum time to buy the stock.

CHAPTER 9

FOLLOW THE LEADERS

OST OF THE BIG MONEY made in bull markets comes in the early stages, during the first 12 to 18 months. However, by the time a big advance asserts itself in the broad market indexes, many of the best stocks may have been running up for weeks in advance. The question then becomes how you know when to jump on board *before* an emerging rally gets away from you and the very best stocks leave you in the dust. The answer: follow the leaders.

Top-performing stocks will lead the broader market averages at important turning points. As a bear market is bottoming, leading stocks, the ones that best resisted the decline, will turn up first and then sprint ahead—days, weeks, or even months before the Dow, S&P, and Nasdaq indexes put on their running shoes. These leading names will break into new high ground while the major indexes are just starting to come off their respective lows. At this point, overall market conditions still look bleak to most investors and the news is still for the most part negative and cautionary. Later, the rally broadens, pushing up the indexes, which propels the front-runners even higher. Then sentiment begins to shift from fear to optimism. By paying close attention to the market's leading names, you can be in the best stocks before they are obvious to the public. This is nothing new to astute stock investors who know what to look for. The legendary Jesse Livermore built his fortune by trading in leading stocks in the 1920s and 1930s. I made 99 percent of my profits in the stock market by trading in leading names.

Market leaders tend to foretell turns to the downside as well. As a bull market enters its later stages (generally after one or two years), many of the leadership stocks that led the market advance will start to buckle while the broad market averages march on toward their tops. Typically, a second wave of postleadership stocks start to perform relatively well as money rotates out of the true leaders and into some of the group's constituents, laggard follow-up stocks, or defensive groups such as drugs, tobacco, utilities, and food stocks that are thought to be less sensitive to an economic downturn. Follow-on stocks and laggards, however, rarely experience the length or, more important, the magnitude of the price move that true market leaders accomplish. When you see this rotation occurring, it's a warning that the market rally may be entering its later stage. The ultimate market top may still be weeks or even months away, but this internal market action is a proverbial shot across the bow that should get your attention.

Getting in Sync

The problem for most investors is that they fail to notice the important nuances and clues from leading stocks near turning points, and that causes them to lose perspective. Why? Investors are gun-shy after the market has been declining steadily. Just about the time the market is bottoming, most investors have already suffered large losses in their portfolios because they refused to cut their losses short. After a market correction, many investors are busy hoping to break even on the open losses they hold or are convinced that the end of the world is coming because they got crushed during the previous decline and refuse to acknowledge the buy signals individual leading stocks are offering.

Making it even more difficult is the fact that leading stocks always appear to be too high or too expensive to most investors. Market leaders are the stocks that emerge first and hit the 52-week-high list just as the market is starting to turn up. Few investors buy stocks near new highs, and fewer buy them at the correct time. They focus on the market instead of the individual market leaders and often end up buying late and owning laggards. Adding to the distraction is the fact that the news media are usually wrong at major turning points. At a market bottom they'll predict the end of the world, and at a top the same people will say you can't go wrong investing in stocks. It can be very confusing if you listen to what people are saying instead of pay-

Figure 9.1 **Pharmacyclics, Inc. (PCYC) vs. the Nasdaq Composite Index,
2009–2010**
Market leader Pharmacyclics emerges into new high ground the same day the
Nasdaq Composite hit a correction low. It then rose 1,500 percent in 33 months.

ing attention to what the stocks are telling you. **More than 90 percent of superperformance stocks emerge from bear markets and general market corrections. The key is to do your homework while the market is down; then you will be prepared to make big profits when it turns up.**

On February 4, 2010, I purchased Pharmacyclics Inc. (PCYC), and also recommended it to our Minervini Private Access clients; this was a day when the Nasdaq Composite Index was hitting a new low. Over the next 48 trading days, PCYC advanced 90 percent, during which time the Nasdaq rallied only about 18 percent. The 90 percent advance proved to be only the beginning; PCYC advanced 1,500 percent in 33 months, a clear example of market leadership.

The Lockout

During the first few months of a new bull market you should see multiple waves of stocks emerging into new high ground; general market pullbacks will be minimal and probably will be contained to 3 to 5 percent from peak to trough. Many inexperienced investors will be looking to buy a pullback that rarely materializes during the initial leg of a new powerful bull market, which from the onset will appear to be overbought.

Typically, the early phase of a move off an important bottom has the characteristics of a lockout rally. During this lockout period, investors wait for an opportunity to enter the market on a pullback, but that pullback never comes. Instead, demand is so strong that the market moves steadily higher, ignoring overbought readings. As a result, investors are essentially locked out of the market. **If the major market indexes ignore an extremely overbought condition after a bear market decline and your list of leaders expands, this should be viewed as a sign of strength.** To determine if the rally is real, up days should be accompanied by increased volume whereas down days or pullbacks have lower overall market volume. More important, the price action of leading stocks should be studied to determine if there are stocks emerging from sound, buyable bases.

Additional confirmation is given when the list of stocks making new 52-week highs outpaces the new 52-week low list and starts to expand significantly. At this point, you should raise your exposure in accordance with your trading criteria on a stock-by-stock basis. As the adage goes, "It's a market of stocks, not a stock market." In the early stages of a market-bottom rally it's absolutely critical to focus on leading stocks if your goal is to latch on to big winners. Sometimes you will be early. Stick with a stop-loss discipline, and if the rally is for real, the majority of the leading stocks will hold up well and you will have to make only a few adjustments. However, if you get stopped out repeatedly, you may be too early.

The Best Stocks Make Their Lows First

To make big money in the stock market, you're going to need to have the overall stock market's primary trend on your side. A strong market trend is not something you want to go against. However, if you concentrate on the general market solely for timing your individual stock purchases, you're likely to miss many of the really great selections as they emerge at or close to a market bottom.

The true market leaders will show strong relative price strength *before* they advance. Such stocks have low correlation with the general market averages and very often act as lone wolves during their biggest advancing stage. The search for these stocks runs contrary to the thinking of most investors, who often take a top-down approach, examining first the economy and the stock market, then market sectors, and finally companies in a specific industry group. As I'll show you in several examples in this chapter, many of the very best leading stocks tend to bottom and top ahead of their respective sectors, whereas specific industry groups can lead a general market turn. **Although it's true that many of the market's biggest winners are part of industry group moves, in my experience, often by the time it's obvious that the underlying sector is hot, the real industry leaders—the very best of the breed—have already moved up dramatically in price.**

In the early stage of a relative strength leader's uptrend, there may or may not be much confirming price strength from its group overall. This is normal. Often there will be only one or two other stocks in the group displaying strong relative strength. Therefore, it requires additional skill to pin-

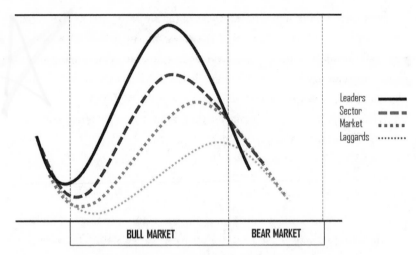

Figure 9.2   **Leading stocks versus respective sector and lagged "follow-up effect"**
Theoretical cycle dynamics shows the leaders, the overall sector, and the laggards during a bull market and then entering a bear market phase.

point these stocks early on. As the leader's trend continues to advance and eventually its industry group and sector begin to show signs of strength, the price advance of the market leader will do one of two things: it will continue its advance while the group propels it even higher, or it will consolidate in a sideways fashion and digest its previous gains while the group and other stocks in the group play catch-up. This does not necessarily mean that the leader's price advance has ended, because leaders can zig while the market zags; this is typical of high alpha stocks. You should look for definite signs that the stock has topped before concluding that the move is over.

YOUR WINDOW OF OPPORTUNITY

Market leaders are the stocks that can increase the value of a portfolio significantly and rapidly, the types of stocks that can produce superperformance. By applying a bottom-up approach to find the best relative performers in the early stages of a bull market, you will put yourself in a position to latch on to some really big winners. **The stocks that hold up the best and rally into new high ground off the market low during the first 4 to 8 weeks of a new bull market are the true market leaders, capable of advancing significantly. You can't afford to ignore these golden opportunities.**

There are countless examples of market leaders that displayed obvious signs of strength before there was a widespread indication of overall market or industry group strength. It's a matter of knowing what to look for. For example, in 2001, Amazon bottomed well ahead of the market and gave investors a year to prepare for the eventual buy point that propelled the stock 240 percent in 12 months.

Figure 9.3 **Amazon (AMZN) vs. the Nasdaq Composite Index, 2001–2003**
Amazon (AMZN) turned into a stage 2 uptrend well in advance of the general market, giving investors ample time to prepare for the buy point, which preceded a 240 percent advance in only 12 months.

Market leaders tend to stand out best during an intermediate market correction or in the later stages of a bear market. Look for resilient stocks that hold up the best, rebound the fastest, and gain the most percentage-wise off the general market bottom. This, too, will identify potential leading names. After an extended bear market correction, look for stocks that hold their ground or, even better, work their way higher while the general market averages trend lower. A series of higher lows during lower lows in the general averages is a tip-off that a potential market leader is in the making. The relative strength line of the stock should show steady improvement as the market declines. **It's important to study carefully the price action of individual companies with new positive developments and strong earnings per share during major market declines. Many of the most strongly rebounding stocks and the ones that hold up the best are likely to become the next up cycle's superperformers.**

Superperformance can be triggered by several factors, including a positive earnings surprise, industrywide regulatory change, governmental policy change, newly awarded contracts, better than anticipated results from a new product launch, and the planned introduction of a unique new product. For a pharmaceutical or biotech company, U.S. Food and Drug Administration approval for a promising new drug or medical device can have an enormously positive effect. On July 20, 2009, shares of the small biopharma company Human Genome Sciences (HGSI) soared, closing up more than 270 percent in just one day, but that was only the beginning. The company unveiled test results on a drug that could become the first new treatment for lupus in 50 years, a drug with truly revolutionary potential. Seven months later, HGSI's stock price was up an additional 165 percent. Similarly, on April 14, 2009, shares of Dendreon Corp soared almost 200 percent after the company said its prostate cancer vaccine Provenge significantly prolonged the overall survival of patients compared with a placebo. Eleven months later, the stock price was up an additional 117 percent.

There was a stark contrast between Humana's stock price trend and the general market price action from June 1977 to August 1978. Humana's stock had been in a stage 2 uptrend and was hitting a new high while the Dow had not even turned the corner yet. Then Humana emerged into new

Figure 9.4 **Humana (HUM) vs. the Dow Jones Industrial Average, 1978**
Humana (data from 1978, adjusted for splits) provides a classic example of an emerging leader, rising 1,000 percent in 38 months.

high ground as the overall market initially came off its lows. Humana's stock price advanced 1,000 percent over the subsequent 38 months.

Humana's action provided the type of subtle sign that few can detect during a bear market bottom. What you are looking for as a sign of a bottoming market is the following:

1. A first wave of market leaders emerge and build bases in a stairstep fashion, as in the Humana example.

2. Stock set-ups proliferate while the original leaders give up relatively little ground and rebound fairly quickly from any selloff. Leading stocks will generally advance 15 to 20 percent and then rest, during which time they may pull back 5 to 10 percent.

3. The majority of leaders should hold their ground. Even though there are bound to be some stocks that emerge and then fail, you don't want to see most of the leaders that broke out come crashing down and not able to rally.

4. Volume on the major averages should also be watched for signs of distribution. If this is accompanied by increasing volume on down days versus up days, it may be too early, and you may need to revert back to cash for protection.

EMULEX

In 2001, I bought shares of Emulex (EMEX). The stock attracted my attention for several reasons. First, as the general market was near a new low, Emulex shot up 100 percent in only one week. This impressive strength was the initial tip-off that something big was about to happen with the stock. Such a surge in demand is often a reaction to a positive development that has recently surprised the Street or an indication that something is being anticipated. Next, the stock pulled back sharply, but it recovered very quickly in only a few days. The stock gave up little ground afterward. The price then moved into new high ground as the general market rallied off its lows. This was the green light to buy.

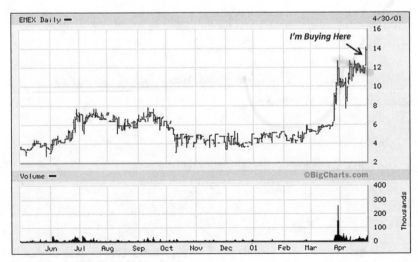

Figure 9.5   **Emulex (EMEX) 2001**

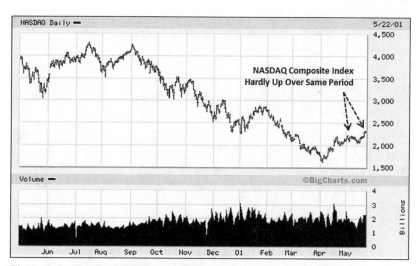

Figure 9.6 **Emulex (EMEX) vs. the Nasdaq Composite Index, 2001**

From the point at which Emulex made a new high, the stock gained 160 percent in only 17 days. The Nasdaq, meanwhile, eked out only a small fractional gain in the same time frame.

W.R. GRACE & CO.

I bought W.R. Grace & Co. (GRA) on August 26, 2004, while the Nasdaq Composite was just starting to rally off its correction low on the ninth day. The stock ran up more than 40 percent in 13 days. Forty-four days later, GRA was up 110 percent. The Nasdaq Composite Index during that period was up only 10 percent.

Figure 9.7   **WR Grace & Co. (GRA) vs. the Nasdaq Composite Index, 2004**

Secular Growth Cycles

Often, stocks that hold up well during bear market corrections are in their own earnings up cycle. These stocks may benefit from strong earnings and sales, new products or services, or industry changes that positively affect the company. However, a stock's price trend may be temporarily held back or muted by the weight of the bearish primary trend of the general market. This causes a stock's price to decline, but not as severely as the prices of other stocks. These stocks are generally very resilient and bounce back into new high ground quickly off their lows. When the bearish market exhausts itself and turns up, stocks in their own earnings up cycle will blast off and advance significantly, in some cases for an extended period. On the flip side, stocks that are in their own bearish cycle may resist even a strong market and go nowhere. Often this is an indication of an unfavorable outlook, and these stocks should be avoided.

Panera Bread (PNRA) advanced an incredible 1,100 percent over 26 months during one of the most devastating bear markets in U.S. stock market history. The Nasdaq Composite, meanwhile, declined approximately 80 percent in that period. This does not mean that you should focus on buying stocks during major declines in the overall market; Panera Bread is clearly not the norm. However, Panera vividly illustrates the power of the earnings cycle when timed correctly.

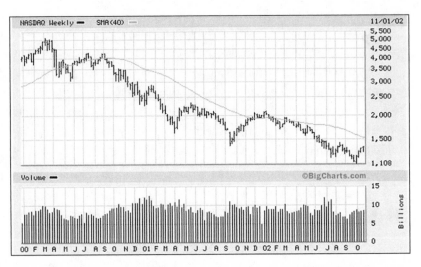

Figure 9.8   **Panera Bread (PNRA) vs. the Nasdaq Composite Index, 2000–2002**
Panera Bread made a meteoric 1,100 percent rise while the Nasdaq Composite
fell by 80 percent.

A Classic Case of Market Leadership

During the entire 1990 bear market, I observed that Amgen's stock price barely dropped below its 50-day moving average for any length of time. As the market continued in a precipitous downtrend, Amgen moved sideways and marked time. This is how a stock can improve its relative strength ranking during a market correction even without the stock rallying very much.

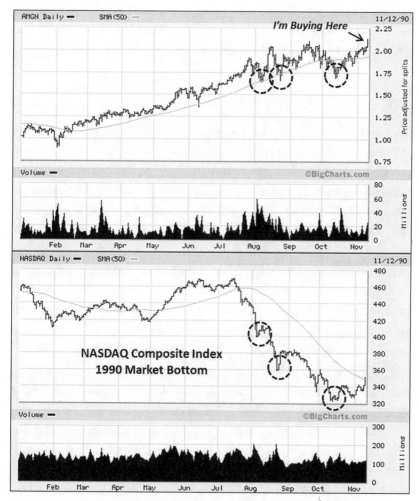

Figure 9.9   **Amgen (AMGN) vs. the Nasdaq Composite Index, 1990**
Amgen held up exceptionally well and displayed strong relative strength while the overall market was declining.

Every time the Dow rallied off its lower lows, Amgen would edge its way into new high ground; this got my attention. Finally, in October 1990, the market reached a bottom. Only 22 days later Amgen hit an all-time price high. The Nasdaq Composite and other popular averages were still 25 percent off their highs. The market indexes, however, did not discourage me. I started to buy stocks in the healthcare group that were displaying the best earnings and price strength. The broader market had been sitting on the stock throughout its correction; however, once the market took off the pressure, Amgen took off. It was one of the first stocks to emerge in the 1990 bull market and gained 360 percent in just 14 months,.

Look for a Technical Theme

Each market cycle has a unique signature in the form of the price and volume action in leading names. Often a similar technical theme will be present. **A growing number of stocks displaying positive, divergent price behavior during a general market decline can tip you off to where the next group of market leaders may emerge or what stocks are likely to blast off first when the market starts to rally.** When you see this type of price action, it's time to tune out the media and the gurus and concentrate on the facts: price, volume, earnings, sales, profit margins, new products, and positive industry changes. Look for the evidence stock by stock and employ the best criteria. Most of the time there will be more than just one stock in a particular industry group displaying this type of behavior. You should try to own the top one, two, or three names in the industry in terms of relative performance and earnings power. Look for the types of patterns and price action that are proliferating in the marketplace. This can help you understand what type of tactic will work best in the current cycle.

In 1990, medical-related stocks were emerging as market leaders one after the other. Stocks such as US Surgical, United Healthcare, Amgen, Ballard Medical Products, and Stryker, among others, were leading the market. For many of these stocks, their relative price strength during the 1990 bear market proved to be a valuable tip-off that they were about to lead the next bull run and score huge returns for investors. I know. I was there at the time, buying them as they emerged.

Also emerging from the 1990 bear market bottom was the market leader American Power Conversion (APCC). Like Amgen, this company caught my attention, and for similar reasons: a stock that was starting to go higher as soon as the market took off the brake. Founded by a group of engineers from MIT, APCC had set out to develop solar power products, but after sharp declines in oil prices and muted government support for solar power, the company quickly shifted to developing uninterruptible power supply (UPS) systems for computers and workstations. The timing was perfect. APCC introduced its first UPS models in 1984 just as the microcomputer market began to blast off. In 1991, APCC introduced models that sold for under $200, which opened up the home PC market for the first time. The rest is history.

It was no coincidence that APCC's stock price emerged off the 1990 bear market low into new high ground on the exact day that Amgen did (22 days into the rally). The two stocks displayed nearly identical price

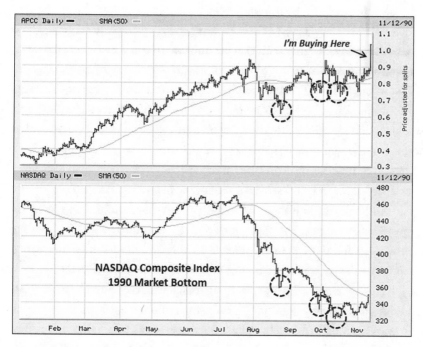

Figure 9.10   **American Power Conversion (APCC) vs. the Nasdaq Composite Index, 1990**
American Power Conversion emerged as the market was bottoming and then gained 4,100 percent in 50 months.

strength, indicating that their up cycles were being suppressed temporarily by the weight of the overall market correction. Selling for its highest price ever on November 12, 1990, proved to be only the tip of the iceberg. APCC advanced a whopping 4,100 percent over the subsequent 50 months.

WHICH LEADERS SHOULD I BUY FIRST?

As you shift into buying gear, the question becomes, Which stocks should I buy first? It's simple. Buy the strongest first. Coming off a market low, I like to buy in order of breakout. The best selections in your lineup will be the first to burst forth and emerge from a proper buy point and into new high ground. The ones that act the strongest are generally the best choices at this point. **Let the strength of the market tell you where to put your money, not your personal opinion, which rarely is a good substitute for the wisdom of the market.** Ultimately, opinions mean nothing compared with the verdict of the market. **The stocks that emerge first in the early stage of a new bull market with the greatest power are generally the best candidates for superperformance.**

At the August 2007 low, oversold conditions dominated many market-timing indicators, which were down to levels equivalent to the 2002 and 2004 market bottoms. Most important and what caught my attention was the fact that an increasing number of fundamentally strong companies were emerging from sound consolidation patterns. New stock breakouts were boosting some industry sectors out of oversold levels.

Adding to my bullish view was the fact that the previous weeks included positive key reversals in the major averages, an improvement in advisory sentiment and put/call ratios, and very impressive up/down volume ratios on the Nasdaq of 9 to 1 and on the New York Stock Exchange of 21 to 1.

There was still a distinct possibility that the market could be hit with an additional wave of selling, which would force another leg down in the major averages. Nonetheless, I started adding many of the best names to my buy list and covered all my short positions. My thinking was that even if the market did sell off again, many of my stops on my longs would probably not be violated. If they were, I would simply sell and cut my losses.

When a market is bottoming, the best stocks make their lows ahead of the *absolute* low in the market averages. As the broader market averages make lower lows during the last leg down, the leaders diverge and make *higher* lows. It's important to watch very carefully at this juncture and stand ready to cut your losses if volatility widens too much in your individual holdings. If more leaders emerge and the overall market strengthens, be ready move to an even more aggressive long bias.

As the following examples show, your objective is to look for the stocks that hold up the best—either declining the least or even moving somewhat higher—during bear markets.

Figure 9.11   Lumber Liquidators (LL) vs. the Nasdaq Composite Index, 2012
Lumber Liquidators emerged into new high ground off the market low and rallied 90 percent. During the same period the Nasdaq was actually down. Note the divergence that took place from late April to early June.

Figure 9.12   **Chipotle Mexican Grill (CMG) vs. the S&P 500 Large Cap Index, 2012**

In September 2010, Chipotle Mexican Grill made an all-time high and then advanced 186 percent in 20 months.

Figure 9.13 **Apple Computer (AAPL) vs. the Nasdaq Composite Index, 2003–2004**

I purchased Apple Computer in March 2004. Shortly afterward, the stock set two follow-up buy points before more than doubling in price.

Figure 9.14   **Wal-Mart (WMT) vs. the Dow Jones Industrial Average, 1982**
Walmart gave investors two spots to buy before the 1982 market bottom. It rose
360 percent in 21 months.

A DOUBLE-EDGED SWORD

Just as the leaders lead on the upside, they also lead on the downside. Why? After an extended rally or bull market, the market's true leaders have already made their big moves. The smart money that moved into those stocks ahead of the curve will move out swiftly at the first hint of slowing growth. When the leading names in leading industry groups start to falter after an extended market run, this is a danger signal that should heighten your attention to the more specific signs of market trouble or possible trouble in a particular sector.

Most stocks experience a relatively severe decline in price after a super-performance phase has run its course. This is due to profit taking and the anticipation of slower growth ahead. Scientific evidence and my personal experience indicate that the chances of a superperformer giving back most or all of its gains are high. You must have a plan to sell and nail down profits when you have them. **History shows that one-third of superpeformers give back all or more of their entire advance. On average, their subsequent price declines are 50 to 70 percent, depending on the period measured.** In a post-bubble-type market such as 1929–1930s and 2000–2003, many leading stocks declined as much as 80 to 90 percent. This is not the type of decline from which a stock investor can recover. For those who do recover, it generally takes 5 to 10 years or more.

LEADERS CAN FORECAST TROUBLE AHEAD

In the later stage of the general market's advance, the same leaders will alert you to weakness in their underlying sectors as well as potential upcoming weakness in the broader market. Your portfolio will be your best barometer. Your watch list of potential stock candidates should bring you into the market early in the bullish phase as leading stocks set up and emerge into new high ground. Later, you will be forced out of the market—stock by stock—as many of the same issues start to churn, buckle, or accelerate their advance over a number of weeks in a parabolic fashion ahead of the inevitable bear phase or market correction. Leaders tend to top around the same time the general market starts to show signs of distribution. It's important to keep your sights on the trees rather than on the forest.

Bull markets sometimes roll over gradually, whereas bottoms often end with a sudden sell-off, followed by a strong rally. As the leaders start to buckle, the indexes can move up farther or start to churn, moving sideways. That occurs because cash stays in the market and rotates into laggard stocks. The indexes hold up or even track higher on the backs of the stragglers. Watch out! When this happens, the end is near and the really great opportunities may have already passed.

Most investors miss these subtle signs, mainly because they become conditioned by the market's uptrend during the bullish phases. What's the big deal if a few stocks start to crack, they tell themselves, as long as the Dow keeps heading higher, right? Wrong!

A bull market is always dominated by at least one sector and several subsectors. Within the top sectors leading a new bull market, the relatively few leading names that dominate the leadership during that market eventually attract the attention of institutional money. Buying enthusiasm for those leaders can push their prices far above realistic valuations. As a result, those issues tend to decline the most during the subsequent bear market. For investors who hold on to the former leaders for too long, the results can be devastating.

Investing in leading stocks is indeed very risky if it is timed incorrectly. The highfliers are great when they're going up; however, the downside can be disastrous. If you don't have a sensible exit plan to minimize losses, it is certain that you will experience a major setback at some point. Big profits can be made during periods of optimism. However, if you're late to the party, look out below. The same stocks that have been going up could be due for a major correction.

For example, the technology stocks that led the 1998–2000 bull market were the biggest losers during the 2000–2002 bear market and recovered at best only about half of their losses during the entire 2003–2007 bull market. History is littered with examples showing that the leaders of one bull market are rarely the leaders of the next. Financials and housing stocks were market leaders in the 2003–2007 bull market and then took the biggest losses during the bear decline in 2008. Therefore, if history is any guide, the leaders of one cycle should generally be abandoned as buy candidates both for bear market recovery rallies and for the next bull market. There is one caveat to this: if the leadership stocks or sectors started to emerge near the end of the bull market cycle preceding the subsequent bear market, in some cases they can lead during the bull market. One thing for certain is that very often the leaders of the next bull market will emerge from the most unlikely areas but quickly reveal themselves through the application of the price analysis techniques discussed in this chapter. Follow the leaders and you will participate in and profit from many of the most exciting entrepreneurial companies this country has to offer.

Learn to Buy Leaders and Avoid Laggards

As a general rule, I buy strength, not weakness. True market leaders will always show improving relative strength, in particular during a market correction. You should update your watch list on a frequent basis, weeding out issues that give up too much price and adding through forced displacement new potential buy candidates that show divergence and resilience. In addition to keeping your lineup of candidate buys current, this practice will sharpen your feel for the overall health and quality of the market and keep you focused on the very best companies. Things begin to get exciting as the broader market indexes start to bottom and begin the first leg up in a new bull market.

At this point, you should concentrate on the new 52-week-high list. Many of the market's biggest winners will be on the list in the early stages of a new bull market. You should also keep an eye on stocks that held up well during the market's decline and are within striking distance (5 to 15 percent) of a new 52-week high. Conversely, every day there is a list of stocks to avoid printed in the financial newspapers: the 52-week-low list. I suggest that you stay away from this list and all of its components.

The 95 best-performing stocks of 1996 and 1997 took just five weeks to surge 20 percent. On average, those stocks gained 421 percent. Among those 95 stocks, 21 jumped 20 percent within a mere week. Those stocks went on to surge on average 484 percent. In 1999, many of the best stocks took just one week to run up 20 percent; some did it in only three days. All of them displayed superior relative strength *before* they advanced significantly.

If the market is indeed bottoming, a growing number of stocks will display improving relative price strength while they go through a comparatively tight price correction. Generally, the correction for a healthy stock from peak to low will be contained within 25 to 35 percent and during severe bear market declines could be as much as 50 percent, but the less, the better. A correction of more than 50 percent is generally too much, and a stock could fail as it reaches or slightly surpasses a new high. This is due to excessive overhead supply created by the steep price decline.

As the overall market is bottoming, your watch list should multiply over a number of weeks. The better stocks start moving into new high ground as the market rallies off its lows. This is a good sign that the market has bottomed or is getting close to a bottom. This is a critical juncture. Each emerging bull market tends to send up its unique set of leaders. **The leaders of the past bull market rarely lead the next rally, so expect to see unfamiliar names. Fewer than 25 percent of market leaders in one cycle generally lead the next cycle.** It's important to recognize the new crop of top-performing companies and industries as early as possible. Remember to listen to what the stocks are telling you, not the pundits. This will be your best early-alert system.

TUNE OUT THE MEDIA

During a market decline the news is always filled with market gurus predicting the end of the world. Pessimism abounds. Inevitably, another group of so-called experts chime in that the bottom may be near. But they'll announce that a real rally cannot take place without getting the nod from their pet technical indicators. There is no shortage of elaborate theories and technical indicators that people use to time the market. This deluge of fear and conflicting advice can paralyze you on the cusp of a powerful rally. Worse still, the media barrage could divert your attention from doing your homework and concentrating on the facts if you let it.

Shut off the TV, close out the media, and start looking for the next wave of market leadership, which is certain to emerge eventually. Concentrate on facts and follow the leaders. I assure you that new companies with new products and new technologies will continue to emerge for as long as the United States operates as a free enterprise system. History shows that with each bull market, new leaders emerge and old ones step aside. Be ready to act quickly; be prepared. Most important, tune out the media and tune in the leaders.

CHAPTER 10

A PICTURE IS WORTH
A MILLION DOLLARS

Although the cheetah is the fastest animal in the world and can catch any animal on the plains, it will wait until it is absolutely sure it can catch its prey. It may hide in the bush for a week, waiting for just the right moment. It will wait for a baby antelope, and not just any baby antelope, but preferably one that is also sick or lame; only then, when there is no chance it can lose its prey, does it attack. That, to me, is the epitome of professional trading.

—Mark Weinstein

ROPONENTS OF THE efficient market hypothesis (EMH), which was developed by Professor Eugene Fama at the University of Chicago Booth School of Business in the early 1960s, consider the stock market to be perfectly priced—or at least nearly perfectly priced—to the extent that the market is "informationally efficient." In other words, it is theorized that stock prices already reflect all known information and that the markets adjust so rapidly to reflect new information that there is no advantage in having it. Therefore, according to EMH, it is impossible to outperform the market by using data that the "market" already knows about except through luck. Defenders of this theory scoff at the notion that price and volume analysis can give an investor a winning edge. Needless to say, I disagree; my career and those of many other traders I know have demonstrated that EMH is a flawed theory. Most of those who subscribe to EMH have never made a living from stock trading, let alone achieved superperformance. Perhaps EMH makes sense to those who cannot outperform the market; since they cannot do it, they believe it's impossible. Highly successful traders know otherwise.

Ultimately, it's people—emotional, imperfect, even illogical—who make buy and sell decisions. Ego, fear, greed, hope, ignorance, incompetence, overreaction, and a host of other human errors in reasoning and judgment create all sorts of discrepancies and in turn opportunity. An invaluable tool to use to discern those opportunities is charting the fundamental battle between supply and demand. **Charts enable us to see what's going on in a particular stock as buyers and sellers come together in an auction marketplace. They distill the clash for emotional, logical, and even manipulative decisions into a clear visual display; the verdict of supply and demand.** If you look at charts in this way, you will appreciate how these images depict all the choices people are making, whether to buy or to sell. In one glance you can see precisely what took place in a particular time frame.

There is nothing new under the sun in regard to charting and using graphs. People have been using charts for centuries. Think of the ship captains who charted the stars for navigation. In a similar way, we use charts to navigate the market. Many investors try to read charts, but few know how to do it correctly. As I pointed out earlier, the argument some people make against charts is that past information cannot be predictive. If you were to utilize that philosophy in life, however, you would never be able to judge a current event by using the evidence of the past: what a drop in barometric pressure signals about the weather or that a 103-degree fever and body aches are symptoms of the flu.

Some people believe that you cannot time the market or time stock trades very effectively, that attempting to do so is a fruitless endeavor regardless of your techniques or available information. I can tell you from experience that I owe much of my success to the precision of my timing, which would be virtually impossible without the use of charts. Many of the best money managers use charts. **My own trading relies on charting to the extent that I would never bet on my fundamental ideas alone without confirmation from the actual price action of the underlying stock.** First, I utilize charts to establish the prevailing trend of a stock's price. In other words, technical analysis enables me to qualify candidates for my watch list. Then I use charts to time the entry of my trades.

Can Charts Help You Achieve Superperformance?

Can charts empower you to predict the market? Of course not. You can't predict the market any more than you can predict where the ball will drop during the next spin of a roulette wheel. Fortunately, to succeed at stock trading, you don't have to predict the market any more than a casino needs to know in advance the outcome of each individual spin of its roulette wheel or each hand at its blackjack tables to make money from its gaming operations. Those who think it's necessary to predict stock prices to be successful are missing the whole point. Savvy traders use price and volume analysis as a mechanism to time their trades, manage risk, and increase the probabilities for profit. Many of the most successful traders know firsthand the value of charting stocks. Their success has nothing to do with prediction or forecasting; rather, they rely on the acquired skill of reading the footprints of the market and then expose their capital to high reward-to-risk opportunities.

Use Charts as a Tool

Broadly speaking, there are three schools of thought about the art of charting stocks, also referred to as *technical analysis*. The first is the purest method, relying *only* on the price and volume action. Pure stock market technicians believe that everything you need to know is in the chart; they essentially regard fundamentals as unnecessary information that is ultimately "discounted," that is, reflected in a stock's share price. At the other end of the spectrum is the second group: pure fundamentalists who believe that everything you need to know lies in a company's fundamentals. To them, squiggly lines, candlesticks, and point-and-figure boxes are irrelevant. These number crunchers disdain chart analysis as something akin to reading tea leaves.

The third group consists of techno-fundamentalists. As the name suggests, these traders exploit both technical analysis and fundamental analysis. If I had to pick, I would put myself in this group. I rely on price and volume as well as fundamentals. In making the decision whether to purchase a stock, there are important characteristics to consider, both fundamental and technical. A healthy hybrid approach exploits charts as well as fundamentals to increase the trader's odds of success.

THE EFFECT, NOT THE CAUSE

Many of the basic chart patterns were discovered in the pre-Depression era, in the early 1900s. You might well ask, Assuming that these trading patterns were effective in the remote past, might they have become so popular or readily available that they should have ceased to bestow an edge many years ago? The answer is simple: **Chart patterns are not the cause; they're the effect. The supply and demand picture does not dictate to the market; human behavior does, and human behavior hasn't changed and isn't likely to change much in the future.** Thus, chart patterns remain powerful tools in timing trade entries and exits.

Today, more information moves faster than ever and trades can be placed in an instant with a click of a mouse. However, that has not changed basic human nature. The charting techniques I explain in this chapter, like everything in this book, are based on what I do in my own trading: my daily work, the product of 30 years of learning, application, refinement, and personal success in the stock market. Not only are these techniques applicable today, historical studies have shown that the techniques I used during my own career would have been effective many decades before my lifetime. For example, let's time-travel back to 1927, when RCA was the AOL of its era, advancing 721 percent in 18 months, or to 1934, when Coca-Cola emerged as a market leader several months before the general market bottomed and then advanced 580 percent. The clues leading up to their phenomenal performance were no different from what occurs in a modern time frame. So, then, are price patterns timeless?

I have dedicated most of my life to the study of superperformance investing, and I can tell you that the same elementary forces of hope and greed, exuberance and panic, that formed the observable price behavior of Microsoft and America Online in the 1990s showed up in the price movements of market leaders decades before that period. Stock prices move in virtually the same fashion today that they followed in the past. That's observed fact, not opinion. For an investor who is willing to commit the time to become educated, charts are a valuable tool, along with fundamen-

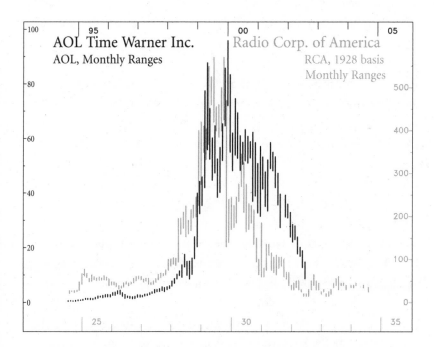

Figure 10.1   **American Online (AOL) 1995–2005 and Radio Corp. of America (RCA) 1924–1933**

Source: Prepared for Tocqueville Asset Management, LP, by Topline Investment Graphics, www.topline-charts.com. Copyright © 2002. All rights reserved.

tal analysis. Bringing all the tools in your tool kit together allows you to use them in a synergistic way in your pursuit of superperformance.

Is the Train on Schedule?

Over the years, people would walk into my office, look at my computer monitors, and ask, "How do you know what all those lines mean? They look so confusing." The answer is that you have to know what you're looking for. When I go into the doctor's office and get an EKG, I have no idea what the lines bouncing up and down on the little strip of paper printouts mean. But to a trained professional, this simple procedure of charting the activity and rhythm of a person's heart can provide valuable information on whether the heart is acting normally or abnormally. Similarly, in examining a graph of a stock's price and volume, we are looking to see if it is acting normally or giving us reason for concern. Therefore, charts provide valuable clues as well as specific information.

Price and volume analysis can help you determine whether a stock is under accumulation or distribution (being bought or sold in size). It can alert an astute chart reader to extreme danger, and it can also indicate when the odds of a potentially profitable situation are relatively high. But only a small number of people who look at charts use them effectively, and only a small percentage know what to focus on to produce really outstanding results. The ultimate fundamental in any auction marketplace is the law of supply and demand. If you learn how to differentiate constructive from faulty price action, you can use charts as a filter to screen your investment candidates to find the best possible selections and improve your odds of success. **The key is not knowing for sure what a stock is going to do next but knowing what it should do. Then it's a matter of determining whether the proverbial train is on schedule.**

Suppose you take the 6:05 train to work each morning. It generally arrives at the station somewhere between 6:00 and 6:10. But today, you look down at your watch and see that it is 6:15 and the train has still not arrived. You don't think much about it and probably say to yourself that the train is just running a little late. What happens at seven o'clock if the train has still not pulled into the station? You are most likely going to think that maybe something is wrong with the train; the more time that elapses, the higher the probability that something has gone wrong. The only reason you can make this educated guess is that you have knowledge of what is normal and what should happen.

When one identifies the proper characteristics for a superperformance candidate, the risks become unambiguous. If a stock doesn't act as expected, that's a major red flag. After all, the stock has already met very elite criteria and has been deemed a strong prospect. If such a stock behaves poorly, that suggests a problem. Learning what to expect allows you to detect when a stock is acting correctly or incorrectly in the prevailing conditions. Because you know how something is supposed to perform, when it doesn't perform that way, it makes the exit decision much easier.

First Things First

The first mistake I see amateurs make time and again when using charts is ignoring the first step: the big picture. The first and most basic information that charts show us is the prevailing trend of a stock. We can see if it's trending up or down or is moving in a sideways pattern (i.e., stage 1, 2, 3, or 4). Once we have established that the longer-term trend is up (stage 2) and see some evidence that a particular name is a candidate deserving of our attention, whether it's a market leader, a turnaround situation, or even a cyclical, it's time to concern ourselves with the best time to purchase the stock. At that point, we want to determine when the moment is right to pull the trigger and make our commitment to the position. Therefore, charting can play an important role in selection and timing.

My first advice about charting stocks is that you should not look at things in a vacuum. Most of the chart work I rely on is based on the continuation of an existing trend. This concept is fundamental to my approach. If you want to maximize compounding, you want to be where the action is and take advantage of momentum. **You should limit your selections to those stocks displaying evidence of being supported by institutional buying. You're not trying to be the first one on board; rather, you're**

looking for where momentum is picking up and the risk of failure is relatively low. To time my entry, I look for price consolidations, which are momentary pauses or periods of rest within the context of a prior uptrend. However, too often an investor will buy a stock because it has a "great" chart base but will overlook the fact that the base is within the context of a long-term downtrend.

Going long a "great base" in a long-term downtrend is like saying you're in good health by focusing on your low cholesterol reading when you have pneumonia. Although the cholesterol reading is good, you face a much more serious problem. **The current chart pattern is only as good as where it resides within the context of its longer-term trend. If you are too early, you run the risk of the stock resuming its downtrend. If you're too late, you run the risk of buying a late-stage base that is obvious to everyone and prone to failure.** Time the trade correctly, though, and you could be on the way to a very sizable gain.

I never go against the long-term trend. I look to go long a stage 2 uptrend and go short a stage 4 downtrend, plain and simple. To be consistent and stack the probabilities in your favor, you need to operate in a systematic fashion. The step-by-step approach I'm showing you here is a process. The first part of that process is to qualify the current chart pattern by filtering stocks on the basis of the prevailing trend and then buying them as they emerge from their consolidation periods before they become too widely followed and obvious. However, the current chart pattern must be put into context. If the long-term trend is not up, the stock simply doesn't qualify as a candidate for purchase. Therefore, don't forget the big picture. As the saying goes, the trend is your friend. If you try to trade against it, the trend becomes your worst enemy. To increase your odds of success, stick to stocks moving in a definite uptrend. If a stock's price is in a long-term downtrend, don't even consider buying it.

Look for Consolidation Periods

Once you have identified a stage 2 uptrend, the next step is to look for the conditions that facilitate a sustainable move higher: a proper base. Notice

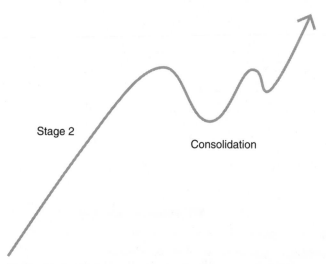

Stage 2

Consolidation

Figure 10.2   **Insist that a stock be in a stage 2 uptrend before you consider buying. The proper time to begin buying is as the price emerges from a proper consolidation.**

that I said a proper base, not just any base. Anyone can look at a chart and identify a stock that is moving sideways. It takes more than that; you need to know precisely what to look for. A constructive price consolidation phase starts as a period of rest or digestion during which the previous movement in the stock is met with temporary profit taking, which leads to an equilibrium or correction mode. The better stock selections generally will correct the least amount percentagewise from absolute peak to trough during their correction phase. Stocks that are under accumulation will rest and consolidate within the context of a long-term uptrend and then continue higher. Most of these situations will show telltale signs. Depending on the particular footprint of the price action over 3 to as many as 60 weeks of price history, there are various nuances that will allow you to make an educated decision about whether the stock should be bought or sold.

THE VOLATILITY CONTRACTION PATTERN

Most investors cannot resist the urge to buy stocks at the wrong time, usu-ally when the price is declining. I'm constantly asked whether I like this stock or that stock, and 99 percent of the time my reply is, "I wouldn't buy it here." The reason for this is that I have a strict discipline that only allows me to buy at a very specific point: the point at which reward outweighs risk. How do I identify this point?

If there is any one commonality or Holy Grail that I follow and practice regularly, it is the concept of volatility contraction. This is a key distinction that I look for in almost every trade. **A common characteristic of virtu-ally all constructive price structures (those under accumulation) is a con-traction of volatility accompanied by specific areas in the base structure where volume contracts significantly.** I use the *volatility contraction pattern* (VCP) concept to illustrate this.

For our purposes here, VCP is part of the supply and demand setup. The main role that VCP plays is establishing a precise entry point at the line of least resistance. In virtually all the chart patterns I rely on, I'm looking for volatility to contract from left to right. I want to see the stock move from greater volatility on the left side of the price base to lesser volatility on the right side.

THE CONTRACTION COUNT

In February 1995, I purchased FSI International (FSII), which was emerging out of a cup-with-handle pattern. The stock displayed perfect VCP charac-teristics in a clear stage 2 uptrend. The consolidation period lasted 10 weeks, corrected 18 percent in the cup, and contracted to just 5 percent in the han-dle area. Note the volume contraction during the tightest portion of the setup on the far right side of the base. I bought the stock as it broke above the high in the handle during week 11. The stock advanced 130 percent from that point.

During a VCP, you will generally see a succession of anywhere from two to six contractions, with the stock coming off initially by, say, 25 percent from its absolute high to its low. Then the stock rallies a bit, and then it sells

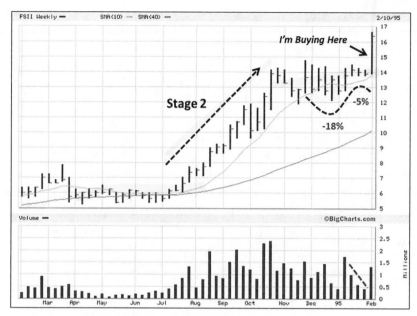

Figure 10.3 **FSI International (FSII) 1995**
In February 1995, I purchased FSI International just as it was emerging from a
classic VCP pattern. It rose 130 percent in seven months.

off 15 percent. Then buyers come back in, and the price goes up some more,
and finally it retreats 8 percent. The progressive reduction in price volatility,
which will be accompanied by a reduction in volume at particular points,
eventually signifies that the base has been completed.

As a rule of thumb, I like to see each successive contraction contained
to about half (plus or minus a reasonable amount) of the previous pullback
or contraction. The volatility, measured from high to low, will be greatest
when sellers rush to take profits. When sellers become scarcer, the price correction will not be as dramatic, and volatility will decrease. Typically, most
VCP setups will be formed by two to four contractions, although sometimes
there can be as many as five or six. This action will produce a pattern, which
also reveals the symmetry of the contractions being formed. I call these contractions Ts.

Not all price patterns display VCP characteristics. There are some variations, such as the square-shaped Darvas box pattern, or a flat base structure

Figure 10.4   **Example of volatility contraction "Ts"**

that is four to seven weeks in duration. With this type of base, there is no real volatility contraction as it remains a tight and narrow pattern or box, moving in a sideways range with about a 10 to 15 percent correction from high point to low point. Or a stock could undergo successive consolidations, with varying degrees of volatility to produce contractions, for example, from a 25 percent correction, to a 10 percent, to a 5 percent, and so forth, which would be indicative of a classic VCP progression.

Figure 10.5   **WR Grace (GRA) 2004**
In 2004, WR Grace & Co. contracted three times (3 Ts) and set the stage for a powerful advance. It rose 147 percent in 55 days.

THE TECHNICAL FOOTPRINT

Each stock makes its own unique mark as it goes through a consolidation period. Similar to a fingerprint, they look alike from afar, but when you zoom in, no two are identical. The resulting signature is what I call the stock's technical footprint. **The immediate distinguishing features of the VCP will be the number of contractions that are formed (typically between two and four), their relative depths throughout the base, and the level of trading volume associated with specific points within the structure.** Because I track hundreds of names each week, I created a quick way to capture a visual of a stock by quickly reviewing my nightly notes and each stock's footprint abbreviation. This quick reference is made up of three components:

1. **Time.** How many days or weeks have passed since the base started?

2. **Price.** How deep was the largest correction, and how narrow was the smallest pullback at the very right of the price base?

3. **Symmetry.** How many contractions (Ts) did the stock go through during the basing process?

In the same way you could get a mental picture of a man if I told you he was 6 feet tall, weighed 230 pounds, and had a 43-inch waist, knowing a stock's "measurements" gives me a visual of its footprint and helps me understand certain key aspects of the price base even without looking at the chart. Let's take a look at Meridian Bioscience (VIVO), which in the middle of a stage 2 uptrend built a series of volatility contractions as it consolidated before continuing its upward run. Meridian Bioscience contracted four times (a **4T**) before it emerged out of its 40-week (**40W**) consolidation and advanced more than 100 percent over the next 15 months.

The following chart shows four periods of volatility contraction within the base that are framed by the dotted lines. The first period started in April 2006, when the stock declined from $19 a share to $13, correcting 31 percent from high to low. The stock then moved higher and consolidated again, falling from just under $17 to below $14 a share for a 17 percent pullback. This is the first sign of contracting volatility. After the second pullback, the stock

The VCP Footprint

40W 31/3 4T

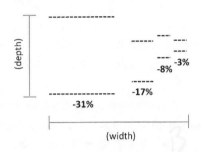

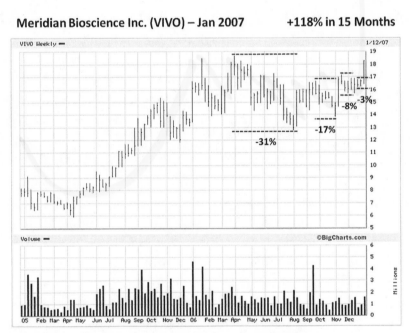

Meridian Bioscience Inc. (VIVO) – Jan 2007　　**+118% in 15 Months**

Figure 10.6　**The VCP footprint with abbreviation: 40W 31/3 4T**

rallied once again, this time to just above $17 a share, and then it pulled back to below $16, a much tighter price range of about 8 percent. At this point, I began getting interested in the stock.

Finally, a short and narrow pullback of just 3 percent over two weeks on very low volume formed the pivot buy point. This told me that selling activity had dried up. Profit taking had exhausted itself as incremental supply coming to market had abated. After putting in four Ts with successive decreases in price volatility and volume, the stock price was primed to spike if buyers came demanding inventory. In January 2007, I jumped on board as Median Bioscience cracked above the pivot buy point at $18 a share on a noticeable increase in volume; it proceeded to advance 118 percent over the next 15 months.

What Does Volatility Contraction Tell Us?

If a stock is under accumulation, a price consolidation represents a period when strong investors ultimately absorb weak traders. Once the "weak hands" have been eliminated, the lack of supply allows the stock to move higher because even a small amount of demand will overwhelm the negligible inventory. This is referred to as the *line of least resistance*. **Tightness in price from absolute highs to lows and tight closes with little change in price from one day to the next and also from one week to the next are generally constructive.** These tight areas should be accompanied by a significant decrease in trading volume. In some instances, volume dries up at or near the lowest levels established since the beginning of the stock's advance. This is a very positive development, especially if it takes place after a period of correction and consolidation, and is a telltale sign that the amount of stock coming to market has diminished. A stock that is under accumulation will almost always show these characteristics (tightness in price with volume contracting). This is what you want to see before you initiate your purchase on the right side of the base, which forms what we call the *pivot buy point.* Specifically, the point at which you want to buy is when the stock moves above the pivot point on expanding volume.

This is a vital concept for successfully timing the continuation of an existing trend. For the best situations, during this contraction in volatility, volume will also contract during specific points that can be identified time and again.

I came up with the VCP concept because I saw so many people rely on patterns that seemed to trace out the general appearance of a constructive

Figure 10.7 **USG Corp. (USG)**
In 2006, USG Corp. consolidated its previous run-up and formed a VCP pattern
before rising 85 percent in four months.

price base, but those people missed some of the most important elements of
the structure, which can make it invalid and prone to failure. **I can assure
you that almost every failed base structure that you experience can be
traced back to some faulty characteristic that was overlooked.** Many books
superficially describe technical patterns. Pattern recognition exercises will
often lead you astray if you lack an understanding of the supply and demand
forces that give rise to high-probability setups as opposed to head fakes. Let's
look a little more deeply at the nature and forces of supply and demand to
understand what is actually taking place.

DETECTING OVERHEAD SUPPLY

As a stock corrects and heads lower, inevitably there are trapped buyers who
bought around the stock's previous high point and are now sitting with a
loss; trapped buyers agonize over their deepening paper losses and, sweat-
ing bullets, look for a rally to sell. As their losses grow and more time passes,

many of these buyers would be delighted just to get even. This is what creates overhead supply: investors who want out around their breakeven point; they can't wait to sell and assuage their egos by thinking that despite the roller-coaster ordeal, they "got out even."

Adding to the supply issue is another group of buyers who, unlike the trapped buyers sitting at a loss and waiting to break even, were fortunate enough to bottom fish the stock and now are accumulating very nice profits. As the stock trades back up near its old high, as the trapped buyers are getting even, the profit takers also feel the urge to sell and nail down a quick buck. All this selling creates a price pullback on the right side of the base. If the stock is indeed being accumulated by institutions, the contractions will be smaller from left to right as supply is absorbed by the bigger players. When a stock traces out a VCP and undergoes a series of contractions, it is simply the law of supply and demand at work, an indication that the stock is changing hands in an orderly manner. You should wait until the stock goes

Figure 10.8 **Theoretical example of supply/demand dynamics**
A significant contraction in volume associated with tightness in price signals supply has stopped coming to market and the line of least resistance has been established.

through a normal process of shares changing hands from weak holders to strong ones. **As a trader using a stop loss, you are a weak holder. The key is to be the last weak holder; you want the other weak holders to exit the stock before you buy.**

Evidence that supply has stopped coming to market is revealed as the trading volume contracts significantly and price action quiets down noticeably. Demanding this attribute will help you avoid a crowded trade, improving the likelihood that the stock is off the public's radar, which increases the odds of success. If the stock's price and volume don't quiet down on the right side of the consolidation, chances are that supply is still coming to market and the stock is too risky.

Why Buy Near a New High?

One of the most common phrases you hear in the stock market is "buy low and sell high." These words have become synonymous with the way most people think about how to make money in stocks. Of course, it's obvious that you have to buy at a price lower than the price at which you sell to make a profit. However, this does not mean that you have to buy at or near the lowest price at which a stock has traded historically. Markets are far more often correct than are personal opinions or even expert forecasts. A stock making a new 52-week high during the early stages of a fresh bull market could be a stellar performer in its infancy. In contrast, a stock near its 52-week low at best has overhead supply to work through and lacks upside momentum; worse still, such a stock may be headed for a series of lower lows. A stock hitting a new high has no overhead supply to contend with. The stock is saying, "Hey, I have something going on here, and people are taking notice," whereas a stock hitting a new low is clearly a laggard that lacks investor interest or is being dumped in size by institutions.

There are those of you who say, "I don't want to wait until the stage 2 criteria are confirmed." You want to try to get in early, when the stock is moving off its lows. The problem here is that there is no confirmation in the early stages. How do you know that the stock is attracting institutions? Even a good start can get derailed if the fundamentals aren't really there, and you end up buying a bounce that fizzles and the stock stays in stage 1 limbo or, worse, breaks down and declines.

When a stock reaches a new high in a confirmed stage 2 uptrend supported by big volume clues, it has been propelled upward by institutions taking positions because they believe that the fundamentals are solid and the prospects for the future are even better. In the following examples you can see how the real excitement doesn't even start until these stocks are hitting all-time price highs.

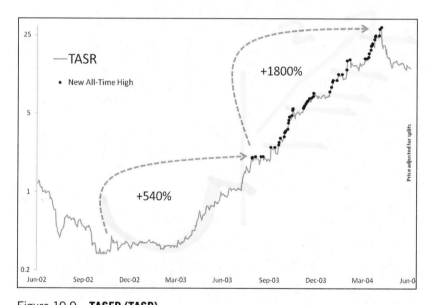

Figure 10.9 **TASER (TASR)**
TASER advanced 540 percent to reach an all-time high, then from that point advanced an additional 1800 percent.

Chart courtesy of Longboard Asset Management.

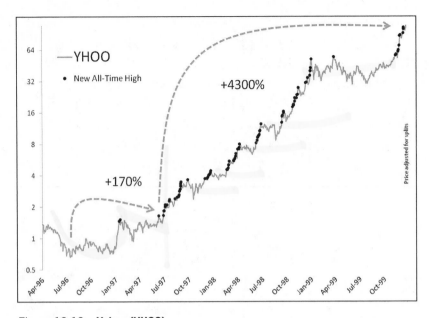

Figure 10.10   **Yahoo (YHOO)**
Yahoo advanced 170 percent to reach an all-time high in price, then advanced an additional 4,300 percent.

Chart courtesy of Longboard Asset Management.

The only way a stock can become a superperformer, moving from, say, $20 to $80, is for that stock to make a series of new highs repeatedly, all the way up. The same thing applies to a stock that's at $50 and doubles to $100 on its way to $300. Monster Beverage (MNST) registered an all-time high in late 2003. If you were afraid to buy the stock because it appeared too high, you would have missed a huge opportunity; the stock price advanced 8,000 percent by early 2006.

Figure 10.11 **Microsoft (MSFT)**

From the point Microsoft hit an all-time high in 1989, it advanced 54-fold.

Chart courtesy of Longboard Asset Management.

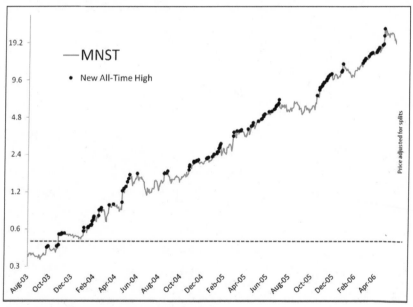

Figure 10.12 **Monster Beverage (MNST)**

Monster Beverage rallied more than 8,000 percent from its all-time high registered in August 2003.

Chart courtesy of Longboard Asset Management.

Deep Correction Patterns Are Failure-Prone

When a stock declines precipitously, it is likely that there is a serious problem in the company, its industry, or perhaps a bear market is unfolding. You shouldn't conclude that a stock is a bargain just because it's trading down 50 or 60 percent off its high. First, such a decline could indicate that a serious fundamental problem is undermining the share price. Second, even if the fundamentals are not problematic yet, a stock that has experienced a deep sell-off must contend with a large amount of overhead supply: the more a stock drops, the more it is burdened by trapped buyers. Finally, the more a stock declines, the more potential profit takers will be waiting to sell if the stock rallies and intersects overhead supply; the larger the profit is, the more likely it is that bottom feeders will sell. During major bear market correc-

Figure 10.13   **Mankind (MNKD) 2009–2012**

Mankind (MNKD) rallied back near its old highs into overhead supply where selling took the stock down precipitously. The following year the same scenario repeated.

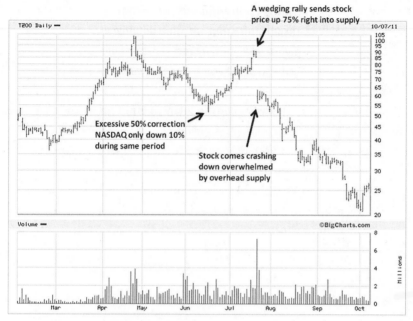

Figure 10.14 **Travelzoo (TZOO) 2011**
Large correction leaves Travelzoo vulnerable to overhead supply and the stock
plummets 80 percent over the next 12 weeks.

tions, some names can decline by as much as 50 percent and still work out.
**I rarely buy a stock that has corrected 60 percent or more; a stock that is
down that much often signals a serious problem. Most constructive setups correct between 10 percent and 35 percent.** You will have more success
if you concentrate on stocks that correct the least versus the ones that correct the most. Under most conditions, stocks that correct more than two or
three times the decline of the general market should be avoided.

TIME COMPRESSION

If a stock advances too quickly up the right side, this forms a hazardous
time compression, and in most cases the stock should be avoided, at least
temporarily. Time compression will show up as V-shaped price action or
the absence of proper right-side development. Constructive price consoli-

dations tend to have a degree of symmetry; a buildup of supply takes time to digest and work through. A quick up-and-down gyration doesn't give the stock enough time to weed out the weak holders; it takes time for the strong hands to relieve the weaker players. You want to give your stock enough time to undergo a constructive consolidation period, which will allow it to continue its primary advance unencumbered by the chains of immediate sellers.

Depending on the depth of the correction, a proper basing period can last anywhere from 3 weeks to as long as 65 weeks. By demanding that the price action display VCP characteristics, you will increase your chances of identifying a stock in which supply is diminishing and a sound point for entry is developing, which will lead to an immediate and sustained advance.

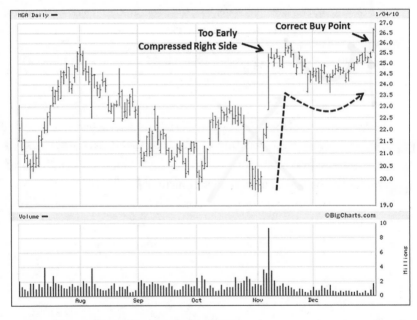

Figure 10.15   **Magna Intl. Inc. (MGA) 2010**

In November 2010, Magna Intl. Inc. ran up the right side too quickly and required more time to set a low-risk buy point. It rose 140 percent in three months.

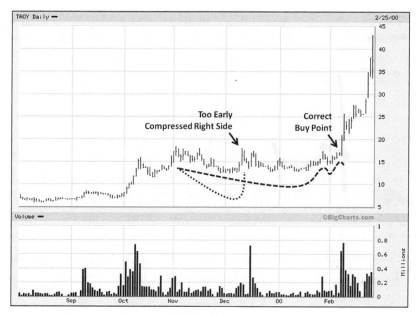

Figure 10.16 **Troy Group Inc. (TROY) 2000**
Troy Group needed time to forge a proper VCP consolidation that set the stage for a very powerful advance. It then rose 146 percent in 14 days.

SHAKEOUTS

In addition to contracting volatility and the absence of time compression, we are looking for price shakeouts within the base structure. Most of us have been on the wrong side of a shakeout at one time or another. Let's say you bought a stock at $40 a share. You noticed that over the past several months it had traded several times as low as $35 a share before bouncing higher. It stood to reason that this was an area of support and that placing a protective stop just below that level would be logical. The problem, however, is that you were not the only one who made that observation. **Always include in your thinking that whatever you're seeing in the marketplace is also visible to everyone else.** Most likely, other traders thought it was obvious to put a stop somewhere under $35 a share. In the stock market, what is too obvious seldom works. Shortly after you purchased the stock at $40, it sold off, and this time it dropped below $35. Sell stops were hit, and that sent the price even lower. You were knocked out of your position, as was everyone else who had a stop just below $35. Once that selling was exhausted, the stock turned around and rallied higher, only you weren't on board. Sound familiar? You were the victim of a price shakeout.

To improve your odds, you want to see one or more price shakeouts at certain key points during the base-building period. This will also allow for the elimination of weak holders and allow a sustained move higher. Remember, as a disciplined stock trader using stop losses to control risk, you, too, are a weak holder. In other words, you will sell during a relatively minor price pullback to protect yourself against the possibility of a larger loss. This is not to delegitimize your stop-loss discipline. A stop-loss regime is essential. Inevitably, however, good stop-loss practice will shake you out of some winning stocks. To the extent that you identify base formations that have exhibited and digested shakeouts before your entry, you are less likely to be thrown from the saddle.

Figure 10.17   **Dick's Sporting Goods (DKS) 2003**
In February 2003, Dick's Sporting Goods undercut its December 2002 low creating a shakeout.

Informed investors who understand price action are on the lookout for evidence of price shakeouts within the base before they buy. Price shakeouts will strengthen the setup at the completion of the base. Major support areas are obvious to amateurs and therefore should be obvious traps to professionals. Like a minefield, they're filled with stops, ready to blow when the share price brushes the trip wire. It's beyond the purview of this book, but there are professional traders who are expert at picking off the amateurs when obvious support areas are breached and trigger the amateurs' standing orders.

Don't get confused; what you may think is just a shakeout is *not* the time to buy a declining stock. We are not forecasters; we are interpreters. When a stock that is seemingly in the process of building a base undercuts a support floor, it may be a price shakeout, or the stock could be entering a precipitous or sustained decline. This is why you wait to see if it results in a shakeout. Ideally, you want to see this occur one, two, or three times,

Figure 10.18 **Meridian Bioscience (VIVO) 2007**
Meridian Bioscience had several key points where the stock price undercut previous lows creating constructive shakeouts.

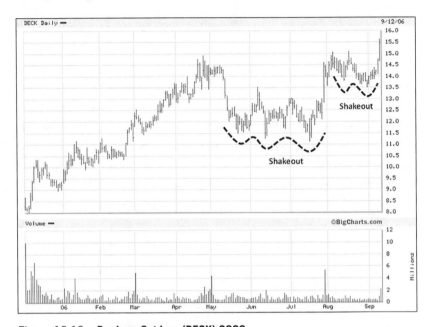

Figure 10.19   **Deckers Outdoor (DECK) 2006**
Deckers Outdoor drifted below previous lows in the bottom of its base and during the handle phase on the right.

depending on the size and magnitude of the price base, before you enter the trade. Shakeouts can occur at the lows of a base, on the right side, and in the handle or pivot area.

LOOK FOR EVIDENCE OF DEMAND

So far we have taken an aerial view to identify candidates that meet our criteria on the basis of the footprint formed by their price action. At this point in our analysis, we have already determined that a stock is in a stage 2 uptrend. As that previous uptrend is digested, people will sell and take profits; therefore, we will look for some correction to occur. When that selling occurs, there will be some people who wish they had taken a profit but did not. When the stock moves up again, they will seize the next opportunity to get out. What we want to see is what comes next. After the selling has slowed, is there still an appetite for the stock? Will big demand come in after a sell-off to propel the stock even higher? Or is the move over? By closely observing price and volume action, we can gain this insight.

At this point, we want to zoom in and look for signs of institutional accumulation. A sign of accumulation is a spike up in price. Price spikes generally occur off the lows of a correction within the base and on the right side of the base; this kind of price action gains credence if it is accompanied by outsized volume. **A spike in price on overwhelming volume often indicates institutional buying, which is exactly what we're looking for. After a price shakeout, it's a good sign if the stock rallies back on big volume.**

A stock may experience big price spikes in the form of gaps. A price gap occurs when the share price prints at a wide increment above or below the previous print; this is most easily observable at the open, but in thinly traded stocks it can also occur intraday. Gaps often occur on big volume. Upward price gaps may result from positive news such as better than expected earnings, a favorable industry development, or a brokerage house upgrade. Ideally, the gap will result from a fundamental change that creates a positive shift in perception and generates buying demand. In many cases, a price gap will show up on a weekly graph as well. What you're trying to determine is whether the stock is under accumulation by large institutional buyers.

The next chart shows Meridian Bioscience (VIVO) as the stock price initially came down and put in a low in May, a level that was undercut in July; after that, the stock came roaring back, followed by a short-term pullback and then a big gap to the upside. Accompanying that gap was a surge of volume, reflecting strong demand. A sideways pattern developed during October, with a sell-off that took out the September low, triggering another price shakeout. Notice how the overall price structure is beginning to tighten up. The combination of the big demand (gap) days, low-volume pullbacks, several price shakeouts within the base, and a contraction in price provided sufficient evidence that this stock was under accumulation. Even as the stock tightened up and formed the handle area in December, it underwent two minor price shakeouts, adding even more strength to the setup. Keep in mind that one aspect alone did not make for a great trade setup. Rather, it was a combination of all these factors.

Figure 10.20   **Meridian Bioscience (VIVO) 2007**
Meridian Bioscience displayed strong demand off the lows before tightening up constructively on the right side.

A big price spike on a surge of volume indicates that institutions are buying in size. At the same time, you'll want to see a dearth of down spikes. In other words, the volume must be much bigger on up days than on down days, and a few of the price spikes to the upside should be large, dwarfing the contractions that have occurred on relatively lower volume.

After undercutting the December low, the stock price of Dick's Sporting Goods came roaring back on big volume. Note the price gap that occurred in February with the biggest volume since the company's initial public offering (IPO). In and of itself, this action was an insufficient reason to buy because the stock had yet to go through the process of putting in a VCP. Later, however, once the VCP was completed, the stock was set up properly as a buy candidate; it soon broke out and went on to advance 525 percent in 54 months.

Figure 10.21   **Dick's Sporting goods (DKS) 2003**
After undercutting its December low, Dick's Sporting Goods came roaring back
on big volume; a sign of institutional support. It rose 525 percent in 54 months.

Look for significant, above-average increases in volume on upward
moves coming off the lows and up the right side of the base. It's not
uncommon to see a surge of several hundred percent or even as much as
1,000 percent compared with the average volume. Look for big up days
that are larger and occur more frequently than big down days. Avoid a
stock that follows a big demand day with even bigger down days on volume. Large up days and weeks on increased overall volume, contrasted
with lower-volume pullbacks, are another constructive sign that the stock
you are considering is under institutional accumulation. Look for these
traits before you buy.

Figure 10.22   **Deckers Outdoor (DECK) 2006**

After shaking out two lows in the bottom of the base, the price ran up the right side on a surge in volume.

Figure 10.23   **Magna Intl. Inc. (MGA) 2010**

After a shakeout occurred in November 2006, a price surge on overwhelming volume was the tip off that Magna Intl. Inc. was under institutional accumulation. It rose 140 percent in three months.

Figure 10.24   **Valassis Communications (VCI) 2010**

Valassis Communications experienced a surge up the right side on a big spike in volume. It rose 80 percent in five months.

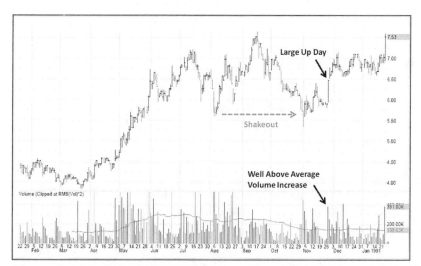

Figure 10.25   **Elan PLC (ELN) 1991**

Elan was able to follow through on increased volume after undercutting its consolidation low. It rose 152 percent in 12 months.

Chart courtesy of Interactive Data, © 2009.

Price Spikes Preceding a Consolidation

Often a price spike will occur on the left side just before a price correction or consolidation begins. This may come on news and cause the stock to become extended and prone to a pullback, particularly if the overall market begins correcting. Cirrus Logic raised its earnings guidance by forecasting better than expected numbers for the upcoming quarter. This caused the stock to shoot up dramatically. Within days of the price spike, the overall market started correcting. This put temporary pressure on Cirrus's stock price, causing it to correct 23 percent off its high, which was an acceptable 2.3 times the market correction. Once the market bottomed, the stock price moved up the right side and set up constructively. Cirrus advanced +162 percent in just four months from the point at which it made a new 52-week high.

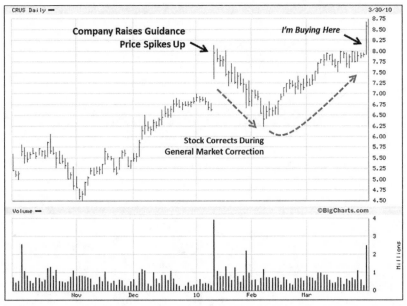

Figure 10.26   **Cirrus Logic (CRUS) 2010**
Cirrus Logic rallied on earnings guidance, leaving the stock price extended and vulnerable to a pullback. After pulling in during an intermediate general market correction, the stock emerged as a market leader.

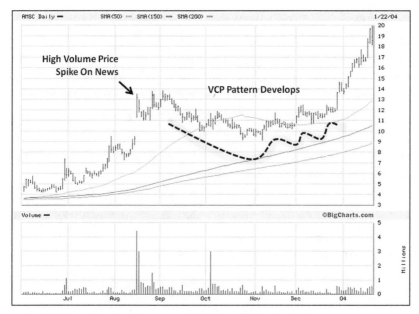

Figure 10.27 **American Superconductor (AMSC)**
American Superconductor digest news and sets up for a powerfull rally by developing a classic VCP pattern from mid-August through mid-December 2003.

The Pivot Point

A proper pivot point represents the completion of a stock's consolidation and the cusp of its next advance. In other words, after a base pattern has been established, the pivot point is where the stock establishes a price level that will act as the trigger to enter that trade. Now the stock has moved into position for purchase. As the stock's price trades above the high of the pivot, this often represents the start of the next advancing phase. A pivot point is a "call to action" price level. It is often referred to as the optimal buy point. A pivot point can occur in connection with a stock breaking into new high territory or below the stock's high.

In the context of a stock's consolidation, a temporary pause allows you to set a price trigger to enter a trade. For example, a trader might put in a limit order to buy 1,000 shares if the price breaks the upper level of the pivot point. You want to buy as close to the pivot point as possible without chasing the stock up more than a few percentage points.

Jesse Livermore described the pivot point as the line of least resistance. A stock can move very fast once it crosses this threshold. **When a stock breaks through the line of least resistance, the chances are the greatest that it will move higher in a short period of time.** This is the case because this point represents an area where supply is low; therefore, even a small amount of demand can move the stock higher. Rarely does a correct pivot point fail coming out of a sound consolidation.

The next chart shows Mercadolibre (MELI), which has a technical footprint of 6W 32/6 3T, meaning that the basing period occurred over six weeks, with corrections that began at 32 percent and concluded at 6 percent at the pivot. In November, the stock underwent a price shakeout and proceeded to tighten up in a constructive fashion. Notice, too, how the last contraction was accompanied with little volume as a dearth of stock changed

Figure 10.28   **Mercadolibre Inc. (MELI) 2007**
In early December 2007, Mercadolibre Inc. emerges from a proper pivot point. It rose 75 percent in 13 days.

Figure 10.29 **American Superconductor (AMSC) 2004**
American Superconductor breaks through the line of least resistence from a classic VCP pattern. It rose 60 percent in 17 days.

Figure 10.30 **Impax Labs (IPXL) 2003–2004**
In January 2004, Impax Labs broke out above a well-defined pivot point. It rose 70 percent in three months.

Figure 10.31   **Netflix (NFLX) 2009**
In October 2009, Netfiix emerged into new high ground from a classic VCP consolidation period. It rose 525 percent in 21 months.

hands during the last (T) pivot point. After charging through the pivot point, Mercadolibre's stock price rose 75 percent in just 13 days. This is the type of rapid price escalation I'm interested in being part of.

Volume at the Pivot Point

Every correct pivot point will develop with a contraction in volume, often to a level well below average with at least one day when volume contracts very significantly, in many cases to almost nothing or near the lowest volume level in the entire base structure. In fact, we want to see volume on the final contraction that is below the 50-day average, with one or two days when volume is extremely low. This may not always occur in the largest-cap stocks, but in some of the smaller issues, volume will dry up to a trickle; viewed as a lack of liquidity, this worries many investors. However, this is precisely what occurs right before a stock is ready to make a big move. Why? Because the

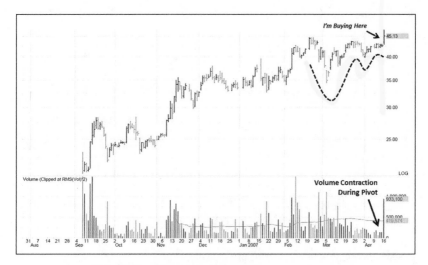

Figure 10.32   **New Oriental Education (EDU) 2007**
Stock emerged from a VCP set-up in April 2007. Note the extreme price and
volume contraction which established the pivot point and line of least resistance.
It rose 105 percent in seven months.
Chart courtesy of Interactive Data, © 2008.

decreased volume means that stock has stopped coming to market. With
very little supply of stock in the market from sellers, even a small amount of
buying can move the price up very rapidly.

During the tightest section of the consolidation (the pivot point), volume should contract significantly. Consider the example of New Oriental
Education. First, take note of the footprint: 8W 22/2 3T, indicating an
eight-week base with successively tighter pullbacks of 22 percent, 8 percent, and then 2 percent. Not only is the last contraction tight in terms
of price (a 2 percent fluctuation), volume dries up considerably as well.
The pivot point that forms is very tight with volume that is dramatically
lower than the average. This is a very constructive sign. Now, just as the
price breaks above the pivot on increasing volume, that's where you want
to place your buy order. New Oriental Education advanced 105 percent in
seven months from the pivot point.

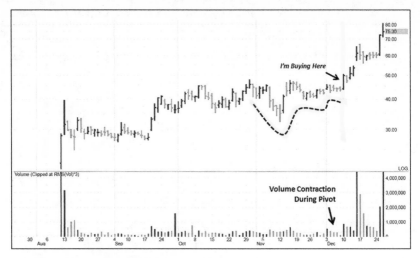

Figure 10.33 Mercadolibre Inc. (MELI) 2007

The day before MELI broke out, volume contracted near the lowest level in the stock's history. It rose 75 percent in 17 days.

Chart courtesy of Interactive Data, © 2008.

Figure 10.34 Cirrus Logic (CRUS) 2010

Prior to the breakout, Cirrus Logic experiences extreme tightness in price on exceptionally low volume. On March 30, 2010, I bought the stock and also recommended it to our Minervini Private Access members at $8.09. It rose 163 percent in four months.

Extrapolating Volume Intraday

After the last narrow contraction in a VCP pattern on light volume, ideally you want to see an upward move in the making on stronger than usual volume. Let's say that a stock normally trades 1 million shares. Two hours into the trading day, 500,000 shares—half the usual volume—has already exchanged hands and the stock is moving up. You still have four and a half hours to go. Therefore, you can comfortably extrapolate that on the basis of the intraday volume thus far, the volume for the day could easily be 300 to 400 percent (or more) of the average daily volume. Now, when the price goes through the pivot point, you can place your trade.

Always Wait for the Stock to Pivot

Some investors will try to get in before the breach of the pivot point to save a few pennies on the trade. Assuming that a stock will break out is dangerous. **If the pivot point is tight, there is no material advantage in getting in early; you will accomplish little except to take on unnecessary risk. Let the stock break above the pivot and prove itself.** The pivot point is only one part of the overall setup, but it's the most important piece of the puzzle before I buy a stock, because it is the final determinant of when I'm going to pull the trigger and risk my capital.

Not all consolidations have tight pivot points. When a flat base occurs with no real pivot other than the high of the base, an investor can look to buy as the stock moves above the highest price at the top of the base provided that the base corrects no more than 10 or 15 percent. Other price patterns, such as a cup completion cheat (3-C), or a cup with handle, can form pivot points below the high of the overall structure.

This step-by-step approach will help you time your trades with accuracy as you determine the optimal place for a low-risk and potentially high-reward trade. If you use the techniques I just described, you will have more precision and a better rationale for placing your trades. This does not mean that you will never have a loss or that the stock will not pull back, hit your stop, and leave you on the sidelines. If your analysis is faulty, or you're attempting to trade on the long side during a bear market, the search for a pivot may result in frustration instead of a significant entry point or possibly an abrupt failure soon after your purchase. The success of the pivot point is related to how well the setup has been established.

SQUATS AND REVERSAL RECOVERIES

Sometimes a stock will break out from a pivot point only to fall back into its range and close off the day's high. This is what I refer to as a *squat*. When this happens, I don't always jump ship right away; I try to wait at least a day or two to see if the stock can stage a *reversal recovery*. This accommodation makes sense especially in a bull market. In some cases it can take up to ten days or longer for a recovery to occur. This is not a hard-and-fast rule; some may take a little longer, and some fail and stop you out.

Of course, if the reversal is large enough to trigger my stop, I sell. If the reversal causes the price to close below its 20-day moving average, it lowers the probability of success and it becomes a judgment call; sometimes I sell if this happens. However, as long as the price holds above my stop loss, I try to give the stock some room.

If the price action tightens and volume subsides, the setup could be improving, and it could be that you've just entered the trade a bit early. That is precisely what happened with Affymax, Inc. I bought the stock on August 20, 2012. It closed off the day's high and even pulled in a bit the very next day. Over the course of the next few days, the price action tightened up and volume contracted. I stayed with the stock and held to my original stop. Ten days after my purchase, the price recovered into new high ground, and I added to my position. Affymax, Inc., then advanced 61 percent in 42 days.

Figure 10.35 **Affymax, Inc. (AFFY) 2012**
Affymax, Inc. held my stop and staged a reversal recovery 10 days after
squatting on the breakout. It rose 61 percent in 42 days.

Figure 10.36 **Magna Intl. (MGA) 2010**
Magna Intl. Inc. recovered a squat in three days. It rose 140 percent in three
months.

Figure 10.37   **Amazon (AMZN) 1997**
Amazon displayed a series of reversal recoveries as it emerged into new high ground after going public less than four months earlier. It rose 1,700 percent in 16 months.

How Do You Know a Breakout Has Failed?

Once a stock breaks out of its pivot area, watch for signs of failure; a failed breakout can quickly lead to a base failure. Once the stock successfully breaks out, the stock price should hold its 20-day moving average and in most cases should not close below it. The pattern should not get wider (meaning up and down movements). Up is good, but wild swings back and forth are not. Although the price may pull back or even squat, don't automatically conclude that the trade is going to fail. You want to give the stock a chance to recover. If it pulls in, holds above the 20-day average, and squats, often the stock will recover the next day or within a few days. However, if it hits your stop, get out and reevaluate.

Dealing with an Early Day Reversal

Another rule of thumb regarding a reversal on the breakout day is the *early day reversal*. This occurs when a stock moves up in the morning and then comes back down to the breakout before noon or 1:00 p.m. Try to give the stock until the end of the day unless the reversal is so severe that it triggers your protective stop. You should not panic and conclude that the breakout has failed just because the early morning rally lost steam and the stock pulled in. This often happens. The stock may even undercut your purchase price. Stick to your game plan and hold to your original stop loss. In a healthy market, often stocks that do this will recover later in the day and close strong.

Putting It All Together

In March 1995, I purchased Kenneth Cole Productions (KCP) because of characteristics that were classic in every sense: a perfect VCP setup. Kenneth

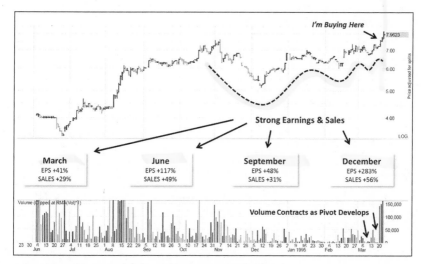

Figure 10.38   Kenneth Cole Productions (KCP) 1995
In March 1995, I purchased Kenneth Cole Productions as it emerged from a VCP pattern backed by solid fundamentals. It rose 102 percent in eight months.
Chart courtesy of Interactive Data, © 2008.

Cole attracted my attention when it displayed healthy earnings and sales. The price and volume action looked great, and the market was starting to recover after a period of correction.

Note how volatility contracts from left to right; the stock corrects and progressively tightens within ranges of 32 percent, 14 percent, 7 percent, and 3 percent. The VCP leads right to an entry point and a successful break-out. This provides an excellent example of constructive volatility contraction. The stock emerged and advanced more than 100 percent in just eight months.

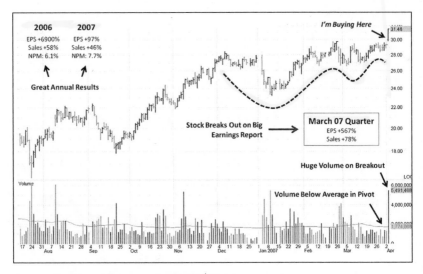

Figure 10.39   **Foster Wheeler (FWLT) 2007**

In April 2007, I purchased Foster Wheeler on a gap fueled by a great earnings report announced in the morning. Note the huge breakout volume and the close right at the high of the day. It then rose 180 percent in nine months from this point.

Chart courtesy of Interactive Data, © 2008.

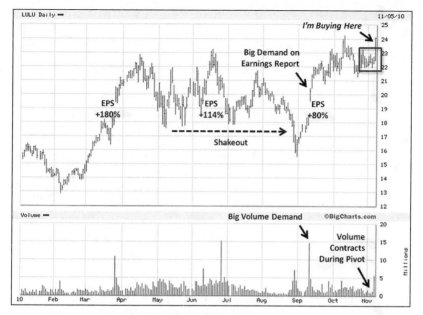

Figure 10.40 **Lululemon Athletica (LULU) 2010**
In November 2010, I bought Lululemon and recommended it to our Minervini
Private Access members as it emerged from a double bottom. It rose 245
percent in 18 months.

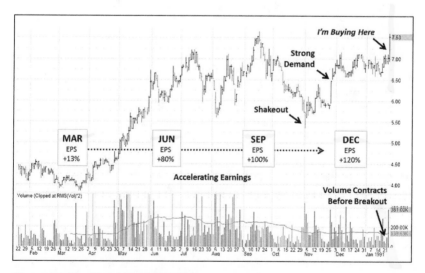

Figure 10.41 **Elan PLC (ELN) 1991**
Strong accelerating earnings and a proper technical setup fueled a successful
breakout from a cup with handle pattern. It rose 152 percent in 12 months.

Chart courtesy of Interactive Data, © 2009.

WATCH LIST ORGANIZATION

An important element for success is how well you can organize your thoughts and analysis. Many traders go through routines, but most of them lack consistency. Planning your trades in advance allows you to conduct research when there are no distractions such as level II systems or blinking quote screens. I conduct my research at around the same time each evening. By the time the opening bell rings at 9:30 a.m., I already know which stocks show the most potential and at what price level. I use a kind of shorthand to indicate the footprint of a stock. I use this shorthand system to get a visual of the stock at a glance. On September 2, 2012, I was interested in a handful of names.

You'll notice that some stocks are circled, two are underlined, some have asterisks after them, and one has a "pb" notation. You can use whatever symbols you like, but here is what this all means to me. Circles, asterisks, and

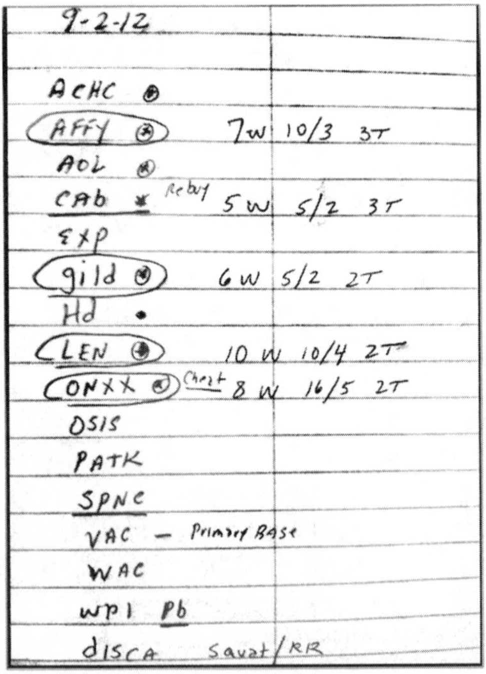

Figure 10.42   **My notepad from September 2, 2012**

"pb" are part of my ranking that allows me at a glance to see how the stocks on my watch list are setting up: which ones appear to be ready for action and which ones need more time to mature.

If I really like a stock, I circle it. If a stock shows potential, I underline it. If a stock has formed a pivot point, I put in an asterisk after the symbol. If the pivot point is immediately buyable, I circle the asterisk. If a stock is setting up in such a way that I would be interested on a pullback, I write "pb" next to it. You will also notice that on the right I use the technical footprint abbreviation for the names I'm most interested in.

Here's how this translates into my trading system. Stocks that have been circled or have asterisks will go on my quote screen for close attention. Those that are underlined do not have setups that are mature enough at this point, but they bear watching. The rest will stay on the watch list to see what develops. I rank them as watch, buy alert, and buy ready. As time progresses, some stocks may become actionable. Some on the watch list will move up (from watch to buy alert and then to buy ready), and some will fall off entirely. Once I have my list of stocks, I can watch how they trade intraday. When a stock hits my predetermined price as it moves through its pivot point, I put on the position.

The Natural Reaction and Tennis Ball Action

In the 1980s, I became intrigued by the methods of the late William M. B. Berger, a fifth-generation money manager and founder of the Berger Funds. Bill Berger was a great money manager. His Berger Fund had a very impressive track record and consistently included some of the market's most dynamic leaders. Bill had a saying about price pullbacks that has stuck with me for decades. He said that price reactions and pullbacks allow you to determine whether your stock is a tennis ball or an egg. He wanted to own tennis balls. This has turned out to be a golden nugget that I am now passing on to you.

Once a stock has penetrated a proper pivot point emerging from a constructive price consolidation, it's time to watch the stock to see how it acts. This will tell you whether to continue holding it. The stock price will experience short-term pullbacks as it makes its way higher. If the stock is healthy and under accumulation, the pullbacks will be brief and will be met with support that pushes the stock to new highs within just days, bouncing back like a tennis ball. This is how you determine whether the stock is experiencing a natural reaction or abnormal activity that should raise concern.

Netflix illustrates a successful breakout coming out of a 27W 27/7 3T VCP setup. You can see the pullbacks are five and seven days, respectively, and the stock subsequently moves right back into new high ground. Volume expanded dramatically on the initial breakout and on the subsequent rally after the first normal reaction. **Often, a stock will emerge through a pivot point and then pull back to or slightly below that initial breakout point. This is normal as long as the stock recovers fairly quickly within a number of days or perhaps within one to two weeks.** Volume should contract during the pullback and then expand as the stock moves back into new highs.

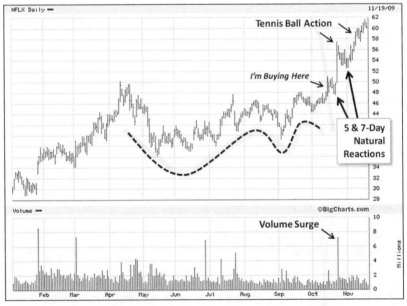

Figure 10.43   **Netflix (NFLX) 2009**
Netfix pulled back to the breakout point but came roaring back on huge follow-through volume just five days later: classic tennis ball action.

There should not be much volatility during the initial rally phase and during the first one or two normal reactions. Minor reactions or pullbacks in price are natural and are bound to occur as the advance runs its course. The best stocks rebound quickly. This is how you know you're on to something worth holding.

Once you have bought a stock emerging from a VCP, look for the following signs:

- At the beginning of the move, volume should expand over a number of days.

- Prices generally should move upward for a few days with little resistance.

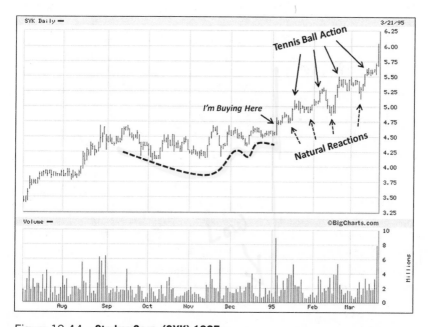

Figure 10.44   **Stryker Corp. (SYK) 1995**
In January 1995, I bought Stryker as it emerged from a VCP consolidation. Over the next couple of months every pullback recovered quickly back to new high ground.

- A *normal reaction* will occur: volume should decrease compared with the volumes observed during the initial trend, and the price may move against the trend somewhat.

- Within a few days or perhaps a week or two of the normal reaction, volume should increase again and the price trend should be resumed.

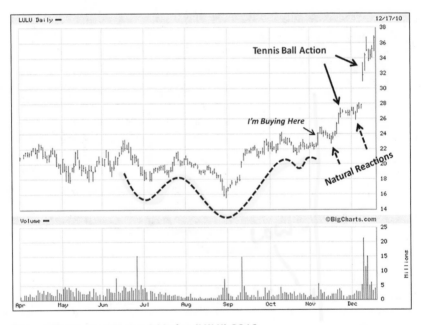

Figure 10.45   Lululemon Athletica (LULU) 2010
After a strong breakout in November 2010, Lululemon stair-stepped higher providing only brief pullbacks.

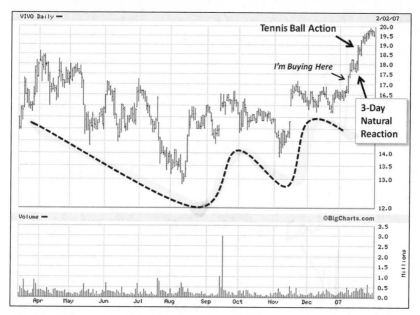

Figure 10.46   **Meridian Bioscience (VIVO) 2007**
After a successful breakout and two days of follow-through, Meridian Bioscience only pulled in 3.5 percent over the course of three days before rallying back into new high ground.

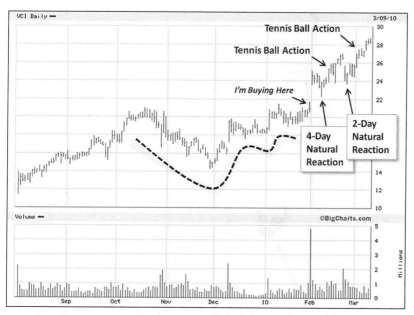

Figure 10.47   **Valassis Communications (VCI) 2010**
Valassis gapped up on earnings but gave little back before moving higher into new high ground.

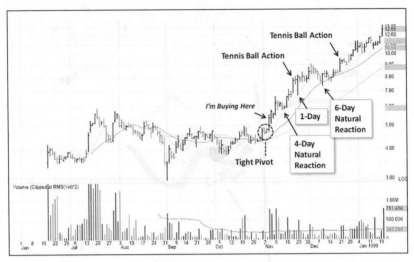

Figure 10.48   **Bebe Stores (BEBE) 1998**
After breaking out in November 1998, each pullback was met with support and subsequently rallied quickly to new highs. Very powerful price action.

Chart courtesy of Interactive Data, © 2009.

SAUCER WITH PLATFORM

In the 1960s, William L. Jiler wrote a book titled *How Charts Can Help You in the Stock Market.* In my opinion, Jiler's work on chart patterns was way ahead of its time and to this day still has valuable findings. I would put it on the must-read list for anyone interested in using charts to improve his or her performance in the stock market. Jiler was the first to highlight the saucer-with-platform pattern, which later became popularized as the cup-with-handle pattern. This pattern without a doubt is the most repeatable and reliable price structure among all the variations that superperformance stocks trace out before they advance dramatically in price. Jiler refers to the saucer pattern as a "dream pattern," citing its ease of recognition and reliability. Although I agree with Jiler, the pattern is prone to misinterpretation. The VCP concept and some education about volume and certain specific nuances to look for can quickly clear up poor analysis and lead you to find the next big superperformer. As was mentioned above,

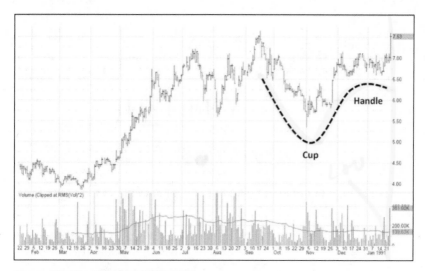

Figure 10.49 **Elan PLC (ELN) 1991**
Elan forms a cup with handle pattern.
Chart courtesy of Interactive Data.

volatility contraction is a key characteristic of constructive price behavior within all patterns.

THE 3C PATTERN

The *cup completion cheat,* or 3C, is a continuation pattern; it is the earliest point at which you should attempt to buy a stock. Some stocks form a low cheat, and some form the cheat area, near the middle of the cup or saucer that precedes it. The key is to recognize when the stock has bottomed and identify when the start of a new uptrend is under way, back in sync with the primary stage 2. The cheat trade gives you an actionable pivot point to time a stock's upturn while increasing your odds of success.

When a handle forms, it usually occurs in the upper third of the cup. If it forms in the middle third of the cup or just below the halfway point, you could get more than one buy point.

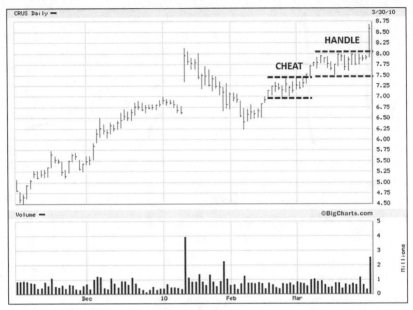

Figure 10.50   **Cirrus Logic (CRUS) 2010**

In February 2010, Cirrus Logic formed a 3C pivot point (cheat area) and then a handle in March.

Figure 10.51   **Valassis Communications (VCI) 2010**

In January 2010, a handle formed just above the cheat area; both provided viable pivot points for entry.

The cheat area is the earliest point at which I attempt to trade a cup pattern. You don't want to be involved any earlier than this point. Like the handle, a valid cheat area should exhibit a contraction in volume as well as tightness in the range of price. This pause presents an opportunity to enter the trade at the earliest point, perhaps not always with your entire position, but you can lower your average cost basis by exploiting cheat areas to scale into trades. Once the stock trades above the high in the pause area, it has made the turn; it probably has made its low and will resume the longer-term stage 2 primary trend.

The cheat setup has the same qualifications as the classic cup with handle because it's simply the cup portion being completed. To qualify, the stock should have already moved up by at least 25 to 100 percent—and in some cases by 200 or 300 percent—during the previous 3 to 36 months of trading. The stock should also be trading above its upwardly trending 200-day moving average (provided that 200 days of trading in the stock has occurred). The pattern can form in as few as 3 weeks to as many as 45 weeks

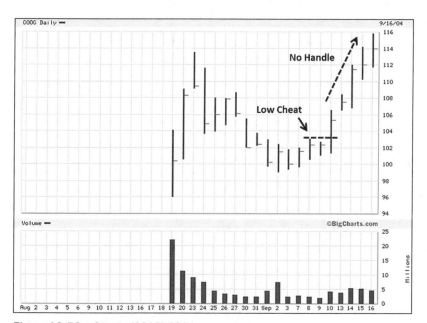

Figure 10.52   **Google (GOOG) 2004**
In September 2004, Google formed a rare low cheat pivot point. It rose 600 percent in 38 weeks.

(most are 7 to 25 weeks in duration). The correction from peak to low point varies from 15 or 20 percent to 35 or 40 percent in some cases and as much as 50 percent, depending on the general market conditions. Corrections in excess of 60 percent are too deep and are extremely prone to failure. It is common for a cheat setup to develop during a general market correction. The most powerful stocks will rally off this pattern just as the general market averages turn up from a correction or at least close to the same time.

Making the Turn

A. **Downtrend.** The stock will experience an intermediate-term price correction that takes place within the context of a longer-term stage 2 uptrend. This leg down can happen over a number of weeks or months, and it is normal to experience large price spikes along the downtrend on increased volume.

B. **Uptrend.** The price will attempt to rally and break its downtrend. You do not want to buy just yet; it's too early. At this point, the price and volume action lacks the necessary confirmation that the stock has bottomed and entered a new uptrend. The price will start to run up the right side, usually recouping about one-third to one-half its previous decline; however, overhead supply created during the intermediate downtrend will typically be strong enough to stall the price advance and create a pause or pullback.

C. **Pause.** The stock will pause over a number of days or weeks and form a plateau area (the cheat), which should be contained within 5 percent to 10 percent from high point to low point. The optimum situation is to have the cheat drift down to where the price drops below a prior low point, creating a shakeout, exactly the same thing you would want to see during the formation of a handle in a cup-with-handle pattern. At this point, the stock is set up and ready to be purchased as it moves above the high of the pause. A typical sign that indicates that the stock is ready to break out is when volume dries up dramatically, accompanied by tightness in price.

Figure 10.53 Cirrus Logic (CRUS) 2010
In March 2010, Cirrus Logic makes the turn as it rallies above the cheat area.

D. **Breakout.** As the stock rallies above the high of the plateau area, you place your buy order. The stock is now deemed to have made the turn, meaning that it probably has made its low and the intermediate-term trend is now up and back in sync with the longer-term stage 2 primary trend.

WHY WAIT FOR THE TURN?

When a stock has been moving in one direction, a trendline can be drawn by connecting significant highs or lows. The typical rationale is that as long as the stock price doesn't break through the trendline—rising above it during a downtrend or breaking below it during an uptrend—the trend continues. Then, when the trendline is "broken" because of a change in direction, a new trend is thought to be in place. Why not just buy when the stock breaks its trendline? Doesn't that mean that a new trend has begun? The problem is that although the trendline has been broken, this could be a temporary phenomenon. Instead of starting a new trend, the stock could just have made a momentary move in the other direction until the prevailing trend resumes, sometimes with even wider volatility, which often happens.

Countertrend volatility is common. This raises the question: How can you tell when a new trend is in force? The answer is to wait for the stock to turn. **The most dangerous time to trade is when a stock is trying to bottom. This tends to be a very volatile period for stocks. When a stock is searching for a bottom, it can whip back and forth violently. Trying to pick a low can be very frustrating and costly.** Repeated triggers of your stop-loss protection during a whipsaw environment inflict repeated small losses that can add up over time. Often a stock will appear as if it is bottoming by breaking its downtrend, only to reverse and then take out the previous low, defining a new downtrend. As volatility widens, this can occur over and over. We want to avoid this. You can increase the odds of success by waiting for the stock to turn, which will lessen the chance of failure (although it won't eliminate it). The odds increase dramatically in your favor if you wait for the stock not only to rally and break its downtrend but for the price to pause and then follow through before you place a trade. This also gives the stock more time to bottom and complete an orderly correction. Don't buy just because a trendline is breached; wait for the stock to turn. The spot to begin buying is just as the high of the pause is taken out. This could occur at the cheat area or the handle.

THE LIVERMORE SYSTEM

The legendary trader Jesse Livermore had a system of buying and selling when a stock changed direction, but only if the stock followed through. Livermore only took positions in the direction of his trade. By waiting for a stock's price to confirm a new uptrend, he avoided being whipsawed on every minor countertrend rally. Instead, Livermore waited for the trend to be broken and two reactionary pullbacks to take place; then, as the stock traded above the second reaction high, he would enter a trade. This was Livermore's version of the turn. Livermore used this technique to make more money than any other trader ever.

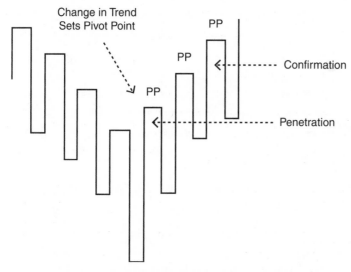

Figure 10.54 **Example of the Livermore trading system**
Jesse Livermore used pivot points (PP) for entry levels. Livermore never bought at the low; he waited for a change in trend and then starting buying on evidence that the trend was continuing (i.e., waiting for the high to be taken out after a natural reaction).

The Failure Reset

The fact that you get stopped out of a stock doesn't necessarily mean the underlying fundamentals are bad or the trade has soured; you may just be the victim of a shakeout. If I am knocked out of a stock, I keep the stock on my radar to see if it resets technically. At times the subsequent setup is actually better than the first chart pattern, with an even higher probability of success than what triggered my first entry. The fact that it had a shakeout could turn out to be constructive for the stock going forward. This is what I call a *failure reset*, which comes in two forms: a *base failure*, which requires building a whole new base before it can be purchased again, and a *pivot failure*, which can reset and recover within a small number of days.

Some of my biggest winners were stocks that stopped me out and then reset. Of course, not all failed setups will reset.

Figure 10.55   **Mercadolibre Inc. (MELI) 2007**

After attempting to emerge from a suspect base in September 2007, in December 2007, Mercadolibre Inc. consolidated and emerged from a failure reset.

Chart courtesy of Interactive Data, © 2009.

In October 2007, MELI emerged into new high ground, coming out of a primary base (the first buyable base after an IPO). Nine days later the stock was down 15 percent, enough to stop out most traders. However, if you kept this name on your watch list, you would have watched it reset in December 2007, and you could have made a very nice profit, as I did. Don't discard a stock just because it stops you out; if the fundamentals remain intact, stay on the lookout for a failure reset.

THE FAILURE (PIVOT) RESET

The failure pivot reset is similar to the base reset, except that it occurs during the formation of the entry point over a shorter period of time than the base reset. A pivot failure doesn't necessarily cause an outright base failure, instead, it can reset a new entry point usually within a number of days or weeks.

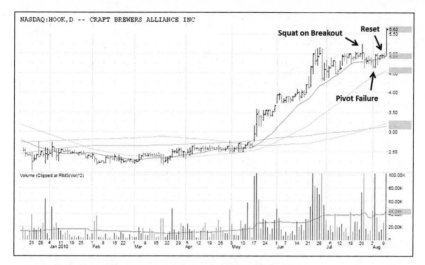

Figure 10.56   **Craft Brewers Alliance Inc. (HOOK) 2010**

In 2010, I bought Craft Brewers and soon after got stopped out. The stock reset and broke out a few days later.

Chart courtesy of Interactive Data, © 2009.

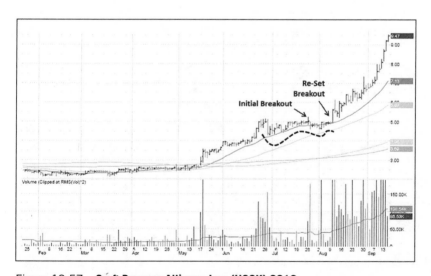

Figure 10.57   **Craft Brewers Alliance Inc. (HOOK) 2010**

Craft Brewers Alliance formed a failure (pivot) reset and then rose 90 percent in 26 days.

Chart courtesy of Interactive Data, © 2009.

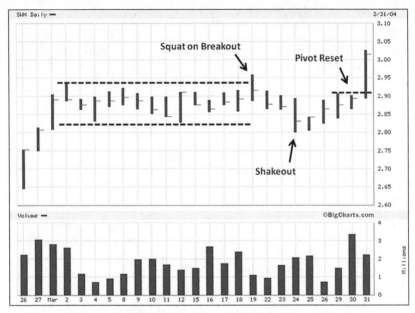

Figure 10.58 **Southwestern Energy Co. (SWN) 2004**
In March 2004, Southwestern Energy attempted to break out from a handle,
squatted, and then undercut the low in the handle creating a shakeout; five
trading days later the stock reset and reemerged.

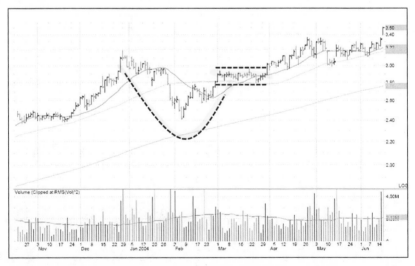

Figure 10.59 **Southwestern Energy Co. (SWN) 2004**
In March 2004, Southwestern Energy emerged from a cup with handle; within
the handle a failure (pivot) reset occurred. It rose 1,400 percent in 53 months.
Chart courtesy of Interactive Data, © 2009.

THE POWER PLAY

One of the most important setups you can learn to distinguish is the *power play*, which is also referred to as a *high tight flag*. This is without a doubt the most misinterpreted price setup among all the technical patterns. However, it is also one of the most profitable. The power play is what I call a *velocity pattern* for two reasons. First, it takes a great deal of momentum to qualify; in fact, the first requirement is a sharp price thrust upward. Second, these setups can move the fastest in the shortest period of time; velocity begets more velocity. This pattern often signals a dramatic shift in the prospects of a company. The rapid price run-up could be induced by a major news development such as an FDA drug approval, litigation resolution, a new product or service announcement, or even an earnings report; it can also occur

Figure 10.60   **TASER Intl. Inc.(TASR) 2004**
A strong prior uptrend, tight price action, and extreme volume contraction formed the perfect setup for an imminent explosion to the upside. Most investors probably thought this stock looked too high and risky. It rose 329 percent in 16 weeks.

on no news at all. Some of the best trades from this setup can develop as unexplained strength. Therefore, this is the only situation I will enter with a dearth of fundamentals. It doesn't mean that improving fundamentals don't exist; very often they do. However, with the power play, the stock is exhibiting so much strength that it's telling you that something is going on regardless of what the current earnings and sales are showing you. The stock is discounting something major. Although I don't demand that a power play have fundamentals on the table, I do require it to display VCP characteristics just as I do with all the other setups. Even the power play must go through a proper digestion of supply and demand.

Figure 10.61   **Quality Systems, Inc. (QSII) 1995**
In September 1995, Quality Systems setup as a power play with classic VCP characteristics and strong accelerating earnings leading up to a successful breakout. It rose 127 percent in 66 days.

To qualify as a power play, the following criteria must be met:

1. An explosive price move commences on huge volume that shoots the stock price up 100 percent or more in less than eight weeks. This generally occurs after a period of relative dormancy.

2. The stock price then moves sideways in a relatively tight range, not correcting more than 20 to 25 percent over a period of three to six weeks (some can emerge after only 12 days).

3. Within the base (usually just days before a breakout), volume will contract considerably.

Figure 10.62   **In December 1997, I purchased shares of Best Buy Co.**
Note the lowest volume and super tight price action the day *before* the stock breaks out. It rose 947 percent in 19 months.

Figure 10.63   **Arena Pharmaceuticals Inc. (ARNA) 2012**
Arena Pharmaceuticals Inc. offered two viable buy points; first at the turn and then emerging from the handle. It rose 70 percent in nine days.

Fundamentally Sound versus Price-Ready

The fact that a company has met all of your fundamental criteria does not mean that you should necessarily run out and buy it right away. Even if your fundamental analysis of the company is spot on, to make big money, your analysis of investor perception also needs to be accurate and timed correctly. Often a company will deliver one or two great quarterly earnings reports while the stock is still in a correction or consolidation. The stock price may have already run up in anticipation, and it simply needs time to digest the advance while earnings catch up, or perhaps the overall market is in a correction, holding it back. Be patient. Keep the stock on your radar and wait for its price and volume characteristics to set up properly. **The key to making big money in stocks is to align supporting fundamentals with constructive price action during a healthy overall market environment.** You want all the forces behind you: fundamental, technical, and market tone. A stock can be fundamentally sound but not price-ready, meaning that supply and demand dynamics have not yet established the line of least resistance. A good company is not always a good stock. It's important that you learn to differentiate between the two.

It doesn't really matter what you think about a stock. What matters is what big institutions think, because they are the ones that can move a stock's price dramatically. Therefore, it's your job to find the companies that institutions perceive as valuable.

After Dick's Sporting Goods (DKS) issued positive guidance, a strong response in its stock price put the stock on my watch list. Once it delivered the strong earnings promised and the stock held up technically, I moved its status up to buy alert. A few weeks later, constructive price action forged the setup I was waiting for, and I purchased the stock as it emerged from a proper consolidation.

Figure 10.64 **Dick's Sporting Goods (DKS) 2003**

CHAPTER 11

DON'T JUST BUY
WHAT YOU KNOW

Let us say that a new stock has been listed in the last two or three years and its high was 20, or any other figure, and that such a price was made two or three years ago. If something favorable happens in connection with the company, and the stock starts upward, usually it is a safe play to buy the minute it touches a brand new high.

—*Jesse Livermore, 1930*

A S A DISCIPLINED TRADER, you must chart a narrow course in your quest to score the richest return in the shortest amount of time. You should buy a stock only when you believe that enough factors have converged into an optimal setup for an imminent explosion in share price. A vital ingredient in my entry setups is *youth*. Some of the most exciting trading opportunities reside in newly public entrepreneurial companies: firms that have gone public within the past few months to a year or two. As a matter of fact, history shows that most superperformers go public within 8 to 10 years before the start of their superperformance phase. But youth alone doesn't cut it; I want youth with character! Along with sound fundamentals, the type of character I'm referring to becomes evident with a price setup termed the *primary base*.

The Primary Base

Every bull market is represented by a handful of leadership stocks that were recent IPOs. Generally, a stock will go public, rally strongly on the initial offering, and maybe even rally for several weeks or months. What usually follows is profit taking by those who made some quick and relatively easy money. This will cause the stock to correct. To attract my interest, a new issue must prove its mettle in the market with at least a couple of months of trading activity. Proof comes in the form of a primary base: the first buyable base after a company has gone public. The base forms during a corrective period of three weeks or longer that is followed by the emergence to an all-time high or from a constructive consolidation near the stock's all-time high.

During the recovery phase in which it recoups lost ground, the stock breaks into new high territory. Over the course of a long advance, a leading stock will form many such bases or consolidations. It will weather the ensuing profit taking and sell-offs and then proceed to new price highs. The primary base is simply the first occurrence of this bullish chart pattern in a stock's trading history. Stocks that began phenomenal advances from primary bases include Yahoo!, eBay, Google, Starbucks, Reebok, Microsoft, and Intel, as well as Amazon.com and Research in Motion, to name a few.

The primary base points to the possible future direction of a stock from its price and volume history, but the primary base has deep roots in so-called corporate fundamentals as well as the stock's market action. The biggest part of a company's growth usually occurs in the first 5 to 10 years after the company issues common stock and goes public. That's when the company's products or services are expanding into new, untapped markets fueled by the cash raised in the public offering. This crucial period is when management tends to be at its entrepreneurial best. As sales expand and economies of scale improve, margins are boosted and profit growth accelerates.

Remember, the fact that a company has recently gone public doesn't necessarily mean that it has been in business only for a short period. Some companies operate successfully as private organizations for many decades before they go public, whereas others are brand new start-ups in new industries. Eighty percent of the stock market winners that drove the tech boom during the 1990s were IPOs within the prior eight years. Amazon went

Figure 11.1   **Amazon.com (AMZN) 1997**
In September of 1997, Amazon emerged from a primary base and rose 2,500 percent in 16 months.

public in May 1997, formed a primary base, and emerged into new high ground less than four months later in September 1997. Sixteen months later, Amazon's stock was 2,500 percent higher than its highest price coming out of its primary base.

ALLOW A PRIMARY BASE TO DEVELOP

Once a stock goes public, it may shoot straight up 25 percent, 50 percent, 100 percent, or even more, sometimes during its very first trading day. Or the new issue may sell off sharply soon after its debut. This was the case for the much anticipated Facebook IPO in 2012. On its first day of public trading Facebook's stock traded as high as $45 a share, but by the end of the day's session the stock closed at $38.23; 12 days later it was trading 43 percent off its high at $25.52. Facebook never set up properly and then corrected excessively, rendering it unbuyable.

Before I buy a recent new issue, a stock must have a minimum trading history: a primary base. Some IPOs can take up to a year or more to form a proper base. In most cases, you should insist that the stock put in a base of at

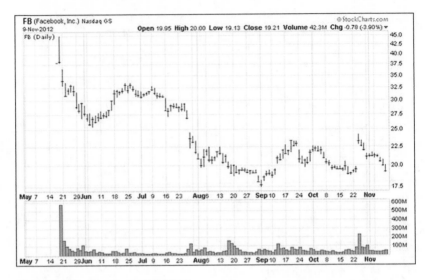

Figure 11.2 Facebook (FB) 2012
After its IPO, Facebook failed to set up properly and corrected excessively,
rendering it unbuyable.

least three to five weeks and not correct more than 25 to 35 percent to be reliable. Corrections that last longer (usually around one year) sometimes result
in a decline of as much as 50 percent, yet the setup can still be sound. Shorter
three-week consolidations should not correct more than 25 percent. Let's say
you spot a promising new issue. The company has an exciting new product
or service. Sales growth and earnings growth are accelerating. Now you must
wait for the market to confirm your fundamental belief. Your opinion about
a company is worthless unless it is verified by the price action of the stock.
As the technical pioneer Jesse Livermore wrote: "Apply strict attention to the
action of the market itself. Markets are never wrong—opinions often are."
That confirmation will display itself in the stock's successful emergence to
new high ground from its first viable consolidation: the primary base.

A PRIMARY BASE FEW WOULD CONSIDER

In 1997, I couldn't get anyone to even consider, let alone buy, Yahoo!.
However, after the stock went up tenfold in 1999, I couldn't get the same

Figure 11.3   **Yahoo (YHOO) 1997**
Yahoo emerged as a market leader in a relatively new industry group called
Internet providers. It rose 7,800 percent in 29 months.

people to sell the stock after they bought late and the story had become obvious to everyone. Suddenly everyone had to own Yahoo!, America Online,
Qualcomm, Nokia, Oracle, and a host of other names that a year or two
earlier had fallen on deaf ears. When the timing was perfect, no one wanted
to hear about them because the names weren't familiar and they were trading at what looked like high multiples. Many of these stocks were emerging when the market had just suffered a bear market decline and the world
was focused on the Asian crisis. In July 1997, I bought Yahoo!. The stock
emerged from a primary base and rocketed 7,800 percent in 29 months.
Yahoo! emerged as a market leader in a relatively new industry group called
Internet providers.

Rambus Offered Multiple Buy Points

California-based Rambus Inc. invented a new design that allowed computer memory chips to speed the flow of instructions to microprocessors.
The technology got a powerful boost from the chip titan Intel, which needed
faster memory chips to keep up with the increasing speeds of microproces-

Figure 11.4 **Rambus, Inc. 1997**

Rambus rose 150 percent in nine weeks and 1,450 percent in 37 months.

sors. Rambus went public on May 14, 1997 (point A). The stock made a huge advance the day of the IPO, closing strong. The price then traded sideways for about five weeks. Rambus broke to a new high emerging from a primary base on June 16, 1997 (point B). The stock blasted off over the next four days. It peaked on June 19 (point C) before settling into a second sideways consolidation, which lasted about six weeks. On July 29, the stock cleared another new high, emerging from a second stage base (point D) which set the stage for another powerful run that sent the price up dramatically once again. Rambus is a classic example of a primary base that provided a stellar investment opportunity for a watchful investor as well as several trading opportunities.

Body Central Corp.

In December 2010, while Christmas shopping in a mall, I spotted the retailer Body Central (BODY/Nasdaq). The trendy store caught my attention as a cookie cutter retailing model. Upon further investigation, I learned it had a solid Internet business as well. Most important, it was delivering the goods; the company reported huge earnings increases in the most recent quarters. Even more interesting was the fact that the stock had gone public only a couple of months earlier. To me, this smelled like opportunity. When I looked at

Figure 11.5   **Body Central (BODY) 2011**
In January 2011, Body Central emerged from a primary base and rose 105 percent in 15 months.

a chart of the stock's price action, I immediately got excited. The stock was setting up perfectly in a primary base. I watched it for a couple of weeks, and on January 5, 2011, the stock started moving up on good volume. The price

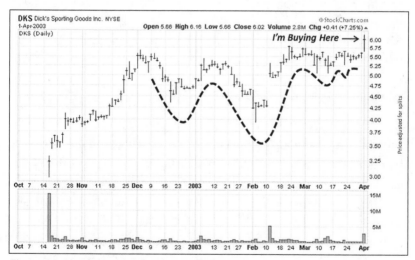

Figure 11.6   **Dick's Sporting Goods (DKS) 2003**
In April 2003, Dick's Sporting Goods emerged from a primary base and rose 200 percent in 15 months.

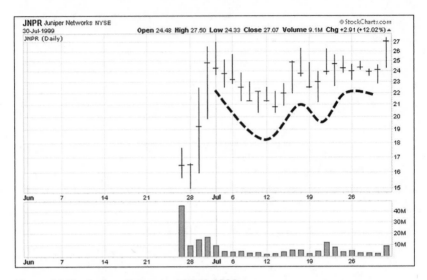

Figure 11.7   **Juniper Networks (JNPR) 1999**
In July 1999, Juniper Networks emerged from a primary base and rose 500 percent in 8 months.

ume. The price consolidation was sound, the earnings were strong, the company was relatively small with a scalable business, and management seemed to be doing the right things, and so I took my position. The stock advanced more than 100 percent over the next 15 months. During the same period, the Nasdaq Composite Index was up less than 10 percent.

NOT EVERY FROG BECOMES A PRINCE

Not every stock that makes a new high from a primary base turns out to be a big winner, and although a proper primary base affords an investor some of the best odds to participate during the majority of a big move, there is no guarantee of catching a stock as it begins a large-scale advance. Therefore, you must always be prepared with an exit plan to cut your losses if a primary base turns against you.

In January 2006, I bought shares of iRobot as the stock was emerging from a primary base. Shortly after that purchase, the stock came off, couldn't rally, and then began to sell off even more. I sold the stock at a small

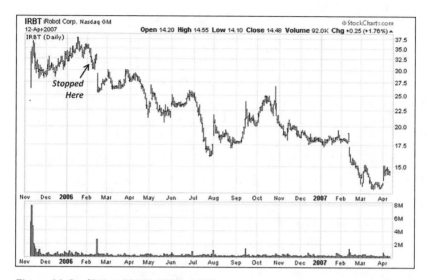

Figure 11.8 iRobot (IRBT) 2005–2007
iRobot's primary base failed and the stock sold off 65 percent from its peak.

loss. Good thing I did, IRBT went into a precipitous slide that took the stock from a peak above $37 a share to just $7. I was able to cut my loss short and avoid a big loss because I followed rules and didn't allow my judgment to become clouded by personal opinions or emotions.

FROM INNOVATOR TO RESPIRATOR

> Just as styles in women's gowns and hats and costume jewelry are forever changing with time, the old leaders of the stock market are dropped and new ones rise up to take their places. In the course of time new leaders will come to the front: some of the old leaders will be dropped. It will always be that way as long as there is a stock market. Keep mentally flexible. Remember the leaders of today may not be the leaders two years from now.
>
> —*Jesse Livermore*

The Richmond, Virginia–based big-box retailer Circuit City filed for bankruptcy in 2008. Circuit City was a pioneer among superstores, and its stock price soared during the 1980s and 1990s, up over 6,000 percent during a 10-year run. In fact, from 1981 through 2000, Circuit City's stock price advanced more than 63,000 percent. Although Circuit City was one of the nation's strongest retailers in the 1980s, it made a series of critical missteps that accumulated over time. Its best growth came during the period when the company was relatively small, and its problems accelerated as it grew much larger. In 2008, Circuit City was still the nation's second largest dedicated consumer electronics retailer after Best Buy, with more than 700 stores. The company planned to close 155 existing stores, open fewer new ones, renegotiate some leases, and cut staff members at its headquarters. This is the opposite of what you see during a company's expansion phase, when the future for growth is promising. Those who held shares of Circuit City watched the stock price go to zero in 2008.

Beware of well-known companies that everyone regards as "official growth stocks." Like Circuit City, these institutional favorites generally have already experienced their best earnings growth and are too obvious once they are officially termed growth stocks. At some point they are so over-owned that the amount of supply that comes to market once a material problem is noticed can bring down the house. Instead, buy the new market leaders; don't be afraid of companies that are unfamiliar to you. Do some detective work and get familiar with stocks that are forming a primary base. This is where many of the next big winners will be found.

CHAPTER 12

RISK MANAGEMENT
PART 1: THE NATURE OF RISK

I N VIRTUALLY EVERY COMPETITIVE ENDEAVOR, there's a championship. In American sports, it's the Super Bowl, the World Series, and the NBA Finals. In entertainment, there's the Academy Awards, the Emmy Awards, and the Tony Awards. Trading is no different. For many years, the best of the best tested their mettle against a host of competitors, from amateurs to professionals, in the U.S. Investing Championship (USIC).

The USIC competition was started in 1983 by Norman Zadeh and quickly became a proving ground for stock, options, and futures traders. Zadeh's career encompassed mathematics, market speculation, and gambling; he authored *Winning Poker Systems* in 1974 and taught mathematics at Stanford University and UCLA. Although a gifted theoretical mathematician, Zadeh understood the inability of static academic theory to grasp the reality of real-life auction markets. His consuming goal was to disprove the efficient markets theory, a point he particularly wanted to bring home to the academic crowd. He would do this by demonstrating that certain individuals could indeed outperform the market. The USIC was just the vehicle to prove it while earning a personal profit!

The U.S. Investing Championship quickly became a prestigious contest, and many of the traders who won it went on to big investment careers. In its early years, the USIC was divided into four divisions: stocks, options, stocks and options, and futures. Through the contest, Zadeh was able to scout trading talent and then sign up a diverse list of individuals to manage money for his clients.

I can remember reading about the winners in the *Wall Street Journal* in the 1980s. A young trader by the name of David Ryan won the contest three years in a row between 1984 and 1986, a magnificent achievement. Another well-known champ was S&P futures trader Martin "Buzzy" Schwartz. Both Ryan and Schwartz would later be profiled by Jack Schwager in his first *Market Wizards* book. To me, it was clear that to win the USIC and join the ranks of these champions was to join an elite circle.

In 1996, at age 31, I decided to enter the contest. I felt confident that my skills had reached the point where I could win. Whoever made the most money during a one-year period was the champion; pretty simple. The account size required for entry was $25,000. I posted the $25,000 and traded in my usual style: aggressively with supertight risk control. Each day, I combed my watch list to determine the best possible moment for executing a trade. Although I was confident of victory, I kept my focus on sticking to my trading plan. My goal, as always, was to make as much money as possible, but only by executing the best trades at the optimal time, never by taking impulsive actions that deviated from my trading regime.

At the end of the first quarter, I was up 49.72 percent and had run the $25,000 account up to $37,430. Quarterly results were not being published publicly at the time, and so I had no idea how well my performance stacked up against those of the other traders. By the end of the second quarter, I really hit my stride. My account was up an additional 93.75 percent, bringing my total return for the first six months to +190.08 percent. My contest trading account was at $72,521, and I had the feeling I was pretty well positioned in the field of competitors.

Shortly after that day I got an unexpected phone call from one of the contest coordinators. He told me that the championship was being suspended because of an inquiry by the Securities and Exchange Commission about an advertisement issue relating to previously published performance results. I couldn't believe it. I had finally decided to enter the USIC, and the SEC was closing it down! "Can you at least tell me where I stand, what place I'm in?" I asked. If nothing else, I would have the satisfaction of knowing how I ranked among the other competitors.

"Mark, you're way in the lead by more than 100 percent," he told me.

I thanked him for the opportunity and hung up the phone very disappointed. Here I was, way out in front so that it would be very difficult for anyone to catch me, and now the contest was closed, probably forever. But as with a bad trade, when disappointment comes, you deal with it and move on.

Later that year, I received another call from the contest organizer, who explained that the issues with the SEC had been resolved and the contest was back on. The competition would resume on January 1, 1997. However, the results of 1996 would not carry over. It was a new contest. If I wanted to enter, I had to start all over again. My 190 percent performance in the first six months would be for my own edification alone. It wasn't official, and although it might make a nice story, nobody would ever see it or care.

New rules were set for the 1997 championship: two divisions, one designed for personal trading accounts ranging from $200,000 to $999,000 and one for combined managed accounts of $1 million and higher, with no restrictions on what could be traded in either division; the contestants were free to trade in stocks, options, futures, or any mixture. Although this seemed incredibly unfair—a pure stock guy like me going up against options and futures traders who could use massive leverage—I decided to enter the first division, putting up $250,000 of my own money.

In the first quarter, I was up just a little over 8 percent; that was not nearly enough to qualify for the top spot, but it was the final tally I was concerned with. This time the contest results were published quarterly in *Investor's Business Daily* and *Barron's*. Quarter by quarter, the world could track the performance of the top competitors. During the first two quarters I was in the top 20, but there were opponents who were far ahead of me. I knew that I must not let being behind affect my trading or cloud my judgment. I had to play the game my way, which meant taking only the best trades according to my criteria and exercising tight control over each execution. There was real money on the line, and so doing something stupid and risky just to win the contest was not an option. I made a commitment to stay with my game plan through the entire year, knowing it was sound.

By the third quarter, things had changed quite a bit. I was now neck and neck with my closest competitor, separated by a mere tenth of a percentage point. I was in first place, up 110.10 percent, and the trader in second place stood at an even +110.00 percent. Then, in the fourth quarter, the market corrected; it was a very tough trading environment. The Dow peaked in October and corrected 10 percent. This was just the scenario I had hoped for. I knew that during a difficult period not only would my discipline avert giving back my profits, I could actually make money trading. This was something that I felt confident few could achieve. Over the next several months I traded fiercely and pulled away from the pack. My final tally was a total return of 155 percent, almost double that of the nearest competitor. I was grateful to be named the 1997 U.S. Investing Champion by Money Manager Verified Ratings.

The point of this story is simple. The uneven playing field of highly leveraged options and futures traders trading against straight stock guys could have pressured me to take on too much risk or overtrade. I also could have gotten flustered when I was significantly behind and tried to make an adjustment, breaking my own rules. But I didn't. Instead, I focused on my trading plan and the two elements that were absolutely critical to winning over the long haul: consistency and risk management.

What Champions Have in Common

People buy stocks in hopes of making money and increasing their wealth. They dream of the great returns that their carefully chosen investments will yield in the future. Before investing your hard-earned cash, however, you'd better think about how you will avoid losing it. If there's one thing I've learned over the years, it's that risk management is the most important building block for achieving consistent success in the stock market. Notice that I said "consistent."

Anyone can have short-term success by being in the right place at the right time, but consistency is what differentiates the pros from the amateurs, the timeless legends from the one-hit wonders. I once bowled a 259 during my very first year playing in a Wednesday night league. It was a bizarre aberration. My average was only 129, and I would never break 200 again. During my career, I've witnessed many people make millions of dollars during good times, only to give it all back and even go broke. I'm going to tell you how to avoid that fate.

IT'S YOUR MONEY ONLY AS LONG AS YOU PROTECT IT

> Whether you are dealing in millions or in thousands the same principle lesson applies. It is your money. It will remain with you just so long as you guard it. Faulty speculation is one of the most certain ways of losing it.
>
> —*Jesse L. Livermore*

To achieve consistent profitability, you must protect your profits and principal. As a matter of fact, I don't differentiate between the two. A big mistake I see many traders make is to consider trading profits as house money, acting as if that money somehow were less their own to lose than their original starting capital is. If you have fallen into this mental habit, you need to change your perception immediately to achieve superperformance.

Let's say I make $5,000 on Monday. I don't consider myself $5,000 "ahead of the game," free to risk that amount shooting for the moon. My account simply has a new starting balance, subject to the same set of rules as before. Once I make a profit, that money belongs to me. Yesterday's profit is part of today's principal.

Don't fall into the faulty reasoning of amateur gamblers. Through consistent play and conservative wagering, a player picks up $1,500 at the blackjack table. Then he starts to make big, reckless bets. In his eyes, he now is playing with house money. This happens all the time in the stock market. Amateur investors treat their gains like the market's money instead of their money, and in due time the market takes it back. Let's say someone buys a stock at $20 a share. It climbs to $27. Then the investor decides he can "give it room" because he has a seven-point cushion. Wrong! Once a stock moves up a decent amount from my purchase price, I usually give it less room on the downside. I go into a profit-protection mode. At the very least, I protect my breakeven point. I'm certainly not going to let a good gain turn into a loss.

At the end of each trading session, when you review your portfolio, ask yourself this: Am I bullish on this position today? If not, why am I holding it? Does your original reason for going long remain valid? End every trading day with a frank appraisal of all your positions.

I'm not suggesting that you not allow a stock to go through a normal reaction or pullback in price if you believe the stock can go much higher. Of course, you should give stocks some room to fluctuate, but that leeway has little to do with your past gain. Evaluate your stocks on the basis of the return you expect from them in the future versus what you're risking. Each day, a stock must justify your confidence in holding it for a greater profit.

Sound Principles Provide Clarity

> My biggest losses have always come after I have had a great period and I started to think that I knew something.
> —*Paul Tudor Jones*

There are certainly times when money can be made very easily in the stock market. Often this leads to carelessness, which in turn can lead to disaster. At the end of the day, success is not decided by your winnings from any particular day, month, or quarter; it's what you *keep* year in and year out. Adherence to sound risk-management principles will not only allow you keep the profits you've acquired but will also keep your feet on the ground when your head is in the sky because you've become overly ambitious after a period of success.

You've undoubtedly heard the phrase "cut your losses and let your winners ride." When I was interviewed by Jack Schwager for his book *Stock Market Wizards: Interviews with America's Top Stock Traders* (HarperBusiness 2001, 2003), I spent a lot of time talking about loss cutting as the key to my success. At one point during the interview, Jack stopped the tape recorder and said, "Mark, this stuff is great, but it's a cliché; it's what all the successful traders say."

"Jack, of course that's what they say," I told him. "That's why they're successful, and that's why I'm successful."

When you have been trading for a long time, you can easily lose perspective as you cultivate new techniques. If you're not careful, the basic fundamentals may come in your mind or, more subtly, in your subconscious to seem remedial. Far from being training wheels to be cast off with maturity, the basics of risk management must be continually refreshed in your mind and perfected. Maybe that sounds unexciting, but as the legendary quarterback Roger Staubach said, "It takes a lot of unspectacular practice to get spectacular results."

A Lesson from Master Jack

Part of my obsession with perfecting the basics goes back to my days as a kid in karate school. I was somewhat gifted as far as being able to do gymnastic-type maneuvers, and after only a short time I could do all sorts of complex karate moves and even a backward no-hand flip. They gave me the nickname Movie Man because of my ability to do the types of moves you saw in kung fu films. Even so, I was still a novice, and my teacher, Master Jack Moscato, knew I needed humbling.

One day, Master Jack told me to assume the basic front stance, which is one of the very first things you learn. He walked around me quietly and then suddenly kicked out my front leg. I fell crashing to the ground. When I looked up in surprise, Master Jack stared down at me and said, "Maybe you should learn to stand before you learn to flip." That lesson has stayed with me ever since. Master the basics. My karate instructor was a stickler for perfecting the basics. Every day, remind yourself that the key building blocks for success include executing the basics better than the other guy and doing it over and over again. Greatness is built on a solid foundation of fundamental principles.

LOSSES MAKE YOU WORK HARDER

When you lose money on a stock trade, you will need a greater percentage gain to get back to even because losses work against you geometrically. For example, if a stock declines 50 percent in price, let's say from $28 to $14, that stock will have to rise by 100 percent (from $14 to $28) to get back to even. That's worth repeating: a 50 percent decline in price requires a double to break even.

What happens if you keep your losses relatively small? A 10 percent loss requires an 11 percent gain to return to even, and a 5 percent loss needs only a 5.26 percent gain. This is why you never want to let your losses get too large. Also, if you lose a big portion of your account, you lose your buying power. Your account will be much smaller when you finally latch on to a big winner. The last thing you want to do is put yourself in a position of losing when your account is large and a position of gaining when it's small; this will accomplish little. By keeping your losses small, you preserve your hard-earned capital for future investments.

The lesson here is never to permit yourself to lose an amount of money that would jeopardize your account. The larger the loss is, the more difficult it is to recover from it. Set an absolute maximum line in the sand of no more than 10 percent on the downside. Your average loss should be much less, maybe 6 or 7 percent. If you can't be correct on your purchase with a 10 percent cushion for normal price fluctuation, you have a different

LOSS	GAIN TO BREAK EVEN
5%	5.26%
10%	11%
20%	25%
30%	43%
40%	67%
50%	100%
60%	150%
70%	233%
80%	400%
90%	900%

Figure 12.1   **Gain needed to break even from loss**

problem to address. Either your selection criteria and timing are flawed or the overall market is hostile and you should be out of stocks.

Two Up and One Down

If I guaranteed you a three year compounded return consisting of two 50 percent up years and one 50 percent down year, that may sound like a pretty good deal, but think again. Regardless of the order, you would have a three-year total return of 12.5 percent, or about 4 percent per year. That's not exactly the type of return you hope for when investing in stocks, especially taking into consideration all the risks you have to take. Actually, there's no good "two up, one down" deal. About the best you can hope for is two 30 percent gains and one 30 percent loss, which results in a return of about 5.75 percent per year; still not very impressive. This demonstrates how losses work geometrically against you. To achieve big results, your gains must eclipse your losses on a risk/reward basis—period!

Year 1	Year 2	Year 3	3-Yr Tot. Ret.	Per Year
10%	10%	-10%	8.9%	2.9%
20%	20%	-20%	15.2%	4.9%
30%	30%	-30%	18.3%	5.8%
40%	40%	-40%	17.6%	5.6%
50%	50%	-50%	12.5%	4.0%
60%	60%	-60%	2.4%	0.8%
70%	70%	-70%	-13.3%	-4.7%
80%	80%	-80%	-35.2%	-13.5%
90%	90%	-90%	-63.9%	-28.8%

Figure 12.2   **Various returns based on three-year compounding**

Convincing Myself: The Loss Adjustment Exercise

> The definition of a great investor is someone who starts by understanding the downside.
>
> —*Sam Zell*

Early in my career, I did not understand the dramatic effect of losses and the importance of cutting them short. Like most traders, I had periods of success followed by some fairly drastic drawdowns because of a few trades gone wrong. I thought loss cutting sounded logical and tried to apply it to my trading, but every now and then I would break the rule, hoping that things would turn around, sometimes holding on to my favorite position for dear life. It got to the point where I was confused, and so I decided to test the effects of cutting my losses on all my trades.

I decided to adjust all of my past losses to an arbitrary level of 10 percent to see what the effect of capping the downside would be. This included adjusting the losses that were smaller up to 10 percent as well as adjusting the ones that were larger down. As I said, occasionally I would hold on to a stock that had fallen, and from time to time I would take 20 percent and even 30 percent losses. When I adjusted those losses and capped them at 10 percent, the effect on my performance was amazing. Capping the losses would have knocked me out of a few of my winners; however, this consequence was overwhelmed by the loss-cutting effect. The hypothetical improvement in the overall portfolio performance seemed too dramatic to be believed. I rechecked the math two or three times, and the numbers were correct. Instead of having a double-digit percentage loss in my portfolio, I would have had a gain of more than 70 percent.

Is it possible that such a small alteration could have such a dramatic impact on performance? Absolutely! This revelation was a pivotal point in my trading. I was convinced that risk management was the key to success. From that point on, I grew very risk adverse, and my results improved dramatically. I religiously cut my losses and as a result attained a whole new level of performance. I call this the Loss Adjustment Exercise. Try it; it's an eye-opener.

Back in the 1980s, my trading account's distribution of gains and losses looked like this:

- **Gains:** (6, 8, 10, 12, 15, 17, 18, 20, 28, 50 percent) **18.40 percent average gain**

Original Account Results   After Losses Adjusted

Trade		% G/L	Cum. Bal.	Tot. Ret %		% G/L	Cum. Bal	Tot. Ret. %
			$ 100.00				$ 100.00	
1		6%	$ 106.00	6.00%		6% $	106.00	6.00%
2		8%	$ 114.48	14.48%		8% $	114.48	14.48%
3		10%	$ 125.93	25.93%		10% $	125.93	25.93%
4		12%	$ 141.04	41.04%		12% $	141.04	41.04%
5	Gains	15%	$ 162.20	62.20%	Gains	15% $	162.20	62.20%
6		17%	$ 189.77	89.77%		17% $	189.77	89.77%
7		18%	$ 223.93	123.93%		18%	223.93	123.93%
8		20%	$ 268.71	168.71%		20%	268.71	168.71%
9		28%	$ 343.95	243.95%		28%	343.95	243.95%
10		50%	$ 515.93	415.93%		50%	515.93	415.93%
11		-7%	$ 479.81	379.81%		-10%	464.34	364.34%
12		-8%	$ 441.43	341.43%		-10%	417.90	317.90%
13		-10%	$ 397.28	297.28%		-10%	376.11	276.11%
14		-12%	$ 349.61	249.61%		-10%	338.50	238.50%
15	Losses	-13%	$ 304.16	204.16%	Losses	-10%	304.65	204.65%
16		-15%	$ 258.54	158.54%		-10%	274.19	174.19%
17		-19%	$ 290.41	190.41%		-10%	246.77	146.77%
18		-20%	$ 167.53	67.53%		-10%	222.21	122.21%
19		-25%	$ 125.64	25.64%		-10%	199.88	99.88%
20		-30%	$ 87.95	**-12.05%**		-10%	179.89	**79.89%**
Bat. Avg. 50%		Average Gain: 18.40% Average Loss: -15.90%				Average Gain: 18.40% Average Loss: -10.00%		

Figure 12.3   **Loss adjustment chart.**

- **Losses:** (7, 8, 10, 12, 13, 15, 19, 20, 25, 30 percent) **15.90 percent average loss**

- **Compounded return: –12.05 percent**

- **Adjust losses to –10 percent** (including the ones that are smaller up to –10 percent)

- **Compounded return: +79.89 percent**

Note: The order in which the trades are compounded doesn't matter; the result is the same.

Accepting the Market's Judgments

Nothing can drag you down if you're not holding on to it.

—*Tony Robbins*

The stock market offers tremendous potential rewards and opportunities for virtually anyone. As a disciplined investor, you have good reason to be optimistic about your chances for success. But the stock market can strike without notice, transforming your lofty dreams into a financial nightmare, a lesson learned by the tens of millions of investors who suffered huge losses during the bear market that began in March 2000 and those who attempted to ride out the storm in the bear market of 2007–2008. Whether you're investing in blue chip stocks or trading pork bellies, any seasoned pro will tell you that there is no room for ego. The market can and will break anyone who ignores the risks and dangers. With each bear market a new group of investors learn this lesson the hard way.

The first discipline you need to learn to be a successful stock trader is simple to comprehend mentally, but for the majority of traders it's the most difficult to perform regularly: the best way to stay clear of the market's wrath is to accept its judgment.

Knowing When You're Wrong

Good trading is a peculiar balance between the conviction to follow your ideas and the flexibility to recognize when you have made a mistake.

—*Michael Steinhardt*

I've been asked, "How do you know when you're wrong?" My answer is always, "The stock goes down." It's that simple. As a matter of fact, I will often sell a stock if it doesn't go up shortly after I buy it. Even though it has not gone down, if the stock doesn't do what I expected it to do, that's reason enough to step aside and reevaluate. When a stock you have bought falls below your purchase price, it is telling you have made an error—at a minimum in timing. Make no mistake, whether you're a short-term trader or a long-term investor, timing is everything. Just as much money is lost on great companies bought at the wrong time as on investments that were poor choices in the first place. **Regardless of your methodology or approach to stock investing, there is only one way to protect your portfolio from a large loss, and that is to sell when you have a small loss before it snowballs into a huge one. In three decades of trading, I have not found a better way.**

Amazingly, no matter how many successful investors advocate this commonsense approach, this advice is followed only by an extremely small group of people even among professionals. Consequently, only a very small number of investors (including pros) achieve outstanding results in the stock market. Without a doubt, the hardest discipline for investors to follow consistently is to cut their losses short because it involves admitting that one's original purchase was a mistake, and no one likes to be wrong.

Avoid the Big Errors

> What vulnerabilities do we have and what can we do to minimize them, to get around them, to survive them—and give ourselves a better chance to win"
>
> —*Bobby Knight*

Recently I had a chance to speak with Itzhak Ben-David, coauthor of the study *Are Investors Really Reluctant to Realize Their Losses? Trading Responses to Past Returns and the Disposition Effect.* The tendency to sell winners too soon and to keep losers too long has been called the *disposition effect* by economists.

Mr. Ben-David and David Hirshleifer studied stock transactions from more than 77,000 accounts at a large discount broker from 1990 through 1996 and did a variety of analyses that had never been done before. They examined when investors bought individual stocks, when they sold them, and how much they earned or lost with each sale. They also examined when investors were more likely to buy additional shares of a stock they had previously purchased. Their results were published in the August 2012 issue of the *Review of Financial Studies.*

The study highlights several interesting conclusions:

- Investors are more likely to allow a stock to reach a large loss than they are to allow a stock to attain a large gain; they hold losers too long and sell winners too quickly.

- The probability of buying additional shares is greater for shares that have lost value than it is for shares that have gained value; investors may readily double down on their bets when stocks decline in value.

- Investors are more likely to take a small gain than a small loss.

Most investors are simply too slow in closing out losing positions. As a result, they hold on until they can't take the pain anymore, and that eats up precious capital and valuable time. To be successful, you must keep in mind that the only way you can continue to operate is to protect your account from a major setback or, worse, devastation. **Avoiding large losses is the single most important factor for winning big as a speculator. You can't control how much a stock rises, but in most cases, whether you take a small loss or a big loss is entirely your choice.** There is one thing I can guarantee: if you can't learn to accept small losses, sooner or later you will take big losses. It's inevitable.

To master the craft of speculation, you must face your destructive capacity; once you understand and acknowledge this capacity, you can control your destiny and achieve consistency. You should focus a significant amount of time and effort on learning how to lose the smallest amount possible when you're wrong. You must learn to avoid the big errors.

Don't Become an Involuntary Investor

Because investors hate to admit mistakes, they rationalize. They fluctuate from being "traders" when they're right—getting in and out of profitable stock positions in the short term—to becoming "investors" when they are wrong. When their trades move against them and start to rack up losses, all of a sudden they decide to hold on for the long term. They become what Jesse Livermore called an "involuntary investor," a person who harvests a bitter crop of small profits and large losses, the exact opposite of what you want to achieve.

Every major correction begins as a minor reaction. You can't tell when a 10 percent decline is the beginning of a 50 percent decline until after the fact, when it's too late. No one can know for sure that a stock will decline only a certain amount and then move higher. If you had known that your stock was going to drop 15 percent or 20 percent, would you have bought it in the first place? Of course not. The fact that the stock is below your purchase price means you made a mistake in timing, which happens 50 to 60 percent of the time on average. The best traders may pick winning stocks about 60 or 70 percent of the time in a healthy market, which means 30 to 40 percent of their stock picks lose money.

In fact, you can be correct on only 50 percent of your stock selections and still enjoy huge success, but only if you keep your losses in check. You can make money by picking winning stocks only one time out of two or even three trades, but only if you sell your losers before they inflict an insurmountable toll on your account. Every dollar saved is a dollar earned, and every dollar saved is more money that can be compounded when you latch on to your next big winner. Don't become an involuntary investor.

How Low Can It Go?

> It would be simple to run down the list of hundreds of stocks which, in my time, have been considered gilt-edge investments, and which today are worth little or nothing. Thus, great investments tumble, and with them the fortunes of so-called conservative investors in the continuous distribution of wealth.
>
> —*Jesse Livermore*

Some investors feel they don't need to trade with a stop loss because they buy only quality stocks. There's no such thing as a safe stock. Many "conservative investors" have gone broke owning and holding on to so-called blue chip companies for a long-term investment with the philosophy that patience is prudence by way of quality. If this is your strategy, I'm afraid you will eventually be in for an unpleasant surprise. This is simply a lazy person's strategy, or lack of strategy.

I can't tell you how many times I've heard "They're not going to go out of business" because it's Coke or Apple or some other well-known name. Maybe they won't go out of business and maybe they will, or maybe the stock will correct 70 percent or more and take a decade to recover. Coke topped in 1973, declined 70 percent from its high, and then took 11 years to get back to even. Sure, investors received a dividend of a few percent per year, but that doesn't even beat inflation, and they were still sitting with a big fat loss. In 1998, Coca-Cola topped again; the stock declined for five years and took an almost 50 percent haircut.

Vast numbers of "high-quality" companies had periods when their stock prices were decimated. After topping out in 1973, shares in Eastman Kodak took 14 years to break even, just in time for the crash of 1987, which tanked the stock again, and then it took another 8 years to reach its 1973 high.

Xerox also topped in 1973, and it took 24 years to break even; during that period the S&P 500 advanced more than 500 percent. In the 1960s, Avon Products became so popular that the stock price ran up way ahead of its earnings, resulting in a price advance that took the stock from $3 in 1958 to $140 per share in 1972. Then the stock topped out and plunged from $140 to $19, an 86 percent drop in only one year. Fourteen years later the stock was still at $19 a share.

In the 32 month period from December 1999 through February 2002, McDonald's fell 72 percent. In August 2000, AT&T began a slide that took its shares down 80 percent in less than four years. Starting in April 2000, Cisco Systems plunged 90 percent in 30 months. In 2000, institutional favorite Lucent Technologies topped and fell 99 percent in 35 months.

No stock can be held forever. Few stocks can be held unattended for even a few months without risk. Good companies can be terrible stock investments if they are bought at the wrong time. Many so-called investment-grade companies today will face new challenges, deteriorating business conditions, or regulatory changes that can materially affect their future earnings potential. Often, before problems become apparent, the price of a stock declines precipitously in anticipation of such developments. But management said everything is great, right? When fundamental problems arise in a public company, management is probably your worst source of information. The executives will try everything in their power legally, and in some cases illegally, to bamboozle the shareholders in an effort to protect the stock price. In 2008, General Motors went to zero. How about AIG and Lehman Brothers, or before them Enron and WorldCom? These are just a few of the market's casualties that were once high-quality names.

How low can it go? To zero!

A Trip to the Casino

> Consistent winners raise their bet as their position strengthens, and they exit the game when the odds are against them, while consistent losers hang on until the bitter end of every expensive pot, hoping for miracles and enjoying the thrill of defeat. In stud poker and on Wall Street, miracles happen just often enough to keep the losers losing.
>
> —*Peter Lynch,* One Up on Wall Street

The first time I saw seven-card stud being played at a casino, it didn't take me more than a few minutes to see the similarities to trading stocks. The ante (the initial bet to see the first three cards of the deal) was $0.50. However, the pot (what the winner pulled in for a winning hand) averaged about $50. Thus, for half a buck, players could get a fair idea of their chances of winning 100 times the ante.

After a night at the table, I was ahead about $1,400. My secret? I played cards the way I trade stocks: immediately folding the ones that didn't work out as expected. If I didn't receive a decent playable hand on the deal, I didn't continue betting against the other players. I tossed in my cards and accepted the small loss of $0.50 as the cost of doing business. I knew that when I had a winning hand, I could make back the amount of my loss many times over. I probably folded 30 hands in a row at times, which at $0.50 an ante meant a $15 loss. But the average winning pot was $50. If I folded 50 times and won only once, I would still win twice as much as I lost.

Why didn't the other players fold when I played a hand after realizing that I went forward only when I had solid cards? Ego! Big ego equals small discipline. Undisciplined players looking for "action" always show up at the poker tables. The stock market is no different except that most stock market investors are even less disciplined than most poker players. **The Achilles' heel of most gamblers and speculators is the desire to play every hand, a common human weakness that allows impatience to override good judgment.**

Folding mediocre cards at the poker table is the same as selling off stocks soon after they fall below your purchase price to protect your account. Losing trades are inevitable. By limiting your losses, you will put yourself way ahead of the majority of investors because most investors lack discipline. The best traders are the ones who recognize mistakes, dispassionately cut their losses, and move on, preserving capital for the next opportunity.

One in a Million

As a trader, which is the better deal, $1,000 guaranteed or $1 million with a 1 percent chance of losing everything? It's really not an either-or answer. Notice the key words "as a trader." Now think about something: If you were a lawyer, would you go to trial just once? If you were a surgeon, would you conduct just one operation? As a stock trader, are your decisions based on a one-time event? Of course not. As a stock trader, you probably will make hundreds if not thousands of stock transactions over your lifetime.

The answer to the question is that if it's a one-time event, take the million. However, if it involves many trades, say, 100 or more transactions, the 1 percent probability will definitely leave you broke; hence, take the sure thing: the $1,000.

If you're going to become a stock trader, you will be trading for years, maybe even decades. **If you regard each trade as just one out of a million over time, it becomes much easier to take a small loss and move on to the next trade.** If you stay disciplined, apply good judgment, and play the high-probability situations, the odds will distribute over time and you will be profitable.

In poker and in the stock market, you're playing probabilities, not certainties; that means you cannot be correct all the time. If you make more on your winners than you lose on your losers over time, that's all you need to accomplish to be successful. I regard each trade as just one of many in a long continuous trading session: one in a million.

What's the Difference?

You buy a stock at $30 because you think it looks good, the fundamentals look great, the future appears bright, and the stock price is acting well. Suddenly, the company announces that earnings per share will come in well below estimates as a result of a manufacturing plant not opening up as scheduled. The next day the stock falls 10 percent below your purchase price right at the open. You're faced with the decision to sell and take a loss or wait it out.

My question is this: What's the difference if you continue to hold the stock that has declined by 10 percent, waiting for it to come back and overcome the negative news, or buy a fresh new name that looks good from the start? The answer is: nothing but your ego. Successful investors can shift gears and accept change. They don't fall in love with a stock and ignore when circumstances take a turn for the worse; the goal is to make money, not to prove you're right and the stock market is wrong. Move on and find another stock. What's the difference whether you make money with stock A or stock B? If your original stock was at $30 and it's now at $27, it has to go up about 11 percent to get you back to even. It's no different if you buy a new stock at, say, $50 and it goes to $56 than if you hold on to your current position and wait for it to go back to $30, except maybe the new company will open its plant on time.

What a Deal

When you play poker, it costs money to see your cards from the deal; you must pay an ante, or post blinds, as well as pay the house "time" to participate in the game. Now imagine you could see every poker hand for free and place your bets only when the cards were stacked in your favor. How could you lose over time? One of the great things about the stock market is that all comers compete in the same ring: skilled and unskilled, professionals and amateurs. This is one of the reasons the market is *not* purely random. **In the stock market, you have the luxury of being able to stay on the sidelines, free of charge, observing and waiting for the most opportune moment to wager. You get to see the market's "cards" before you bet, free of charge. This is a wonderful advantage, yet few exploit it.**

You don't have to involve yourself in every market movement. In fact, you should not attempt to. Be an exacting opportunist. Be selective and pick your entry spots very carefully. Wait until the probabilities are stacked in your favor before you act. With patience and discipline, you can profit from market opponents who are less disciplined and less capable than you are. While you do nothing, less skilled opponents are laying the groundwork for your success, and you get to wait and watch for free. What a deal!

When a Mistake Becomes a Mistake

> The difference between successful investors and unsuccessful investors is how they react to being invested in a losing stock. There is absolutely no reason to allow a mistake to become an ego shattering experience. Being wrong is not the problem. Making a mistake is not the problem. The problem is being unwilling to accept the mistake. The problem is staying wrong.
>
> —*Dan Sullivan*

No matter how smart you think you are, I guarantee you will make an abundance of mistakes over time. We all do. Many of your failed trades may not even be mistakes on your part, just changes in circumstances that were impossible to forecast. The real mistake comes when you refuse to make an adjustment after things change. **No one will ever be so good that he or she will never take a loss. Being wrong is unavoidable, but staying wrong is a choice.** Staying wrong can be deadly; it can take both a physical and a psychological toll on your health. When you deny reality, you are no longer trading: you've sacrificed your principal to the fates. The linkages between stress and effects such as heart disease and ulcers are well known. To protect your health, your confidence, and your money, you must learn to release a bad hand and move on.

IF YOU'RE NOT FEELING STUPID, YOU'RE NOT MANAGING RISK

Sometimes after you sell a stock to cut short a loss, the stock will turn around and move up in price. This has happened to me thousands of times. Do I feel dumb or get angry? No. Investing and trading stocks is a business of playing probabilities so that the profit from winners outweighs the losses over time. It is completely unrealistic to think you're going to be right all the time or think that you can hold losses and they will never leave you broke. **Making you feel stupid is the market's way of pressuring you to act foolish. Don't succumb. Remain disciplined and cut your losses. The alternative to managing risk is not managing risk, and that never turns out well.**

This concept should be obvious, but in fact it is too often overlooked. Although it's certainly not a secret (it's the most frequently mentioned subject in most books written by successful speculators), it's difficult to do because it goes against human nature and requires strict discipline and a divorce from one's ego. I can't make you cut your losses any more than I can make you diet and exercise to lose weight; that's a personal choice. All I can do is share with you what I know from my own success and tell you that the stock market is no place for someone who is easily discouraged by mistakes. Mistakes are lessons, in other words, opportunities to improve. These experiences are the greatest part of the learning process. Although cutting your losses won't guarantee that you will win in the stock market, it will help ensure your survival.

WHY MOST INVESTORS FAIL TO CUT THEIR LOSSES

Investors usually become emotionally attached to their stock holdings. They may put in many hours of careful research building a case for a company, scouring financial reports, and maybe even trying the company's products. Then, when their proud pick takes a dive, they can't believe it. They make excuses for the stock's decline; they call their broker and search the Internet looking for favorable opinions to back up their faith in the company. They ignore the only opinion that counts: the verdict of the market.

As the stock keeps sliding, their losses mount. Usually, what happens is that the stock's decline becomes so huge and unbearable that they finally throw in the towel and feel completely demoralized. Don't allow yourself to get caught in this lethal trap. **To have lasting success in the stock market, you must decide once and for all that it's more important to make money than to be right. Your ego must take a backseat.**

Sounds like a simple decision to make, but think again. Many people speculate in stocks without getting this one straight. Their self-image rides on the success or failure of their trades. As a result, they make excuses for obvious losers rather than admit mistakes. Ultimately, the success of cutting losses rests on your ability to remove emotion—hope, fear, pride, excitement, and the like—from your investment decisions, at least to the point where it doesn't override good judgment.

Most investors fall into psychological traps. Feelings of hope and greed confuse their decisions to sell their stock holdings at a loss or, for that matter, at a profit. They find it difficult to sell, and so they rationalize a losing position. They convince themselves that they haven't taken the loss until they sell it. **Losses are a part of trading and investing; if you are not prepared to deal with them, then prepare to eventually lose a lot of money.**

As you can see, I devoted two chapters to risk management. That's because in trading and in life, how you deal with losing is the difference between mediocrity and greatness. **Individual stocks are not like mutual funds, they don't have a manager and they don't manage themselves; you're the manager.** When investing in stocks, everything is not necessarily going to be "OK" if you just hang in there and wait it out. For a speculator, small losses are simply the cost of doing business, just as marked-down merchandise is to a retail store operator. A good retail merchant doesn't hang on to dead merchandise, hoping a particular style or product will come back in vogue a year later. If he's smart, he marks it down, gets it off the shelf as quickly as possible, and then looks to restock the shelves with something that everyone wants to buy.

CHAPTER 13

RISK MANAGEMENT

PART 2: HOW TO DEAL WITH AND CONTROL RISK

I have two basic rules about winning in trading as well as in life:
(1) If you don't bet, you can't win. (2) If you lose all your chips, you
can't bet.

—Larry Hite

FOR THREE DECADES, enjoying eight bull markets and enduring eight bear markets, I have traded stocks; I have accumulated my personal wealth almost exclusively through stock speculation. After learning the hard lessons of experience, I have been fortunate to relish consistent success, preserving not only my original starting capital but the bulk of the gains. How will you do the same thing? In other words, how will you endure the test of time, not only winning during bull markets but preserving your gains in bear markets? The secret is neither hidden nor really a secret. The key is risk management.

Risk is the possibility of loss. When you own a stock, there is always the possibility of a price decline; as long as you are invested in the stock market, you are at risk. The goal with stock trading is to make money consistently by taking trades that have more reward potential than risk. The problem for most investors, however, is that they focus too much on the reward side and not enough on the risk side. Simple as this sounds, few will follow the advice I'm about to impart to you.

In the stock market, everyone's goal is to make money. To win in an environment where everyone has the same objective, you must do the things that most investors are consciously unwilling or subconsciously unable to do. If you succeed, when you look back on your career, you will see that an instrumental difference between you and them was discipline. Over time I have learned that investors don't lose money or fail to achieve superperformance because of bear markets or economic hazards but because of mental hazards, the types of personal failings that cause you to say to yourself in retrospect, why didn't I sell that stock when I was only down 10 percent? As you're sitting there down 30 or 40 percent, suddenly a 10 percent loss doesn't look so bad.

Does the following sound familiar? You bought a stock at $35 a share and were reluctant to sell it at $32; the stock then sank to $26, and you would have been delighted to sell it at the original price of $35. When the stock then sank to $16, you asked yourself, Why didn't I sell it at $26 or even $32 when I had the chance to get out with a small loss? The reason investors get into this situation is that they lack a sound plan for dealing with risk and allow their egos to get involved. A sound plan takes implementation, which takes discipline. That part I cannot do for you, but what I can do is teach you how to do it.

Develop Lifestyle Habits

The difference between mediocrity and greatness lies in the fundamental belief that discipline is not merely a principle of trading but a principle of greatness. Managing risk requires discipline. Sticking to your strategy requires discipline. Even if you have a sensible plan, if you lack discipline, emotions will creep into your trading and wreak havoc. Discipline leads to habit. They can be good habits or bad ones; it's a matter of what you discipline yourself to do over time. Like most people, when you get up each morning, you brush your teeth, right? You don't say to yourself, I'm tired of brushing my teeth over and over, so this month I'm taking a vacation from dental hygiene. To the contrary, brushing your teeth has become automatic and ingrained from years of repetition and the belief that it's worth taking the time to do. This same type of psychological conditioning applies to such things as exercising and eating healthy, which are lifestyle habits that some people choose to make priorities in their daily lives.

If you manage your portfolio with your emotions and without discipline, prepare for a volatile, exhausting ride, probably without anything worthwhile to show for your efforts in the end. **Good trading is boring; bad trading is exciting and makes the hair on the back of your neck stand up. You can be a bored rich trader or a thrill-seeking gambler. It's entirely your choice.** With intelligent repetitive work, you can cultivate successful trading habits. Making a habit of doing the things that produce positive results is worthwhile, but it requires the principle of greatness: discipline.

Contingency Planning

Success is never final.

—*Winston Churchill*

In the stock market and in life, risk is unavoidable. The best anyone can do is to manage risk through sensible planning. The only way to control risk when investing in stocks is through how much we buy and sell, when we buy and sell, and how we prepare for as many potential events as possible. As a stock market investor, you must learn to sell for your own protection because you have no control over the forces that move stock prices. **Your goal is not risk avoidance but risk management: to mitigate risk and have a significant degree of control over the possibility and amount of loss.**

I don't like to leave anything to chance in my trading. If I go into a casino and play blackjack, I know what the odds are, and if I feel like taking a chance, that's the best I can hope for. But I don't gamble with stock trading, which would be rolling the dice with my livelihood and my security. The best way to ensure stock market success is to have contingency plans and continuously update them as you learn and encounter new scenarios. Your goal should be to trade without hassles and surprises. To do that, you need to develop a dependable way to handle virtually every situation that is thrown at you. Having things thought out in advance is paramount to managing risk effectively.

The mark of a professional is proper preparation. To execute, you must be prepared. Before I invest, I have already worked out in advance responses to virtually any conceivable development that may take place. I can't think of an event that I'm not prepared for. If and when new circumstances present themselves, I add them to my contingency plans; as new unexpected issues present themselves, the contingency plan playbook is expanded.

By implementing contingency planning in advance, you can take swift, decisive action the instant one of your positions changes its behavior or is hit with an unexpected event. You should also be prepared to deal with profits when they come to fruition. **Before the open of each trading day, mentally rehearse how you will handle each position based on whatever could potentially unfold during that day. Then, when the market opens for trading, there will be no surprises; you already know how you will respond.**

You should run your portfolio the way an airline pilot operates a 747 jumbo jet. To ensure the safe passage of the flight, the pilot has advance plans for every possible contingency: engine failure, severe weather conditions, hydraulic malfunction, and hundreds of other mechanical or electronic problems. The pilot has considered possibilities ranging from an electrical storm to trouble with one of the passengers. When a problem occurs, there is no debate or delay. For every eventuality, the pilot has a procedure or countermeasure. This comes from training and preparation. When we're not prepared, we're vulnerable. September 11, 2001, was a grim reminder of the importance of proper preparation. As a result, cockpit doors are now fortified, and the sky marshal program put into place during the 1960s has been expanded. Some pilots are even armed. Learning from our past mistakes and being properly prepared allow for safer travel and for safer investing as well.

I have the following four basic contingency plans for my stock trading.

THE INITIAL STOP-LOSS

Before buying a stock, I establish in advance a maximum stop loss: the price at which I will exit the position if it moves against me. The moment the price hits the stop loss, I sell the position without hesitation. Once I'm out of the stock, I can evaluate the situation with a clear head. The initial stop loss is most relevant in the early stages of a position. Once a stock advances, the sell point should be raised to protect your profit with the use of a trailing stop or back stop.

THE REENTRY

Some stocks set up constructively and may even emerge from a promising base and attract buyers but then quickly undergo a correction or sharp pullback that stops you out. This tends to occur when the market is experiencing general weakness or high volatility. However, a stock with strong fundamentals can reset after such a correction or pullback, forming a new base or a proper setup. This show of strength is a favorable sign. Often, the second setup is stronger than the first. The stock has fought its way back and along the way shaken out another batch of weak holders. If it breaks out of the second base on high volume, it can really take off.

You shouldn't assume that a stock will reset if it moves against you. You should always protect yourself and cut your loss. However, if a stock knocks you out of your position, don't automatically discard it as a future buy candidate. If the stock still has all the characteristics of a potential winner, look for a reentry point. Your timing may have been off. It could take two or even three tries to catch a big winner. This is a trait of professional traders. **Amateurs are scared of positions that stop them out once or twice or just weary of the struggle; professionals are objective and dispassionate.** They assess each trade on its merits of risk versus reward; they look at each trade setup as a new risk or a new opportunity. Some believe that selling a stock and then reentering the same stock soon afterward is amateurish. I believe missing opportunity because of emotion is as amateurish. Managing risk with the use of stop losses, particularly in a whipsaw market, can sometimes give a trader the feeling of chasing one's tail. Recognize the feelings of frustration and then remind yourself not to let ego override good risk management. So you got it wrong the first time—big deal. So you got it wrong the second time—clever fish! Laugh and keep your rod and reel ready. It's the long-term results that count. Some of my best trades were in stocks that previously stopped me out several times and then reset.

Selling at a Profit

Once a stock amasses a percentage gain that is a multiple of your stop loss, you should rarely allow that position to turn into a loss. For instance, let's say your stop loss is set at 7 percent. If you have a 20 percent gain in a stock, you shouldn't allow that position to give up all that profit and produce a loss. To guard against that, you could move up your stop loss to breakeven or trail a stop to lock in the majority of the gain. You may feel foolish breaking even on a position that was previously a decent gain; however, you will feel even worse if you let a nice gain turn into a loss.

At some point you have to close out a trade. There are two ways you can sell:

- Into strength, which means cashing out shares while the share price is rising
- Into weakness, which means selling while the share price is declining

Selling into strength is a learned practice of professional traders. It's important to recognize when a stock is running up rapidly and may be exhausting itself. You can unload your position easily when buyers are plentiful. Or you could sell into the first signs of weakness immediately after such a price run has broken down. You need to have a plan for both selling into strength and selling into weakness.

The Disaster Plan

The fourth contingency may not be one you run into often; however, it's one that can save your portfolio and protect all your hard work. It would be a shame to see years of work building up your account trade by trade compromised by a random black swan simply because you were ill prepared. The disaster plan could turn out to be the most important part of your contingency planning. In fact, that's probably a safe bet; the disaster plan deals with such issues as what to do if your Internet connection goes down or your power fails. Do you have a backup system? What will your response be if you wake up and learn that the stock you bought yesterday is set to gap down huge because the company is being investigated by the Securities and Exchange Commission and the CEO has skipped the country with embezzled funds? What will you do?

The importance contingency planning plays is that it enables you to make good decisions when you're under fire, when you need it the most. To survive in the stock market over the long term, I run my portfolio as if something really bad were going to happen every day. I am always prepared for the worst-case scenario.

Contingency planning allows you to have a psychological strategy that is as robust as your trading strategy as well as a trading strategy that has built-in responses to potential situations that could, if you are not prepared, lead to competing thoughts at the precise time you need to implement instant unbiased action. Contingency planning is an ongoing process. As you experience new problems, a procedure should be created to deal with them, which then becomes part of your contingency plans. You're never going to have all the answers, but you can cover most of the bases to the point where your reward outweighs your risk, and that's the key.

LOSSES ARE A FUNCTION OF EXPECTED GAIN

> Speculation is nothing more than anticipating coming movements. In order to anticipate correctly, one must have a definite basis for that anticipation.
>
> —*Jesse Livermore*

Life insurance companies run their operations in accordance with mortality tables that are based on population samples, showing the percentage of people who are likely to die by a certain age. From these tables, insurance companies can predict with a high degree of accuracy the number of people at any particular age who probably will be alive a certain number of years in the future. Although they cannot tell a particular person how long he or she will live (just as we don't know if the next trade will be successful), the average can be estimated with enough accuracy to set premium levels accurately. By setting premiums correctly, insurance companies can assure themselves of having enough money in any year to cover the payments to beneficiaries and the cost of doing business and secure a decent profit.

Just as an insurance company utilizes mortality tables, you can use a similar method for your trading as I have done for for mine for many years. **You have no control over how much a stock goes up, but you can, however, control the amount you lose on each trade. You should base that amount of loss on the average mortality of your gains.** This is similar to the insurance company having control over how much it charges in premiums, which are a direct function of the mortality tables. Similarly, your losses are a direct function of the mortality tables of your gains and where they tend to expire on average.

To make money consistently, you need a positive mathematical expectation for return; you need an edge. That is, your reward/risk ratio must be greater than one to one (net of costs). To achieve this, your losses obviously need to be contained on average to a level lower than that of your gains.

During my 30 years trading tens of thousands of stocks, I have been correct on winning trades only about 50 percent of the time. I'm wrong just as often as I'm right as far as wins and losses go; however, though the losses may be the same or at times even greater in number, the dollar amounts the profitable trades have been much larger than the losses on average. Imagine: being wrong just as often as being right allowed me to amass a fortune. This is because I follow a very important rule: always keep your risk at a level that is less than that of your average gain.

At What Point Should You Cut a Loss?

As I've just discussed, the level at which a trader should cut his losses is not arbitrary. Loss cutting is a function of expected gain. The more accurately you can predict the level of gain and the frequency at which you can expect it to occur, the easier it is to arrive at where you should be cutting your losses. Your maximum stop loss depends both on your batting average (percentage of profitable trades) and on your average profit per trade (expected gain).

Let's assume that a trader is profitable on 50 percent of his trades. Therefore, he must on average make at least as much as he loses to break even over time. Although going forward these numbers can only be based on assumption, it's the average gain from your actual trades that's the key number. After you have calculated these numbers, you will be able to get a much clearer picture of where you should be cutting your losses. A rule of thumb could be to cut your losses at a level of one-half of your average gain.

In the words of Warren Buffett, "Take the probability of loss times the amount of possible loss from the probability of gain times the amount of possible gain.... It's imperfect, but that's what it's all about."

Avoid the Trader's Cardinal Sin

Allowing your loss on a trade to exceed your average gain is what I call the trader's cardinal sin. You must make more on your winners than you lose on your losers, remember? How can you possibly make money over time unless your winners return more dollars than your losers lose? The fact is that most traders don't even know what their average gain is. When setting a stop loss, I have a rule of thumb that the amount of loss should be no more than one-half the amount of expected gain based on one's real-life trading results. For example, if your winning trades produce a gain of 15 percent on average, you should sell any declining stock at no more than 7.5 percent off the purchase price. If you buy a stock at $30 a share, you would set your initial stop loss at $27.75.

I also suggest that most investors, no matter how large their average gains, not allow any stock to fall more than 10 percent before selling. If you can't time a purchase well enough that you need more than 10 percent fluctuation from your point of purchase, something is wrong with your timing and selection criteria. Let's say that you sell your winners for an average gain of 30 percent. I would not recommend allowing losses of 15 percent even though that would be half of your expected gain. In my experience, a 10 percent decline signals that something is wrong with the trade, assuming that you purchased it correctly in the first place.

Over time your average gain will improve as you learn how to trade more effectively. You should monitor your average gain on a regular basis and make adjustments to your stop loss accordingly. However, keep in mind that there's also an absolute level at which you need to cut your loss: the "uncle point." When you were a kid, someone would twist your arm until you couldn't take it anymore and said "uncle," meaning, "Okay, I've had enough; I surrender." Next time you allow a loss to grow larger than your average gain, ask yourself how you can be profitable if your losses are bigger than your gains.

The best thing you can do is to keep your losses small in relation to your gains. With more experience, you will become a more effective trader. You'll realize larger gains on average and have more money to reinvest. Improved trading skills will compound your trading account, but only if you keep your losses small and avoid the trader's cardinal sin. Never let a loss grow larger than your average gain.

Building in Failure

I have always lived by the following philosophy: expect the best and plan for the worst. Systems that rely on a high percentage of profitable trades never impressed me very much; they expect the best and plan for the best. I always felt that they were too risky if something went wrong and they lost their edge. The end result may be the same during periods when things are going along normally. However, if a trader has to be right on 70 or 80 percent of his trades and that's his edge, what happens if he's right only 40 or 50 percent of the time during a difficult period? What about during a really difficult period? **The problem with relying on a high percentage of profitable trades is that no adjustment can be made; you can't control the number of wins and losses. What you can control is your stop loss; you can tighten it up as your gains get squeezed during difficult periods.**

I like to keep my risk/reward ratio intact so that I can have a relatively low batting average and still not get into serious trouble. It's a concept that I call building in failure. My goal is to maintain at least a 2:1 win/loss ratio with an absolute maximum stop loss of no more than 10 percent. I shoot for 3:1, and I'm elated if I can attain this ratio with even a 50 percent batting average. This means I'm making money three times faster on my wins than I'm losing when I'm wrong. At a 2:1 ratio, I can be right only one-third of the time and still not get into real trouble. At a 3:1 ratio, even a 40 percent batting average could yield a fortune. If I'm able to be profitable with such a low percentage of winning trades, I've built a lot of failure into the system.

ALWAYS DETERMINE YOUR RISK IN ADVANCE

The time to think most clearly about where you will exit a position is *before* you get in. By the time you purchase a stock, the price at which you will sell at a loss should already be determined. When a stock drops to your defensive sell line, there is no time for vacillating or second-guessing. There is no decision to be made; it's been decided ahead of time. You just carry out your plan; you should write down your sell price *before* you buy each stock. Put it on a Post-it and attach it to your computer screen. If you don't write it down, it's very likely that you will forget about it or start rationalizing why you should hold on. **Not defining and committing to a predetermined level of risk cost traders and investors more money than any other mistake.**

HONOR THY STOP

Letting losses run out of control is the most common and fatal mistake made by virtually every investor, including professionals. Trading without a stop loss is like driving a car without brakes, it's just a matter of time before you crash. As far as I'm concerned, if you aren't willing to cut losses, you should not be managing your investments or anyone else's. Most investors can't stand to take losses. Unfortunately, as a result, they suffer much bigger losses that do lasting damage to their portfolios. This is ironic; they won't take a small loss because their egos won't let them accept that they have made a mistake, but in the long run they take larger losses.

My trading results went from mediocre to outstanding once I finally made the decision to draw a line in the sand and vowed never again to let a loss get out of control. I suggest that you make that same commitment right now.

You should handle a falling stock in your portfolio the way a doctor treats an incoming patient in the emergency room. If an accident victim just got rushed into the ER and had lost a great amount of blood, the doctor would act quickly to stop the loss because the more the patient bleeds, the more likely it is that he will not recover. As with stocks, the larger the loss is, the more difficult it is to recover because losses work against you geometrically.

Your predetermined stop-loss point should be used as an absolute maximum. Once the stock has declined to your stop, sell it immediately without exception or hesitation. Nothing must prevent you from getting out of the position. Unfortunately, most investors don't have a stop, even fewer write it down, and many do not sell when the stop is triggered. Typically, a stock declines and the investor says, "On the next rally I'll get out." Then one of two things happens. The stock rallies and in many cases these investors still don't sell because they feel comfortable that the stock is fine again, or the stock never rallies but keeps falling and becomes even more difficult to sell.

If you want to achieve superperformance in stocks, praying and hoping for a stock to recover from a loss has no place in your psychology. The market doesn't care about what you hope will happen. Inevitably, traders who think this way continually repeat the error of holding losses "just this once" and end up with mediocre or losing records of performance in the market. In fact, such traders frequently go bust. Concentrate on your plan and stick to your rules; the money will come as a result of sticking to your discipline and maintaining a positive reward/risk ratio.

HANDLING STOP-LOSS SLIPPAGE

At the time you purchase a stock, the price at which you expect to sell at a loss should be written down and then executed as soon as the stock trades at that price. At this decisive moment, you execute the trade as quickly as you can. Sooner or later, however, one of your stocks will dive under your sell price before you can react; this is called *slippage*. My advice is to get out immediately. Take whatever the next bid price is. Such a hard-falling stock is sending a warning.

One money manager I know badly mishandled this type of scenario with a large position. A stock dropped quickly on news and shot well below her predetermined sell price; she was quickly down 15 percent on the position. She called me and asked my opinion. Of course, I told her I would have already sold if the stock had gone through my stop loss. She instructed her portfolio manager to wait for the stock to come back and then sell when they were down only 5 percent. The stock never came back. In fact, it fell further, and they ended up taking a 60 percent thrashing before they finally threw in the towel. Does this sound familiar?

Sure, there are going to be many times when you sell a stock that's down and it comes right back up. So what! Stop-loss protection is about protecting yourself from a major setback or, worse, devastation. It has nothing to do with being right all the time or getting the high or low price. Success in the stock market has nothing to do with hope or luck. Winning stock traders have rules and a well-thought-out plan. Conversely, losers lack rules, and if they have rules, they don't stick to them for very long; they deviate. **The old adage holds true: your first loss is your best loss.**

How to Handle a Losing Streak

A losing streak usually means it's time for an assessment. If you find yourself getting stopped out of your positions over and over, there can only be two things wrong:

1. Your stock selection criteria are flawed.

2. The general market environment is hostile.

Broad losses across your portfolio after a winning record could signal an approaching correction in a bull market or the advent of a bear market. Leading stocks often break down before the general market declines. If you're using sound criteria with regard to fundamentals and timing, your stock picks should work for you, but if the market is entering a correction or a bear market, even good selection criteria can show poor results. It's not time to buy; it's time to sell or even possibly go short. Keep yourself in tune with your portfolio, and when you start experiencing abnormal behavior, watch out. Jesse Livermore said, "I'm never afraid of normal behavior but abnormal behavior."

If you're experiencing a heavy number of losses in a strong market, maybe your timing is off. Perhaps your stock-selection criteria are missing a key factor. If you experience an abnormal losing streak, first scale down your exposure. Don't try to trade larger to recoup your losses fast; that can lead to much bigger losses. Instead, cut down your position sizes; for example, if you normally trade 5,000-share lots, trade 2,000 shares. If you continue to have trouble, cut back again, maybe to 1,000 shares. If it continues, cut back again. When your trading plan is working well, do the opposite and pyramid back up.

Following this strategy will help keep you from trading yourself into the ground when things turn sour, which they definitely will at some point. When you take a large loss or get hit repeatedly, there's a tendency to get angry and try to get it back quickly by trading larger. This is a major mistake many traders make and is the complete opposite of what should be done. Don't do it; trade smaller, not bigger. If you keep trading the same size over and over, even making small mistakes can lead to a death by a thousand cuts. Instead, scale back your trading size and raise the cash position in your portfolio.

A Practice That Will Guarantee Disaster

It would be bad enough to sit and watch your wealth disappear and do nothing to protect yourself by not using a stop loss, but it is even worse to put more money into a losing investment. Throwing good money after bad is one of the quickest ways to the poorhouse. This is called *averaging down.*

Brokers often talk their clients into buying more shares of a stock that shows a loss in an effort to sell more stock or rationalize the poor recommendations they made in the first place. They tell the client that it will lower their cost basis. If you liked it at $50, you're going to love it at $40, right? Double up at $40 and your average price is now $45. Wow, what a deal! You now own twice the amount of stock, and you've doubled your risk. Your loss is still the same; you didn't gain anything except maybe a double-size loss if the stock keeps sliding. How about buying at $30, then $20, and then $10? How ridiculous! **There is no shame in losing money on a stock trade, but to hold on to a loss and let it get bigger and bigger or, even worse, to buy more is amateurish and self destructive.**

High-growth stocks that fall in value after you purchase them at a correct buy point do not become more attractive; they become less attractive. The more they fall, the less attractive they are. The fact that a stock is not responding positively is a red flag that the market is ignoring the stock; perception is not going in your direction. Maybe the general market is headed into a correction or, even worse, a major bear market.

For many investors, it's tempting to buy a pullback because you feel you're getting a bargain compared with where the stock was trading previously. However, averaging down is for losers, plain and simple. If this is the type of advice you're getting, I suggest you get a new broker or advisor. This is simply the worst possible advice you can receive. **Remember that only losers average losers.**

Learn to Pace Yourself

When I come out of a 100 percent cash position, generally after a bear market or intermediate-term correction, I rarely jump right in with both feet. I think of each trading year as the opener of a twelve-inning game. There's plenty of time to reach my goal. Early on, I take it slow with my main focus on avoiding major errors and finding the market's theme. This is like an athlete warming up and assessing the competitive environment. Themes can come in the form of how prices are acting in general, industry group leadership, overall market tone, and economic and political influences. I try to establish a rhythm and set my pace during this time. Like a golfer who has found his swing groove, once I find a theme and establish my trading rhythm, then and only then do I step up my exposure significantly. I wait patiently for the right opportunity while guarding my account. When the opportunity presents itself with the least chance of loss, I'm ready to strike. Patience is the key. My goal is to trade effortlessly. **If your trading is causing you difficulty or stress, something is wrong with your criteria or timing or you're trading too large.** To trade with ease, you must learn to wait patiently until the wind is at your back. If you were going sailing, you wouldn't go out on a dead calm and sit there floating in the water all day waiting for the wind to pick up. Why not just wait for a breezy day to set sail?

BUILD ON SUCCESS

> I view the objectives in trading as a three-tiered hierarchy. First and foremost is the preservation of capital. When I first look at a trade, I don't ask, "What is the potential profit I can realize?" but rather, "What is the potential loss I could suffer?" Second, I strive for consistent profitability by balancing my risk relative to the accumulated profits or losses. Consistency is far more important than making lots of money. Third, insofar as I'm successful in the first two goals, I attempt to achieve superior returns. I do this by increasing my bet size after, and only after, periods of high profitability. In other words, if I have had a particularly profitable recent period, I may try to pyramid my gains by placing a larger bet size assuming, of course, the right situation presents itself. The key to building wealth is to preserve capital and wait patiently for the right opportunity to make extraordinary gains.
>
> —*Victor Sperandeo*

To make big money in the stock market you do not have to make all-or-nothing decisions. Stock trading is not an on-off business; moving from cash into equities should be incremental. As emerging stocks multiply on your watch list and the market tries to rally off its apparent lows, the time will come to test the water with real money. Prudence is the order of the day here. You should start off with "pilot buys" by initiating smaller positions than normal; if they work out, larger positions should be added to the portfolio soon thereafter. This toe-in-the-water approach helps keep you out of trouble and building on your successes. **If you're not profitable at 25 percent or 50 percent invested, why move up to 75 percent or 100 percent invested or use margin?** Wait for confirmation and require that at least a few trades work out before getting more aggressive.

Conversely, if your trades are not working as expected, cut back. There's no intelligent reason to increase your trading size if your positions are showing losses. **By pyramiding up when you're trading well and tapering off when you're trading poorly, you trade your largest when trading your best and trade your smallest when trading your worst. This is how you make big money as well as protect yourself from disaster.** Before stepping up my exposure aggressively, I look to my portfolio for confirmation. If the market is indeed healthy, I should be experiencing success with my trading. In addition, you should see additional stocks setting up behind the first wave of emerging leaders. Be incremental in your decision-making process. Build on success. Subtract on setbacks. Let your portfolio guide you.

Scaling In versus Averaging Down

A key difference between professionals and amateurs is that professionals scale into positions whereas amateurs average down. What do I mean by this? Let's assume that both the professional and the amateur decide to risk 5 percent of their capital on a trade. The pro may scale in with 2 percent on the first buy, 2 percent on the second, and maybe an additional 1 percent on the third. He then might put his stop at 10 percent from the average cost of his three buys, risking 0.50 percent of the total account capital.

The amateur buys his position, usually at one price, and if the trade goes against him, he may decide to average down, doubling up on a losing position. Often amateurs double up several times. Do this three times and you've gone from what started out as a 5 percent position to a 20 percent position. If the stock keeps sinking, it becomes even more difficult to sell because you kept committing to the stock with additional buys. In my trading, I try to buy or add to a position in the direction of the trade only after it has shown me a profit; even if I'm buying a pullback, I generally wait for the stock to turn up before going long. **The lesson: never trust the first price unless the position shows you a profit.**

WHEN TO MOVE UP YOUR STOP

I have some basic general guidelines: Any stock that rises to a multiple of my stop loss should never be allowed to go into the loss column. When the price of a stock I own rises by three times my risk, I almost always move my stop up to at least breakeven. Suppose I buy a stock at $50 and decide that I'm willing to risk 5 percent on the trade ($47.50 stop loss for a $2.50 risk). If the stock advances to $57.50 (3 × $2.50), I move my stop to at least $50. If the stock continues to rise, I start to look for an opportunity to sell on the way up and nail down my profit. If I get stopped out at breakeven, I still have my capital; nothing gained but nothing lost. You may feel dumb breaking even on a trade that was once at a profit; however, you'll feel a lot worse if you turn a good-size gain into a loser. Move your stop up when your stock rises by two or three times your risk, especially if that number is above your historical average gain. This will help guard you against losses and protect your profits and your confidence.

NOT ALL RATIOS ARE CREATED EQUAL

You may have heard that in setting a stop loss you should allow more room for volatile price action; you should widen your stops on the basis of the volatility of the underlying stock. I strongly disagree. Most often, high volatility is experienced during a tough market environment. During difficult periods, your gains will be smaller than normal and your percentage of profitable trades (your batting average) will definitely be lower than usual, and so your losses must be cut shorter to compensate. It would be fair to assume that in difficult trading periods your batting average is likely to fall below

50 percent. **Once your batting average drops below 50 percent, increasing your risk proportionately to compensate for a higher expected gain based on higher volatility will eventually cause you to hit negative expectancy; the more your batting average drops, the sooner negative expectancy will be achieved.**

As the next figure illustrates, at a 40 percent batting average your optimal gain/loss ratio is 20 percent/10 percent; at this ratio your return on investment (ROI) over 10 trades is 10.2 percent. Note that the expected return rises from left to right and peaks at this ratio. Thereafter, with increasing losses in proportion to your gains, the return actually declines. Armed with this knowledge, you can understand which ratio at a particular batting average will yield the best expected return. This illustrates the power of finding the optimal ratio. Any less and you make less money; however, any more and you also make less money.

If your winning trades were to more than double from 20 percent to 42 percent and you maintained a 2:1 gain/loss ratio by cutting your losses at 21

% Gain	% Loss	G/L Ratio	@ 30% Bat. Avg.	@ 40% Bat. Avg.	@ 50% Bat. Avg.
4.00%	2.00%	2:1	-2.35%	3.63%	10.00%
6.00%	3.00%	2:1	-3.77%	5.16%	14.92%
8.00%	4.00%	2:1	-5.34%	6.49%	19.80%
12.00%	6.00%	2:1	-8.89%	8.55%	29.34%
14.00%	7.00%	2:1	-10.86%	9.27%	33.95%
16.00%	8.00%	2:1	-12.93%	9.79%	38.43%
20.00%	10.00%	2:1	-17.35%	**10.20%**	46.93%
24.00%	12.00%	2:1	-22.08%	9.80%	54.71%
30.00%	15.00%	2:1	-29.57%	7.71%	64.75%
36.00%	18.00%	2:1	-37.23%	4.00%	72.49%
42.00%	21.00%	2:1	-45.01%	-1.16%	77.66%
48.00%	24.00%	2:1	-52.52%	-7.55%	**80.04%**
54.00%	27.00%	2:1	-59.65%	-14.88%	79.56%
60.00%	30.00%	2:1	-66.27%	-22.90%	76.23%
70.00%	35.00%	2:1	-75.92%	-37.01%	64.75%
80.00%	40.00%	2:1	-83.67%	-51.02%	46.93%
90.00%	45.00%	2:1	-89.56%	-63.93%	24.62%
100.00%	50.00%	2:1	-93.75%	-75.00%	0.00%

Figure 13.1 **Total compounded return per 10 trades at various batting averages**

percent instead of 10 percent, you would actually lose money. You're still maintaining the same ratio, so how could you be losing? This is the dangerous nature of losses; they work geometrically against you. At a 50 percent batting average, if you made 100 percent on your winners and lost 50 percent on your losers, you would do nothing but break even; you would make more money taking profits at 4 percent and cutting your losses at 2 percent. Not surprisingly, as your batting average drops, it gets much worse. At a 30 percent batting average, profiting 100 percent on your winners and giving back 50 percent on your losers, you would have a whopping 93 percent loss in just 10 trades.

If the optimal result is achieved by having a 48 percent/24 percent win/loss ratio at a 50 percent batting average, what do you think happens when your percentage of profitable trades drops to only 40 percent? The following figure may surprise you by showing that the optimal level drops to 20 percent/10 percent.

If you're trading poorly and your batting average is dropping off below the 50% level, the last thing you want to do is increase the room you give your stocks on the downside. This is not an opinion; it's a mathematical fact. Many investors give their losing positions more freedom to inflict

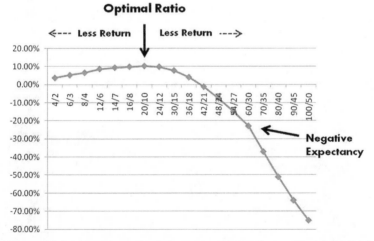

Figure 13.2   **Total compounded return per 10 trades at 40 percent batting average**

deeper losses. Their results begin to slip, and they get knocked out of a hand-ful of trades; then they watch the stocks they sold at a loss turn around and go back up. What do they say to themselves? "Maybe I should have given the stock more room to fluctuate; I'd still be in it." This is just the opposite of what you should do.

In a difficult market environment, profits will be smaller than normal and losses will be larger; downside gaps will be more common, and you will most likely experience greater slippage. The smart way to handle this is to do the following:

- Tighten up stop losses. If you normally cut losses at 7 to 8 percent, cut them at 5 to 6 percent.

- Settle for smaller profits. If you normally take profits of 15 to 20 percent on average, take profits at 10 to 12 percent.

- If you're trading with the use of leverage, get off margin immediately.

- Reduce your exposure with regard to your position sizes as well as your overall capital commitment.

- Once you see your batting average and risk/reward profile improve, you can start to extend your parameters gradually back to normal levels.

DIVERSIFICATION DOES NOT PROTECT YOU

I've always felt that if I was enthusiastic about an industry or a company, then I would concentrate in it. It causes commentators to consider me risky. I never thought that was risk; I thought that was opportunity.

—*Kenneth Heebner*

Diversification is a tactic used to distribute investments among different securities to limit losses in the event of a decline in a particular security or industry. The strategy relies on the average security having a profitable expected value. Diversification also provides some psychological benefits to single-instrument trading since some of the short-term variation in one instrument may cancel out that from another instrument, resulting in an overall smoothing of short-term portfolio volatility. **You will never achieve superperformance if you overly diversify and rely on diversification for protection.** During a bear market, almost all stocks will go down. By having your money spread all over the place, you accomplish three things:

1. Inability to follow each company closely and know everything you should know about the investments

2. Inability to reduce your portfolio exposure quickly when needed

3. A smoothing effect that will ensure average results

Depending on the size of your portfolio and your risk tolerance, you should typically have between 4 and 6 stocks, and for large portfolios maybe as many as 10 or 12 stocks. This will provide sufficient diversification but not too much. You should not hold more than 20 positions, which would represent a 5 percent position size if they were equally weighted. All during my trading career I've heard over and over, "You have to be diversified." If Ken Heebner of CGM Funds can move around billions of dollars in just 20 names and still manage to beat the market, a personal portfolio can surely be managed sufficiently with a maximum of 10 to 20 stocks. If you're a true 2:1 trader, mathematically your optimal position size should be 25 percent (four stocks divided equally). As a result, a stock that is a big winner will make a real contribution to your portfolio. In keeping track of 4, 5, or 6 companies, it is much easier to know a lot about each name than it is to follow and track 15 or 20 companies. If you're holding many positions, it's going to be difficult to raise cash and move quickly when the market turns against you. Instead of spreading yourself all over the place in a feeble attempt to mitigate risk through diversification, concentrate your capital in the very best stocks—a relatively small group—that have exciting things going on. Watch your stocks carefully and be prepared to move if things take a turn for the worse.

In my career, I have had many periods in which I put my entire account in just four names. This of course corresponds with some of my most profitable periods. Yes, there is risk, but you can mitigate that risk with the use of a sound methodology. In the words of Warren Buffett, "Risk comes from not knowing what you're doing." If you are strict with your selection criteria and demand the best for your portfolio, it should be difficult to find a lot of names that are worthy to be included among your elite group. Bottom line: diversification does not protect you from losses.

My Walking Barefoot in Four Feet of Snow Story

At some time in your life, you've heard a story like this, probably from your parents or grandparents: how they had to walk barefoot six miles uphill each way to school in four feet of snow, carrying their brother on their back. Well, I'm going to leave you with my own "in my day" story.

When I started trading in the 1980s, I had no quotes, no charts, and no research tools to speak of. There was no such thing as an Internet connection (at least one that I could connect to), no online trading, and no level II system for the average trader to find out where the market was. All I had was closing prices printed in the newspaper each day and some graph paper to hand plot charts.

Making matters worse, stock commissions were extremely high: more than $100 per trade versus $5 or $10 today. Even when discount commissions were introduced, they were still around $60 per side. At the time, however, that seemed like quite a bargain. Finding out where the market was at any particular moment was just about impossible for a small-time trader like me in those days. I had to be resourceful and a little audacious to make up for the tools I didn't have.

When commissions finally came down to a reasonable level, I opened a trading account at a local discount brokerage house. That brokerage office offered a very useful feature: a stock quote machine in the lobby. These were not streaming real-time quotes but rather snap quotes that you could pull up static one stock at a time.

The machine was meant to be a courtesy for customers who stopped by the brokerage office and didn't invite frequent use. The computer terminal sat on a table without a chair. The message was clear: look once and move on. That, however, did not discourage me. I stood outside that branch office every trading day, rain or shine, reading the newspaper. Then I'd go in every 10 minutes or so to check the quotes. Sometimes I'd take a break across the street for a hot dog or a soda. Otherwise, I didn't leave my spot for the entire six-and-a-half-hour trading day. How else could I know where the market was?

Eventually, I purchased a computer to get market data, but there was no Internet trading in those days, no point-and-click two-second execution the way there is today. In those days, I made my money by picking up the phone and paying hefty commissions.

When people tell me that trading today is too difficult, that the market is too complex and the pros have all the edge, it makes me chuckle. It's a much more level playing field today between the amateurs and the professionals. Even casual investors have tools at their disposal—from online trade execution to free charts—that I couldn't imagine in the old days. Today you have the equivalent of a fully equipped F-16 fighter jet at your fingertips.

Don't say the deck is stacked against you, retail players can't win, or only the professionals make money in the market. These are simply excuses. I dropped out of school at age 15 with virtually no money and no education. If I could make big money in the stock market, think about how well you can do. There is no reason you shouldn't be able to achieve far more than I have.

I've always felt that smart people learn from their mistakes but really smart people learn from other people's mistakes. I have tried to follow this philosophy by carefully studying the great traders and innovative thinkers of our time. I have made my share of mistakes and have learned the hard lessons. In this book I have presented to you a sound plan that is based on my experience. It's now up to you to execute it and stick to the discipline. If you do, it will be well worth it.

Best wishes!

ACKNOWLEDGMENTS

Special thanks to the following people:

Patricia Crisafulli for your valuable guidance and unconditional patience. Loren Fleckenstein for your editorial advice, your friendship, and your unwavering confidence in my abilities over the years. Bob Weissman for your dedication, loyalty, and most important your friendship. Mary Glenn and her team at McGraw-Hill for total professionalism and integrity; thank you for allowing me to write this book the way I envisioned. My literary agent, Jeffery Krames (even though we yell at each other from time to time); Jeffery is a great agent. David Ryan for taking the time out of his busy schedule to write a foreword, as well as being a great inspiration for me early in my career. Linda Ludy for your editorial suggestions, friendship, and support. Patricia Wallenburg for doing a wonderful job with the book layout and getting it in "under the wire"; thank you. Dennis Maggi who early in my life exposed me to great classic books like *Think and Grow Rich*, *The Power of Positive Thinking*, and many others that were instrumental in my growth in business and in life. To all my friends and family who supported my efforts over the years.

Thank you all.

INDEX

References to figures are in italics.

10 Secrets for Success and Inner
    Peace (Dyer), 9
3C pattern, 243–247

acceleration, Code 33 situation,
    158–159
accumulation, 70–72
    signs of, 217
advancing phase, 70–72
    how to pinpoint, 79
Affymax, Inc., 230–231
age of company, 37
AIG, *42*, 47, 117
Amazon, 167, *232*, 261
America Online, 101, 193
American Power Conversion,
    177–178
American Superconductor, *223*,
    225
Amgen, *76*, *81*, 128

as a market leader, 175–176
in stage 1, *67*
in stage 2, *71*
in stage 3, *73*
in stage 4, *75*
transitioning from stage 1 to
    stage 2, 68–69, *70*
analysts, tuning out, 86–87
"The Anatomy of a Stock Market
    Winner" (Reinganum),
    28–29
annual earnings, 134–135
anticipation, 120
Apollo Group, 49–50, 62, 128,
    134–135, 173
    net margins, 146
Apple Computers, 98, 105–106,
    181
    net margins, 146
Arena Pharmaceuticals Inc., *256*

ABOUT THE AUTHOR

Starting with only a few thousand dollars, Mark Minervini turned his personal trading account into millions. To demonstrate the effectiveness of his SEPA® trading methodology, in 1997 Minervini entered the U.S. Investing Championship posting $250,000 of his own money; he won with a 155 percent return, a performance that was nearly double the next nearest competing money manager.

Using his SEPA trading strategy, in a five-year period Minervini generated a towering 220 percent average annual return with only one losing quarter. To put that in perspective, a $100,000 account would explode to over $30 million with those returns.

Mark Minervini is a 30-year veteran of Wall Street. He is featured in Jack Schwager's *Stock Market Wizards: Conversations with America's Top Stock Traders.* Schwager wrote: "Minervini's performance has been nothing short of astounding. Most traders and money managers would be delighted to have Minervini's worst year—a 128 percent gain—as their best."

Currently, Minervini educates traders about his SEPA trading methodology through a service called Minervini Private Access, a streaming communication platform that allows users the unique experience of trading side-by-side with Minervini in real time. He also conducts a live Master Trader Program, which is an investment workshop where he spends two days teaching his SEPA strategy and techniques.

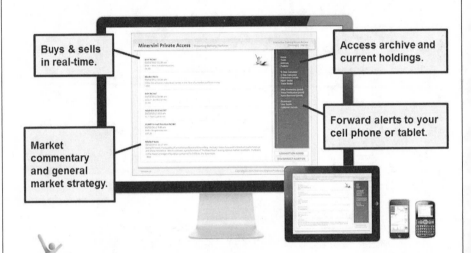

Better Investing.

Minervini Private Access

A Click Away

www.minervini.com

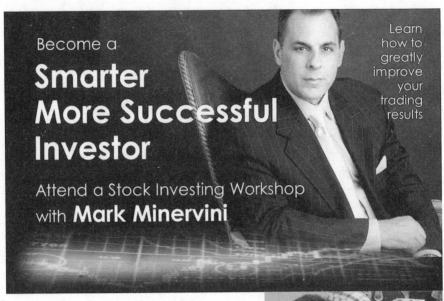

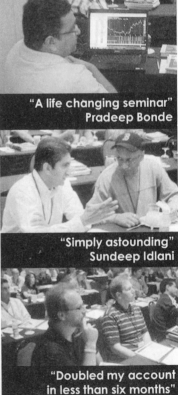